THE BEGGAR

THE
BEGGAR

~~~~~~~~~~~~~~~~~

HARLAN W. GILMORE

1940

THE UNIVERSITY OF NORTH CAROLINA PRESS

CHAPEL HILL

FOR

R. C. G. and M. J. G.

FOREWORD

BY E. T. KRUEGER

To the casual observer the beggar is only a human derelict or a clever malingerer tricking the benevolently minded, but to the trained social scientist he and his kind form an aspect of human society, not a thing apart and unrelated, but a phase of human relations. It is from this viewpoint that elements of population find a fruitful setting which makes their description and explanation something more than a romantic tale or an essay in ethical and social reform.

In the animal and plant world parasitism is a relationship between living forms, to the entomologist and botanist a familiar pattern of adjustment in the competitive-coöperative organization of the world below man. In like manner begging may be considered a form of human parasitism, as "natural" in the interrelationships of the human world as its counterpart in the sub-human realm. To think of begging in this way, as an expression of social organization and as a pattern of relationship in society, permits us to view this phenomenon scientifically and to write its natural history. This is the admirable task to which Harlan W. Gilmore has set himself in this present volume.

The story of begging is, hence, a part of the story of human nature as fashioned in the crucible of culture and society. Whatever its origin, whether in the mutual aid customs of kin and clan groups of earlier mankind, or, as the author of the present volume sees it, in the primitive practice of placating the magic of the stranger, four things are seemingly apparent. In the first place, in human society some individuals are always found who cannot fend for themselves. Here are the sick, the maimed, and the helpless. Here, too, are the inefficient, those whom misfortune has defeated, and those who are misfits. All of these form a dependency class, and no society has ever been without them.

In the second place, the unattached and unsettled individual, and his family, has become an element in human society. One can readily understand that migration, war, slavery, trade, travel, industrialization, the growth of cities, occupational mobility, and other phenomena have been a source whereby individuals have broken from their social and cultural moorings, have found a means of surviving without participation in the ordered ways of society, and have learned to take toll of the fears, hospitality, or humanitarian impulses of settled folk.

In the third place, each culture group fashions its own approved behavior patterns and modes of making a livelihood, and not every individual, or every family, is capable, or able, or willing to follow these patterns when survival becomes difficult or when economic resources become limited and hard to achieve. In modern industrial societies especially the means of livelihood are not always readily attainable and one may see, as one reads this volume, that not all individuals can be provided with economic opportunity, that the degree to which such provision can be made, inside of the institutional structure, fluctuates with industrial crises and changes. Under these conditions the less competent individuals are generally subjected to severe strain in the effort to secure the essentials to living and often even the more competent cannot find adequate economic opportunity. Thus the pressure to some form of parasitic behavior becomes understandable.

In the fourth place, in the centuries which cover the struggle of man to survive under conditions of greater population den-

sity and greater scarcity of resources, there has grown up a humanitarian sentiment which impresses the more fortunate to extend some bounty to the less favored and to those whose lives have been made difficult by the ills common to man. The great religions, all of them, have stressed this humanitarian attitude; social organizations have incorporated it in extensive programs of amelioration, and government has undertaken the task of succoring its dependent classes.

What then? Parasitism, and by this we need not impute anything invidious, becomes a phase of human relations. The human nature of some individuals is molded to beg, to steal, to feed on other individuals or on organized society. And likewise the human nature of countless other individuals is molded to extend aid, to relieve suffering, and to cast their bread upon the waters so that the hungry may not famish. Moreover, if it so happens that some individuals come in time to expect aid, and even to demand it, so also it happens that other individuals cannot escape the compulsions of religious and humanitarian sentiment to give of their substance. For these latter the very values of the human personality, as culture has fashioned it, are at stake if they do not give. In a world so governed even those whose personal interests sharply override their welfare sentiments feel compelled to respond to the begging hand lest they fall in disrepute with those who are humanly minded. Thus the stage is set and thus it is that the age-old practice or custom of begging continues, though its evils are recognized and deplored. Thus, too, the problem of control seems insoluble.

The reader will find in Dr. Gilmore's volume a fascinating exploration of this neglected phase of social relations. There he may learn why begging is both an old and a new problem, how the beggar applies his art, why he gets results, where he lives and why he thrives, and what may or may not be done about him.

Vanderbilt University.

PREFACE

BEGGING as an object of research seems to have been largely neglected by modern social scientists. While crime, juvenile delinquency, poverty, prostitution, and transiency have been given much attention, mendicancy has been given little. The need for research on begging, however, seems to be as great as on any of these other fields, for, like them, it is a product of social process, a parasitic profession, and a severe financial drain on the rest of society. Also, beggars are a more direct annoyance to more people than any of the other parasites. Interestingly, however, the public has not taken a vindictive attitude towards beggars, as it has towards members of these other groups, particularly criminals and prostitutes. It may be just the lack of a crisis situation which has caused social scientists so largely to overlook beggars in their research efforts. It seems to the author, however, that the very fact that a large parasitic group can, over a long period, secure from the public large sums, by peaceful means and without arousing serious public ill-will, indicates a sociological problem which may profitably be explored.

The belief that mendicancy deserved more careful study than it had received led the author to undertake the task of writing this book. Since mendicancy is an integral part of the larger social structure and since it differs from time to time and place to place, it was necessary to limit the scope of this study to modern, urbanized, Western society, including only such historical data as seemed necessary for the understanding of this phenomenon in the modern period. Begging in societies dominated by state capitalism or communism and in oriental societies, where the phenomenon may take very different forms, has not been included. Even within this prescribed scope, however, the author has no illusions that he has done a perfect and complete job. The field is too large to be treated adequately in one volume or even to be covered adequately by one research student. If this volume succeeds in outlining the subject matter and in calling attention to this subject as a field of research, the author will have accomplished his aims.

As may be observed, the data for the study came from a number of different sources. Much of the field data was collected several years ago when the author served for two years in a research capacity with the Davidson County Welfare Commission to study the problem of begging in Nashville, Tennessee. This has been supplemented by data which the author has collected since that time and by data collected by others.

The author acknowledges his indebtedness to Dr. E. T. Krueger of Vanderbilt University, who first aroused his interest in this subject and who has given many valuable suggestions; to the late Mr. W. S. Bixby, formerly Executive Secretary of the Davidson County Welfare Commission, for extending to the author the facilities of that agency for research purposes; to the Big Brothers of Nashville, Tennessee, for research funds provided; and to the Tulane University Council on Research for financial assistance in publishing this study.

In addition to those specifically named, numerous others have given help on various phases of the subject and to these the author is indebted. Finally, to the numerous beggars who have been so generous and patient in giving information the author wishes to express indebtedness and gratitude.

HARLAN W. GILMORE

The Tulane University of Louisiana
June, 1940

ACKNOWLEDGMENTS

THE AUTHOR GRATEFULLY ACKNOWLEDGES permission from the following persons and firms to reprint from material controlled by them:

American Journal of Sociology (John L. Gillin, "Vagrancy and Begging"; and Harlan W. Gilmore, "Five Generations of a Begging Family"). The American Mercury (Jim Tully, "The Lion Tamer"; H. Tascheraud, "Passenger Stiff"). The American Magazine (Edgar Albert Guest, "10,000 People a Week Ask Henry Ford for Gifts"; and J. D. Godfrey, "A Capable Beggar Makes from $15 to $500 a Day"). D. Appleton-Century Company (G. H. Mullin, "Sidewalks of New York; Further Adventures of a Scholar Tramp," from Century Magazine; and J. W. Thompson, An Economic and Social History of the Middle Ages). Asia (J. W. Bennett, "China's Perennially Unemployed"; A. O. Stott, "Chinese Knights of the Open Palm"; N. B. Parulekar, "Brahmans and Beggars"). The Atlantic Monthly (A. Repplier, "Beggar's Pouch"). The Ford Motor Company (Courtenay Savage, "Beggars Collect Fortunes from the Public," in the Dearborn (Michigan) Independent). Funk and Wagnalls (Hutchins Hapgood, Types from City Streets; "Cheerful Dead-beats Who Go Around the World Without a Cent," and "Panhandlers Who Thrive in Manhattan Crowds," from The Literary Digest). The Living Age (H. D. Irvine, "Leisured Class"; "Hosts of a Tramp"; and G. Coleridge, "Little Brothers of the Pavement"). The Nation ("Begging as a Fine Art"). The New Statesman and Nation (H. Belloc, "The Blind Beggars Guild"). The Outlook Publishing Company, Inc. (A. Edwards,

"The Beggars of Mogador," from *Outlook;* Harrison Rhodes, "Business of Begging," and J. J. Goodwin, "Beggars of New York," from *Harpers Weekly*). *Overland Monthly Magazine* (W. Saroyan, "Portrait of a Bum"). *The Quarterly Review* (J. Cooke, "Vagrants, Beggars, and Tramps"). Russell Sage Foundation (Alice W. Solenberger, *1,000 Homeless Men: A Study of Original Records*). Charles Scribner's Sons (T. M. Lindsay, *A History of the Reformation*). *Social Forces* (A. Morris, "Some Social and Mental Aspects of Mendicancy"). Survey Associates (Graham Taylor, "On the Vagrant 'Elusive'"; J. N. Tillard, "The Criminal Mendicant"; F. H. Wines, "Max Müller on Beggars"; and James Forbes, "Jockers and the Schools They Keep," from *Charities;* and F. Z. Youmans, "Childhood, Inc.; Child Beggars," from *Survey*). The University of Chicago and author (Roger Henry Freund, "Begging in Chicago"). The University of Chicago Press (Nels Anderson, *The Hobo;* H. W. Zorbaugh, *The Gold Coast and the Slum;* and excerpts from *American Journal of Sociology*).

CONTENTS

THE BEGGAR

CHAPTER I

~~~~~~~~~~~~~~~~~~~~~~~~~

OUR MENDICANT HERITAGE

FEW social phenomena are more interesting and less understood than that of begging. For centuries, beggars by the
wayside, at fairs, and on city streets have been familiar figures.
Among us today street beggars, peddling mendicants, child
beggars, begging tramps, hoboes and transients in general,
residence beggars, store beggars, and small town beggars are
well known. Literature contains numerous fictions of the un-
penetrated recesses of the beggar's life, and folklore abounds
with myths of the beggar's reckless squanderings, his immoral
debauches, his associations, and his fabulous earnings.

To the average person, however, the private life of these
persons is a deep mystery. Like ghosts from the dark, they come
to garner their alms and into the dark they return. Where they
stay, how they live, and what they do, one can only glean from
authors' dreams and gossipers' uncanny tales. But the beggar's
greatest mystery is the almost magical spell which he casts
over the rest of society. Unknown as these people are, century
after century they live a parasitic existence on the rest of
society. Without the use of force or coercion they get their
subsistence through the gratuities of other people. Govern-
ments legislate against them; yet so strong is their spell that
the legislator in a fit of emotion tosses a coin into the beggar's
coffer.

The origin of this peculiar practice is largely cloaked in mystery. Certainly begging is a very old phenomenon though it is
impossible to say just how old. Like many social practices,
it is apparently the result of a long process of evolution which

1

had its beginning far back in the preliterate period of human development.

Because of its antiquity, science gives us no real basis for determining the first steps in its development. To reconstruct the prehistoric stages in the development of such a phenomenon results at best in an over-simplification based on scanty evidence; at worst, in a pure fiction of the imagination. Since, however, the imagination has usually preceded the facts in the development of science, it may not be amiss to indicate a possibility as to the early stages in the development of begging.

It seems to be frequently assumed that begging evolved from the customs of mutual aid and responsibility of relative for relative, tribesman for fellow tribesman, and neighbor for neighbor. However, the early glimpses of begging indicate a marked resemblance between begging practices and the customs of treating strangers found in present-day preliterate societies. While such preliterate societies differ greatly from each other in their culture, to most of them numerous happenings in the world are a mystery, and a prominent method of controlling happenings in this mysterious world is through magic. Everybody is considered to have access to magical powers which he may use not only to benefit himself but also to aid or to harm others. To most of these people, the stranger is a mysterious person and represents a mysterious magic.[1] Such people are often at a loss to know whence the stranger comes, and they often suspect that he may be a god or a spirit of some sort walking the earth in human form. His magic is something to be feared because it is one with which they have had no experience and do not know how to control, and, if he be a god, his magic may be much more powerful than their own. To protect themselves from this magic, therefore, they treat the stranger well, for by such treatment they not only hope to prevent the stranger from using his magic for evil against them but also they hope that if he is pleased he may use his magic to bestow good fortune on them. There are

[1] For an extensive study of customs relating to the treatment of the stranger see Margaret Mary Wood, *The Stranger* (New York, 1934).

in most tribes, therefore, customs which, having the force of law, require that the stranger be accorded the most royal hospitality the household or tribe can afford. To protect this hospitality from abuse there usually is a time limit, in many tribes three days, beyond which the guest should not expect and cannot receive this hospitality.

The similarity of these customs to almsgiving is striking when we note that the beggar is almost universally a stranger to those from whom he receives alms. Regardless of the plight of the beggar, the giver feels that he has done his duty when he has given the customary alms. In addition, from time immemorial and under one philosophy or another, the giver has felt that he was giving for his own benefit and not entirely, and often not at all, for the benefit of the beggar. If we assume a marked similarity of the customs of prehistoric people to those of preliterate people today, we can easily imagine how begging practices might have evolved from these customs and this may aid our understanding whether or not it augments our knowledge.

On this supposition, begging and giving to beggars might have evolved from the customs of hospitality as a result of the situation created by an increase in the mobility of people. The hospitality prescribed under primitive conditions was a lavish and expensive hospitality which most people could afford only if there were very few strangers to entertain. In a situation where there were many strangers the host would soon be reduced to poverty and want if he tried to abide by such customs. Under these circumstances, therefore, it became necessary to decrease the amount of hospitality, curtail it entirely, or differentiate among strangers, and the latter seems to be what was done. Since in semi-primitive societies there were no hotels or public lodging houses, all sorts of travelers had to get their food and shelter from the people in the country through which they traveled. At later periods even traveling royalty had to billet themselves on the countryside; because little or no money was in use they usually were unable to buy these services on a commercial basis. For practical as well as superstitious reasons, therefore, customs of hospitality were continued, but as the number of strangers increased, people did begin to distinguish among guests. To personal friends and guests of high esteem, lavish hospitality was extended, and to those of lower estate less pretentious treatment. To the most lowly there was doubtless a tendency to reduce the hospitality to a minimum. In time this probably took the form of a token of hospitality, perhaps bread and water or, if money was in circulation, a small coin.

In small towns and rural areas it was doubtless only migratory persons who could secure even these tokens of hospitality, because no local person could long be regarded as a stranger; as long as conditions of travel were hard it was probably only those who were forced to travel who availed themselves of this hospitality. However, as population became less sparse and travel became less difficult, certain people probably found that by continuing to travel they could live on the hospitality of others, and with less effort than they could by work in a settled abode. Thus was born the habitual or professional beggar.

So long as people's superstitions regarding the treatment of strangers held fast, the migrant had little trouble in getting a livelihood, but he had hopes of getting much more. Guests were not only given hospitality according to their rank but were often given gifts according to the host's estimate of their rank, and the gift for a guest of high estate might be of considerable value. The regular beggar, therefore, wished to be ranked as high as possible in the estimation of his host. To attain this end he might invent all sorts of stories regarding his origin and his past, usually claiming to have been of noble birth.

As towns grew larger and became cities, with so many people living in one community, it became impossible for each person to know all of the others. The stranger, therefore, no longer had to be a migrant. The beggar could settle in a fixed abode and live on the hospitality of those in his community to whom he was a stranger. The growth of cities was a great boon to the comfort of begging.

In the *Odyssey*, Homer gives us a very good picture of the customs of hospitality during what was perhaps a period of transition from tribal life to urban civilization. As traveling royalty Odysseus was extended lavish hospitality and expensive gifts. When he was transformed by the goddess Athena into an apparently wretched and poverty-stricken old man we see him go through the experiences of an ordinary beggar. In this role he first visited Eumaeus, the swineherd, who undoubtedly lived in the country, was of lowly station, and probably had few guests. From Eumaeus he received hospitality according to the ancient pattern: as comfortable lodging and as sumptuous food as his host could provide. And when Odysseus started telling the swineherd big stories about his past and his travels we get the swineherd's point of view regarding hospitality. Then it is that Eumaeus says, "Seeing that some god hath brought thee to me, seek not my grace with lies, nor give me any such comfort; not for this will I have respect to thee or hold thee dear, but only for the fear of Zeus, the god of strangers, and for pity of thyself." [2]

Later, when Odysseus appears as a beggar in his own household in town, we see the treatment of beggars in homes of the noble rich. Here Odysseus appears not to have been seated at a table and served as a regular guest. Rather he was allowed to circulate among the guests who had been served and beg them to share their food with him. The reaction to him is very revealing. His presence was resented, he was verbally abused, and one Antinous even struck him with a stool. At this point one of the lordly wooers rebuked Antinous, saying, "Antinous, thou didst ill to strike the hapless wanderer, doomed man that thou art,—if indeed there be a god in heaven. Yea and the gods, in the likeness of strangers from far countries, put on all manner of shapes, and wander through the cities, beholding the violence and the righteousness of men." [3]

Homer even gives us a brief picture of a local beggar, Irus,

[2] S. H. Butcher and A. Lang, trans., *The Odyssey of Homer* (New York, 1912), p. 234.
[3] *Ibid.*, p. 290.

who visited this same feast and had a fight with Odysseus. Irus apparently was recognized as a greedy, habitual beggar who begged regularly in those parts. He was apparently much disliked, but in spite of the fact that he was not a traveler he seemingly was able to hide under the cloak of the gods and get alms.

The *Odyssey* gives us an indication that even at that early period there were some who habitually lived by the hospitality of others. Furthermore, the people in the towns seemed to recognize that their hospitality was being abused and they resented this abuse, but because of their beliefs they were helpless to refuse.

Since during the early history of civilization society was primarily rural and beggars tended to be migratory or semimigratory, the number of beggars was greatly influenced by the degree to which the local community was able to provide for and hold its own people, preventing them from becoming foot-loose migrants. There have always been persons who, because of physical limitations, mental limitations, or strokes of ill fate, are unable to produce a livelihood under the prevailing economic system. If difficulties of travel are not too great these persons particularly are likely to enter into the ranks of beggars.

Early society had various practices which tended to provide in one way or another for these economic incompetents and keep them from becoming dislodged from their locality. The systems of obligation of mutual aid of tribesman for fellow tribesman, relative for relative, and neighbor for neighbor, which have been characteristic of primitive and rural societies, usually provided for the majority. In addition, in some societies the system of slavery and the system of concubinage gave many the right to receive care from their masters during periods of incompetency. For some the socially disapproved occupations offered an alternative to begging. Prostitution and, under some circumstances, even crime might be engaged in as a way of gaining a livelihood without becoming a migrant. And, of course, even if the person became a migrant these modes of livelihood might be chosen in preference to begging.

In spite of the fact, however, that early societies made diverse provisions for the local care of people, there were a good many migrants. Since each locality was primarily dependent on its own food supply, famine due to crop failures often made it impossible for a community to feed all of its population, and part or sometimes all had to migrate. War and the hunt sometimes resulted in individuals' becoming disconnected from their community. In addition, there were some individuals who left of their own accord: occasionally a person who had committed a crime would flee his community rather than face punishment; travel on holy or semi-holy missions of various kinds is a very old practice; even travel because of curiosity or so-called wanderlust was probably more common than many believe. The traveler, once set loose for any of these reasons, sometimes found it almost impossible to get attached again to a locality. Thus the wanderer tended to continue to wander.

As towns began to develop and people moved around more, the kinship group and the neighborhood found it more and more difficult to care for their own dependents. As a result, other methods of caring for these economic incompetents began to supplement and replace the kinship and neighborhood folk practices. Even government care of the needy appeared rather early. While perhaps not the first to adopt such measures, ancient Athens had a system of state aid for the needy of which it was very proud. In fact, it was the boast of the city that none of its citizens ever had to beg. And apparently this boast was justifiable with the exception of a few periods of disorganization following wars. However, it must not be overlooked that this state aid applied to citizens only, and that in Athens citizenship was primarily a hereditary matter; by no means all who lived in Athens were citizens and assuredly migrants were not. Therefore, while the citizens of Athens did not beg, they probably did not want for beggars at their door.

At a later period, Rome likewise made certain provisions for the needy through its free distribution of corn. Here again, however, we find limitations similar to those of Athens. Free corn was available only to Roman citizens. In Rome citizenship was not so closely restricted as it was in Athens, and the distribution of citizenship rights was continually changing, but it never was based merely on residence in Rome. Some who lived in Rome were citizens while others were not; some who lived away from Rome but in the empire were citizens and others not, and those who migrated to Rome might be citizens or not depending on their status before migration. Therefore, at any given time there were doubtless many people, some of them local residents and some visitors, some needy and others not, who for lack of citizenship rights could not qualify to receive free corn.

These tendencies to limit community relief efforts to those who were, according to various criteria, regarded as members of the community seem to have been quite general in both ancient and modern times. This is not surprising since the kinship and neighborly obligations out of which these arose carried similar restrictions. While community assistance undoubtedly kept many from entering begging, there were many others who could not qualify for aid under these provisions, and some of these were forced to resort to begging.

As Rome declined and the center of western civilization shifted to the primarily rural Europe of the early Middle Ages it is interesting to see the transition which almsgiving, begging, and relief underwent in their transfer from an urban to a rural habitat. In the confusion which marked this transition period, it is difficult to tell just what customs people followed in almsgiving and what philosophy prompted their actions. Most of the people, however, were very close to their tribal days, and it is probably safe to assume that their response to the beggar was closely related to the folk culture of their primitive ancestors, which meant that the beggar was treated as a stranger and accorded warm hospitality. As this pattern was altered through the years, it apparently was replaced by the patterns sanctioned by the Catholic church. These in turn strongly supported almsgiving but for somewhat different reasons than those of the primitive folk culture.

"The early Christian churches cared for their own poor, but took great pains to prevent pauperization. However, there grew up in the course of time the theory of the religious merit of almsgiving. Charity became a means of securing forgiveness of sin to the giver, a means of grace. Almsgiving, no longer the means primarily of helping a fellow-man in need, became fundamentally a method of washing away one's sins.

"With the rise of monasticism in Christendom the religious basis of begging in the cleansing grace of charity was completed in the theory that those were of superior sanctity who forsook all their worldly possessions and depended entirely upon the charity of God's people. Thus, the religious basis of beggary had its roots deep in man's desire to free himself from sin by giving to a beggar, and on the other hand got its justification from the desire to attain salvation by becoming a beggar. From both points of view religion sanctified begging." [4]

The process of displacing the primitive folk culture with the philosophies of the Catholic church was primarily a process of civilizing a barbaric people, and this took centuries. It cannot be said, therefore, just when people ceased to respond to one philosophy and began to respond to another. But for the beggar it made little difference, because both approved almsgiving and he received a favorable response under either.

As has been said, during the early centuries of the Middle Ages life was mostly rural. The chief economic pursuit was agriculture and the prevalent mode of organization was the feudal manorial system. The manor was the farm unit, the feudal mansion was the home of the overlord and the fortress, and the serfs and various freeholders composed a village near

---

[4] John L. Gillin, "Vagrancy and Begging," *American Journal of Sociology*, XXXV (1929), 425-26.

the mansion. There were no towns of great size and few isolated farm homes. Most of the people, therefore, lived in these
small manor towns which tended to be independent social and
economic units with a rather stable population. For the most
part they produced what they needed, buying little from the
outside world and selling little to it. Travel was difficult and
dangerous and hence was seldom engaged in. News from the
outside was rare, and a wandering beggar, as well as a visiting
potentate, might bring news. In addition, a wandering beggar
might bring new stories, new songs, or new tricks to amuse
the semi-shut-in townsmen. The beggar, therefore, tended to
wander from one castle-town to another, staying perhaps a few
days at each, and he always managed to keep in stock jokes,
stories, tricks, stunts, and songs which might help to make his
welcome in each place last a little longer. In such towns the
lord was chief host whether the visitor was a beggar or a
prince.

"But daily life in a medieval castle was pretty dull except in war time, especially for the women, who did not
see so much of the outer world as the men. Before the
literary awakening of the twelfth century few of the laity
could read or write; hence books were not to be found.
The lord's wife and daughters had their separate routine
tasks of supervision and administration of the household,
but beyond these time hung heavy on their hands. Consequently the blowing of his horn by the watchman on a
tower to notify of the approach of a stranger was a welcome event, unless mayhap it was that of an enemy. Be
he who he might, bishop or monk, baron, pilgrim, traveling merchant, vagabond, minstrel, strolling player, or ac-
robat with a dancing bear, one and all were welcomed and
given hospitality according to their rank." [5]

The urban influence, as far as begging is concerned, which
carried over from Rome into this primarily rural world was

[5] James Westfall Thompson, *An Economic and Social History of the
Middle Ages* (New York, 1928), p. 720.

represented mostly by the Catholic church, and it was chiefly this that differentiated this rural world from those preceding it. The Catholic church took over much of the relief which in Rome had been carried by the government. While it did not distribute free corn, it did give relief, and in its monasteries particularly it rendered services of great significance to beggardom. Many monasteries took charge of and cared for physically and mentally handicapped people who had no source of support and were unable to travel. Of equal importance, the monasteries were hostelries or havens for travelers of all sorts, rich and poor. Beggars as well as princes could stop at monasteries and get food and a place to rest, and the beggar could abuse this hospitality as easily as he could that of an individual.

While, as has been said, there were no real cities during this period, there were certain occasions which simulated the urban phenomenon. The most important of these was the periodic fair. The fair was a substitute for permanent commercial towns. The manor came so near to being entirely self-sufficient that there was not enough trade in any one place to keep merchants busy the year round. Yet there was need for some trade with the outside. As a consequence, at certain suitable points fairs were established. Here, usually at the same time each year, merchants of various kinds, many of them from distant points, would assemble and people from a considerable distance would come to sell to these merchants and to buy from them. During the short duration of the fair most of the buying and selling for a year, or at least a season, might be done for a large area. Along with the merchants came grafters and racketeers of all sorts to ply their trades. Fortune tellers, prostitutes, gamblers, thieves, and beggars flocked to these centers in great numbers. In describing the larger fairs of the period, Thompson says, "There were gathered as in modern fairs the thief, the pickpocket, the cut-purse, the thug, the prostitute, beggars. Often the sergeants were hard pressed to maintain order in this heterogeneous mob." [6]

Another type of assemblage which occasionally brought to-

[6] *Ibid.*, p. 602.

gether large numbers of people was the church councils. Besides the church officials who participated in these councils, great numbers of people attended because of their interest in church affairs. In addition, these assemblies of people attracted much the same nondescript elements as the fairs and were especially favorable to beggars, who benefited by the stress which the church placed on almsgiving.

The highways of this period also served in a way to take the place of the city street for beggars. Some writers of the past have pictured the highways of this period as infested with beggars. However, it is doubtful that any of the highways had enough travel to support a large number of beggars. Along most of the highways there may have been occasional beggars, some of whom were used as lookouts by robber bands to inform them of the approach of likely looking travelers. On special occasions when a large fair or other large gathering was under way the highways in the immediate vicinity may have been more or less "infested" with beggars. But on the whole the highway was perhaps one of the least used places for begging.

That the beggar had little trouble in securing alms in the form of food and lodging during the Middle Ages there seems little reason to doubt. This, however, does not necessarily mean that beggars were plentiful. It is difficult in fact to tell just how prevalent they were. Since the beggar got his alms as a stranger and not merely as a beggar, most of them were indistinguishable, probably, from other poor travelers, and some of them, perhaps, posed as traveling nobility. Furthermore, the difficulties of travel were such that "the maimed and the halt and the blind" could not endure the hardships, and in most cases they stayed in their own community or became the charge of a monastery. Most beggars, therefore, were not distinguishable by any physical defects, and in many cases only the beggar himself knew that he was a beggar.

If we look at the well-known difficulties of travel during this period, bad roads, robber-infested highways, and toll bridges, or if we consider the relationship of lord and serf, we may get the impression that there were almost no beggars in this feudal era. On the other hand, if we look at the sources of recruits for beggardom, we may get the impression that there were more beggars than there were. Nevertheless we must run this risk.

The sources of recruits for begging were no different, of course, from those for robbery, prostitution, or any of the other outcast occupations. All of these were modes of securing a livelihood used by people who were not connected with the regular economic system. While the origin of the feudal system is not exactly clear, there is evidence that there was a floating population from the very beginning. Whatever the method was by which serfs originally became serfs and lords became lords, there were some apparently who never became either. Thus in certain areas, which today we would call marginal, there were groups which corresponded more or less to our southern "poor whites" during slavery. We know also that from the beginning there were robber bands and women camp followers with the armies, and all of these elements presumably produced children, who, like themselves, were unattached.

This originally unattached group was continually being augmented by persons dislodged from the regular feudal system. While conditions of life were hard and the death rate was high, the population did undoubtedly increase and this meant a gradual overcrowding of the older settled areas, which necessitated some leaving the older manors. The tendency of natural increase to produce an oversupply of nobility has been widely recognized and blamed for many of the ills of the period, such as the mercenary armies and the robber gangs. While less obvious, this same process undoubtedly deprived many in the lower classes of their birthright. As a result of this overcrowding, some of the serfs might have found it impossible to meet their tenure obligations and been forced to surrender their right to the use of the land. Thus they were dispossessed of their source of livelihood and forced to migrate unless some substitute could be found.

While this forced migration due to overpopulation was more

or less continuous, there were mass migrations which occurred occasionally. As has already been indicated, each locality was an almost completely self-supporting unit. Land transportation methods were crude and the movement of any great quantity of goods was practically impossible. A prolonged drouth or in some cases even a short one could force the complete evacuation of the population of an area. And, as is usually the case, some would return while others would not. In addition, as has been mentioned earlier, there were individuals who for personal reasons fled the manor or were forced off. Criminals, socially disgraced persons, maladjusted individuals, and even some insane persons departed for many reasons other than economic ones.

Besides these foot-loose groups there were the bona fide travelers who might take to the road for any of a number of reasons. Merchants, persons on pilgrimages, and people en route to fairs or church councils were the most common kinds of travelers, but other people also traveled in connection with business and war, and later the crusades led thousands onto the road. While many had to travel for one reason or another, there was probably a goodly number for whom the reason was an excuse. Life on the manor was monotonous and for some boring. In contrast the beggars and travelers brought, in all probability, fabulous tales of their experiences, tales which were part truth and part fiction. To many "wild bloods," with strong curiosity and with a lively imagination stimulated by these tales, the road became a dream path to a world about which they knew little but believed much. Therefore they trumped up a reason to travel and thereby made an honorable exit from their home community and set forth in search of a golden grail.

Travel was difficult and dangerous, and the traveler who set out on any long journey was never sure what fate awaited him. With primitive modes of transportation and with very little money in use, the traveler could not carry much wealth with him. Since the highways were infested with robbers and even robber barons, and since each feudal estate had the right to charge him taxes and tolls, he might soon lose what little he started with and be reduced to the poverty of a traveling beggar. To make matters worse, he might in this manner lose letters or other forms of identification and have to resort to the same tale of woe which the beggar used. If he were really unfortunate he might even lose his life. Many a traveler, therefore, had to rely on the good graces of the people through whose country he traveled and probably often found himself treated as a beggar, even though he might be of noble birth.

It is thus clear that there were travelers and what one would today call vagrants during the Middle Ages, and many who set out as travelers became vagrants temporarily or permanently. We should not make the mistake, however, of assuming that all who got into this class stayed in it, and their descendants after them. While it was difficult to escape, it was not entirely impossible. There were various ways by which new persons could be taken into an established manor system and some of the more capable of them were in this way able to get relocated. The greatest possibility of escape, however, was to go to the frontier and make a new home in the wilderness as did our American pioneers, and in this process the church was of help. Many monasteries were, when founded, essentially frontier settlements. But with crude implements, crude methods of agriculture, and crude methods of transportation the life of the pioneer offered more hardships than were faced by our own frontiersmen. It was not an easy escape for any, and for some it was impossible.

About the eleventh century there began a gradual development of trade and growth of towns, which was destined eventually to transform the rural feudal world into a very different society. The social and economic changes then beginning were in a few centuries to throw huge numbers into the ranks of vagrancy and begging, and early in this drama the begging friars set the stage for these unfortunates by raising begging almost to the status of a sanctified calling.

The begging friars came into being through an effort to accomplish what the monks for centuries had sought but failed to do. To renounce worldly goods and adopt a life of poverty, holiness, and good works was the ideal on which monasteries were founded, and every man becoming a monk took a vow to seek this end in his own life. To separate themselves from the temptations of the world they entered monasteries and on this hinged their downfall. There grew up a fiction that what belonged to the monastery did not belong to the monks in it, and though a monastery might have immense wealth, as many of them did, the monks in it were still in poverty. Nevertheless the monks had the use of this wealth. The result was a deterioration of most of the monks into what many considered an arrogant and pleasure-loving, if not dissipated, group. To correct this situation there would arise periodically a new order of monks, again devoted to poverty, and this one in turn would degenerate.

This search of the monks for poverty without finding it led in the thirteenth century to the establishment of the Franciscan order, which was an epochal event for beggardom. Believing that the monasteries had been the cause of the failure of the monks, St. Francis of Assisi established an order which would have no monasteries. Adopting begging as a mode of living, he set out to travel among people and render unselfish services no matter how humble. He taught his followers to do likewise. Traveling in pairs, always on foot, kind, humble, and helpful, the Franciscans were in such contrast to the other monks that they experienced great popularity. They were loved and supported everywhere they went. The sincerity and humility of these friars gave a status to beggars and to almsgiving such as has seldom existed.

The life adopted by the Franciscans was too idealistic for most human beings and the order tended to experience rapid deterioration and decay. Increasingly they gave more attention to the gathering of alms and the chasing of legacies and less to the doing of good works, until many of the friars became little more than whining alms-seekers. In the wake of the Franciscans came various other imitative orders, which in most cases never manifested the sincerity of the early Franciscans

and deteriorated even more rapidly. In addition, as the number
of such friars increased, professional beggars were able to play
the role of a friar either as an actual member of an order or as
an outright impostor. By this means all beggars profited, directly or indirectly, by the activities of the mendicant friars.
And, while the orders themselves rapidly deteriorated, the halo
which they had brought to begging did not so quickly vanish.

"The very fact of begging seemed to raise those who
shared in it to the level of members of a religious association. St. Francis, the 'imitator of Christ,' had taught his
followers to beg, and this great example sanctified the
practice. It is true that the begging friars were always the
butt of the satirists of the close of the fifteenth century.
They delighted to portray the mendicant monk, with his
sack, into which he seemed able to stuff everything: honey
and spice, nutmegs, pepper . . . new clothes, milk, butter,
and cheese; cheese especially, and of all kinds—ewe's
milk and goat's milk, hard cheese and soft cheese, large
cheeses and small cheeses—were greedily demanded by
these 'cheese hunters,' as they were satirically called. On
their heels tramped a host of semi-ecclesiastical beggars, all
of them with professional names—men who begged for a
church that was building, or for an altar-cloth, or to hansel
a young priest at his first Mass; men who carried relics
about for the charitable to kiss—some straw from the man-
ger of Bethlehem, or a feather from the wing of the angel
Gabriel; the Brethren of St. James, who performed continual and vicarious pilgrimages to Çompostella, and
sometimes robbed and murdered on the road; the Brethren
of St. Anthony, who had the special privilege of wearing
a cross and carrying a bell on their begging visits. These
were all ecclesiastical beggars. The ordinary beggars did
their best to obtain some share of the sanctity which surrounded the profession; they carried . . . the picture of some
saint, or placed the cockle-shell, the badge of a pilgrim, in
their hats, and secured a quasi-ecclesiastical standing." [7]

[7] T. M. Lindsay, *A History of the Reformation* (New York, 1913),
I, 142.

During the time that the orders of friars were creating a highly favorable atmosphere for begging and almsgiving, the change started in the eleventh century was going forward. In addition to the development of trade and the growth of towns, the most notable outward aspects of this change were the decline of serfdom, the growing strength of the central government, and the decline in the power of the Catholic church. While these developments were due to a very complex causation, there were three factors which seem to have been of paramount importance. The growth of population had been going on and the clearing of land proceeding until eventually most of the usable land had been put under cultivation, and still there was a surplus of workers who could not be used on the land. There thus became available numbers of able-bodied men who were willing to sell their labor for any kind of work there was to be done. At approximately the same time there was a marked increase in the amount of money in circulation in England and Europe, due probably to the increase in silver mining in Germany. This money provided a medium by which temporary laborers could be paid. And finally, there was a marked increase in trade which was in part the result of the fact that those who went on crusades became acquainted with products used in different parts of the world and developed new tastes and new modes of living. When they returned home they desired to buy such of these as they could not themselves produce. Then, of course, as trade developed and other forms of travel increased, still other commodities were introduced through these channels.

With money available the feudal lord found that he could hire labor which would be much more efficient than the serf who was fulfilling a traditional obligation. Instead of requiring so many days of labor a year from the serf, the lord let the serf pay him rent equal to the wages for that many days of labor and the serf with money available was usually glad to do this. It was through this process that the serf became a renter, and the lord began to use hired labor to tend his part of the manor. The growth of trade and towns came about in a similar way.

With a demand for goods and with money available there was a market to be supplied, and the surplus laborers could be employed in any of the processes involved in manufacturing, transporting, and merchandising.

About the time those changes got well under way in Europe and when they had little more than started in England, that great pestilence, the Black Death, swept across Europe striking England in 1348 and other European countries a little earlier, and leaving wholesale death in its wake. It created general economic disorganization and social demoralization. Besides killing a sizable proportion of the population, it caused thousands to flee their homes and whole areas to be temporarily deserted. So complete was the demoralization that production was completely stopped for a year or so and seriously disrupted for much longer.

The first phase in the recovery from this catastrophe was a period in which there was as much money, as many houses, as much furniture and other goods as before and a much smaller population. In addition there were large stores of various commodities. Everyone, therefore, seemed to have more than he had had before the catastrophe. There was, as a result, a short period of seeming prosperity which was based principally on the consumption of reserves and was accompanied by very little production.

This period soon passed and was followed by a period of attempted revival of production, and with this many problems arose. Scarcely ever has there been such an apparent shortage of people. From the top down this was the paramount problem. There were not enough government officials, and new, untrained recruits had to be put in; there were not enough noblemen, and new titles had to be bestowed; and there were not enough workmen, and wages rose rapidly.

While all of these shortages of people created corresponding problems, the shortage of laborers released changes of far-reaching consequence. For a number of years the lower classes were released from their attachment to the soil as they had not been for centuries. With land lying idle in many places serfs could bargain with lords with the assurance that they could move to another manor and get land on their own terms. Both the manors and the towns were bidding for laborers and wages went up and up. With jobs to spare, therefore, both the serfs and the laborers tended to move around the country freely and go to those places where they could obtain the most favorable terms or the highest wages. With this migration added to the earlier movement accompanying the Black Death, thousands were removed from the traditional homestead of their family and many fell into the mode of existence characteristic of a semi-migratory labor group. As always happens under similar circumstances, some workers doubtless got an exaggerated opinion of the value of their labor and refused to work unless they were paid a wage higher than they could command. Pending work such persons could live by begging and, having learned to beg, some of them probably preferred that to work at any price.

This shortage of workers caused severe resentment against those who were able to work but refused to, and one of the objects of this resentment was the able-bodied beggar. Many an able-bodied beggar who had never worked in his life and whose ancestors before him may not have worked, for the first time found himself seriously blamed for his idleness. But being both habitually and philosophically opposed to working, he was little tempted by high wages and not greatly influenced by criticism.

As a result of the high and rising wages and the shortage of laborers, the government in England enacted the Statute of Labourers which was issued as a Royal Ordinance of Labourers in 1349 and confirmed two years later. This ordinance set wages at the level prevailing before the Black Death, compelled those offered work at these wages to accept with penalty of imprisonment for refusal, provided that food should be sold at "reasonable prices," penalized those accepting more than the specified wages, and outlawed the giving of alms to able-bodied beggars. The primary purpose of this law, of course, was to solve the wage problem. However, its success in this was only nominal. Employers ran little risk by paying wages higher than those prescribed by law, and thus they continued to bid against each other for laborers. However, the laborers accepting these higher wages were open to punishment and actually many of them were imprisoned. Many others fled rather than accept their punishment, and thus they became outlaws. As outlaws their position was not enviable. If they took a job at legal wages there was danger that the law might "catch up with them"; if they were offered work and refused it they were liable for arrest; and if they begged they were likely to be offered a job. During this period of labor shortage there were many who attained just this status, and because of their peculiar position they banded together for self-protection and were often forced to turn to illegal acts of a more serious nature as a method of making a living. In addition, since the legal wages were usually so low that the worker could not live on them, many workers fled their parish to prevent having jobs offered them. One of the major effects of this law, therefore, was the creation of a large vagrant class.

For various reasons the law was not so stringently enforced in the towns and the vagrants tended to migrate to the towns in large numbers. Often there were no jobs to be had in the towns and they had to devise other ways of securing a livelihood. Many of them turned to begging and others turned to crime.

The Statute of Labourers coupled with later laws designed to strengthen the original enactment, usually by more severe penalties or by prescribing machinery for enforcing the law, created such dire problems of poverty, vagrancy, begging, crime, and revolutionary unrest that it marked the beginning of nearly five centuries of legislative experimentation in dealing with these problems. For nearly two centuries after the passage of this original law the chief aim of legal enactments was to suppress vagrancy and everything associated with it. The methods prescribed by the various statutes were almost uncanny in their variety and the punishments provided were often so severe as to be gruesome. Rewards were offered for the apprehension of vagrants and periodical hunts were prescribed.

Among the punishments prescribed were imprisonment, whipping, and branding, and able-bodied vagrants who had no master could be bound to an employer in a relationship not greatly different from slavery. Runaway workers or serfs could be returned to their masters just as slaves were later returned in America and by much the same method. During all of this period the legislation was of a repressive or negative nature. The government left all the relief of the poor and the care of indigent individuals to the church and to the generosity of individuals.

The revolutionary unrest under these laws of repression became so great that in 1536 the government began what was to be several centuries of experimentation with government relief and preventive programs. In that year legislation was enacted which placed the responsibility of relief on the unit of local government, the parish. Each parish was to appoint an Overseer of the Poor and to levy a tax for the care of the poor. This did not replace, but merely supplemented, the previous laws. Maximum wages, punishment for vagrancy, and enforced servitude continued as before. Indeed the Overseer of the Poor was supposed to care for the able-bodied poor by placing them in servitude.

As the shortage of workers caused by the Black Death gradually disappeared and was replaced by an over-supply of laborers, the problem of caring for the poor became increasingly serious. Even the problem of placing the able-bodied poor in bondage to employers became more difficult and in many cases impossible, and the mounting poor rates became more and more irksome. As a result, many parishes apparently tried to alleviate their relief problem by making the relief allowances so skimpy that the poor would leave the parish. This merely swelled the ranks of vagrancy and created a vagrancy problem of such vast proportions that there was enacted in 1662 the first of a series of laws which attempted to define residence requirements for relief. The fundamental concept of the law was that the person who became in need of relief was not necessarily the responsibility of the parish where he happened to be when relief became necessary. And by the same token, a parish was not necessarily responsible for the relief of all of the poor people in it but might be responsible for some of the poor in other parishes. It was necessary, therefore, to send those who needed relief in parishes which were not responsible for them back to parishes in which these people had fulfilled residence requirements and hence could receive relief. With the amount of vagrancy which had been in existence for three centuries, this law left many in dire straits. They could not secure work because there were no jobs to be had; they could not secure relief because they could not prove that they had fulfilled the residence requirements in any parish; and as wandering thieves or beggars they were liable for arrest and punishment under the vagrancy laws. The only alleviating circumstance was that the laws were poorly enforced.

The failure to enforce these various laws stringently was due in part to the weakness of the central government. While most of the laws were enactments of the central government, the parish was the unit of enforcement and it often did about as it pleased. But part of the failure was probably due to the definitions of the poor which had been built up around almsgiving. Through all the preceding centuries from tribal days, through the domination of the Catholic church, the dependent poor had been looked upon as God's children and especially was this true of the traveler who was now called a vagrant. And the traveling begging friars had raised this group to an almost sanctified status. As a result, giving to beggars had not only become a part of the habits of most individuals but it was also imbedded in the etiquette of most occasions and even in the customs of the household. Every castle seems to have had an alms dish or basket into which were put bread parings, gravy, and food morsels, and this basket was regularly placed at the castle gate. Such long established beliefs and customs could not be banished suddenly by the outburst of an enraged king trying to secure laborers for harassed landlords or even by the enactments of a parliament. It is even probable that while the lords were in parliament passing laws against begging, almsgiving, and vagrants, their wives or servants were setting the alms basket out at the castle gates for the wandering beggars. It is also probable that the law enforcement officers had strong qualms of conscience against the enforcement of such stringent measures against the wandering poor. Thus it is quite likely that begging and giving to beggars continued as little disturbed by the law as it is today; such is admitted in the preamble of practically every one of the numerous edicts and laws against vagrants and beggars, for each new law is justified on the ground that the old law had failed to eliminate these problems.

It was not until the Reformation in the seventeenth century that a philosophical basis for the new system was established. The changes had come as emergency measures to meet practical situations and not as the result of any new religious, economic, or political philosophy. Vagrancy and forced labor laws were passed to try to provide workers, especially for the manors; and relief laws were passed to prevent the unrest of the poor from growing into revolution. However, when the Reformation finally came there were certain implications of its philosophy which tended to make the new system seem more rational and tended to undermine the almsgiving on which many of the poor had been depending. The reformers, especially the Calvinists, laid great stress on work as a religious duty. It was implied that if a person would live properly and work hard he would not only be rewarded in the next world but he would be prosperous in this. The point of this philosophy was that if the person was not prosperous it was either because he did not live as he should or did not work hard, or both. In any case, he was to blame. The poor had only themselves to blame for their poverty, and to give to able-bodied beggars was to give to one whom God Himself would not favor. Only the maimed, and the halt, and the blind might be righteous and yet dependent. Instead of considering indiscriminate almsgiving a meritorious act, the Protestant leaders vigorously opposed it. Martin Luther edited and wrote an introduction to a book exposing the fakery of professional beggars.[8] Relief, except to the physically impotent, was religiously unnecessary. Forcing people to work, therefore, was only forcing them to do what they should be anxious to do as a religious act, and if relief of those able to work was necessary at all, it was for political, not religious, reasons.

Protestantism did not stop almsgiving and probably never will, but it did make it harder for the poor, beggar or not, to rationalize his lot and it did make it harder to secure alms. Protestantism also made it easier for the conscientious citizen to view with equanimity the hardships which the poor suffered at the hands of the law.[9]

Thus bolstered philosophically, this rather gruesome English system of laws, with few significant changes except in methods of providing the minimum relief at the least price, continued in force until after the Industrial Revolution was well under way. The trend of affairs, however, was against it. With the growth of trade and the development of factories, the settlement laws and vagrancy laws got increasingly in the way of the movement of people to points where labor was needed. And with the growth of free competition in trade and the formulation of the laissez-faire philosophy, the maximum wage law became increasingly untenable. Therefore, the whole system was due for eventual revision or repeal.

By the time the Industrial Revolution came, begging and almsgiving had lost most of the halo which the Catholic church and the begging friars had given them and both were held in low esteem. However, the social and economic changes which accompanied this period and have followed it were such as to encourage many to enter the ranks of begging. A part of these changes has consisted in the movement of peoples which has been almost continuously under way. Movement from

[8] *Liber Vagatorum, The Book of Vagabonds and Beggars,* edited by Martin Luther in 1528; republished by J. C. Hotton (London, 1860).

[9] It may at first appear that these effects of Protestantism contradict the supposed relation of Protestantism to philanthrophy. Actually, however, giving for the social welfare involves the idea of stewardship and is in a way a substitute for almsgiving.

rural areas to cities, from city to city, from old countries to new lands has been much in evidence. And always in such movement many get dislodged socially and economically and fall into the disorganized classes. Along with the movement of peoples have gone rapid changes in economic methods and changes in occupations. Old occupations have been wiped out overnight and new ones have been established, and many people have been thrown into poverty because their occupations were obsolete and they were unable to find new ones.

The rapid growth of cities, both in number and in size, and the development of that unearthly monstrosity, the huge metropolis, have done much to promote begging. The anonymity prevailing in the large city, the ease with which beggars may find prospects from whom to beg, and the general ease with which persons may become disorganized and fall into poverty, all make it a very favorable place for beggars. Therefore, with more and bigger cities we have tended to get more and better beggars. We have received the practice of begging through the hands of many generations as a disgraced but by no means decadent profession, and we seem on our way to bequeath it, well preserved, to those who succeed us.

CHAPTER II

~~~~~~~~~~~~~~~~~~~~~~~~~~~~~~~~

THE MENDICANT ART

THE stock in trade of beggars is their art of getting something for nothing. It is this art which has enabled hordes of beggars through the centuries to garner a livelihood through specific means from the giving public. Save perhaps the art of medicine, it is doubtful that any other art has had a wider clientele, or has brought to its artists a more dependable return. Indeed, the total income of all the beggars in any period might well equal or exceed the income of any other class of contemporary artists. Such a remunerative art merits a more careful analysis than it has thus far received.

Any true art reflects the spirit of the age in which it lives. Being an intangible art, mendicancy has left no accumulation of pictures or statuary in which its history is reflected. Its attainment in each period consists of new devices which the mendicants evolve to play on the moods of their public. Each generation of beggars receives this body of techniques from the generation which precedes it, sorts, modifies, and adds to the accumulation, and passes its knowledge to the succeeding generation.

There is a tendency for each generation of beggars to change this art to fit the times in which it lives. The spirit of each age is recorded, therefore, in the art of its contemporary mendicants. Thus the beggars of India make capital of the intellectual and spiritual status which the profession enjoys, while the beggars of China play heavily on the superstitions of the Chinese people. Likewise the beggars of the Middle Ages were not oblivious to the religious sanctions which almsgiving had in their day; it was a common practice for beggars of the Middle Ages to carry "a stone from the tomb of Christ" or a "feather from the wing of Gabriel" and frequently beggars posed as friars. So apt are beggars at adjusting their art to the moods of the public that some of them change their tactics almost daily to capitalize to the fullest local circumstances. A war, a drouth, a flood, or any other disaster produces hordes of refugee-beggars who were in no way connected with the tragedy.

"Times Square now harbors the elite of the mendicants of the East, who have applied modern publicity methods to their professions. Most of them just got out of the hospital after being in some disaster which has figured largely in the news. Many limp or have their arms in slings as a result of the Washington theatre disaster. Hundreds of others just recovered from pneumonia or the influenza. A few date their bandages and crutches to the Wall Street explosion. A new disaster or epidemic changes a thousand stories." [1]

With the decay of earlier beliefs regarding almsgiving and begging and the loss in status of the profession, mendicants were forced to discard many of the clever devices of their crafty forerunners. To pose as an apostle of learning or of piety was no longer to gain favor, it was rather to appear profane and to arouse the indignation of the conscientious citizenry. Many of the devices of early beggars, therefore, have been discarded in evolving the art of modern beggardom. No American beggar would think of using the snake-throwing act, which is considered by Chinese beggars a valuable and legitimate device. In the words of a Chinese King of Beggars, "Often the tao-fan has to throw a snake round a woman's neck before she will drop her grudging gift. The act invariably arouses in those who behold it so great a degree of terror they quickly avoid similar inconveniences." [2]

[1] "Panhandlers Who Thrive in Manhattan Crowds," *Literary Digest*, LXXIII (1922), 52. Statement by Roy P. Gates.
[2] Amelia O. Stott, "Chinese Knights of the Open Palm," *Asia*, XXVII (1927), 831.

There is one motive for giving, however, which has been universal throughout the ages. Everywhere and in every period men have felt responsible for a fellow in need. The appeal to pity has never been void of response. Being the chief surviving motive to which beggars appeal, devices for appealing to pity have been passed on for centuries, and new ones are devised by the clever of each generation. The begging of today, therefore, is largely an art of depicting misery and misfortune for the purpose of arousing sympathy in the giver.

The appeal to pity, however, is often camouflaged by a more respectable veneer. To outline the scope of begging, therefore, is no simple task. When one person frankly appeals to another for aid, solely on the basis of a physical handicap or other misfortune, there is no question but that that is begging. Not all beggars, however, are so frank or so direct in their appeal. In sundry ways, beggars work in a more subtle fashion.

One of the cloaks under which mendicants commonly work is that of salesmanship. Beggars sell matches, pencils, shoestrings, and other relatively valueless articles; "poor hungry children" sell newspapers and magazines; and college students solicit subscriptions for periodicals. The beggars of London carry this salesmanship to its logical conclusion when they offer for sale earthenware containers of ferns too large for any pedestrian to carry away. One of the appeals combining begging and selling is that used by the "ex-service man," for example. He sells for ten cents some trifle in an envelope bearing an inscription like the following: "OVER THE TOP. For the Benefit of a WORLD WAR VETERAN. I am not looking for sympathy or charity from you. Just selling these items to see my way through! Stand By the Ex-Service Men!"

The problem of determining where begging ceases and legitimate salesmanship begins is a difficult task. However, as a working hypothesis it is safe to say that where an article is sold on a basis of the real or imagined needs of the seller, the transaction is begging. When on the other hand, an article is sold on the merits of the goods or on a basis of the needs of the buyer, the sale is legitimate.

That the cloak of salesmanship often soothes the conscience of the beggar as well as the giver is not to be questioned. Many an amateur beggar could not bring himself to appeal outright for alms, but, though making his appeal as pathetic as possible, he could bring himself to sell matches or shoestrings, and in his own mind feel that he was a legitimate salesman. Likewise many conscientious donors will be immune to the most pitiful appeal of a candid beggar but will drop a quarter in the box of a pseudo-salesman and take a pencil in return. The cloak of salesmanship thus shields the conscience both of the beggar and the giver and secures for beggars many gifts which they would not otherwise receive.

Beggars also work under the shield of borrowing, and here the beggar fades imperceptibly into the petty swindler. Pretending to be stranded in the city because of having been robbed, claiming to have work in another city but no money for transportation, feigning to have work but no tools to work with, or any other possible circumstance for needing cash may be used as a pretext to "touch" a stranger for a loan. The "loan" turns into a gift through sheer default of payment. Many such beggars have a studied cleverness in making their stories seem genuine. As a fortification against any doubt, they often pose as an acquaintance of some friend of the person solicited, and their ability to muster facts which will substantiate such friendship is phenomenal. The writer speaks of these swindlers with the mature wisdom gained from a three-dollar experience with one of their number.

About 10:30 one midwinter evening, the writer was sitting peacefully in his room when suddenly he was brought to earth by the sound of knocking at a professor's room next door. Knowing that the occupant was out, the writer proceeded to give this information to the caller. The stranger was found to be a well-clad young man of polished appearance. When told that the professor was out for the evening, he appeared somewhat puzzled and slightly embarrassed. Upon being properly encouraged, he told his informant that he was a former student in the university and a special friend of the said professor. In "old grad" fashion he inquired about the welfare of various faculty members and of certain "landmark" personalities among the clerical force. Finally reaching his "present predicament," he disclosed that he lived some fifty miles from the university, that he had been to a dance in the city, had car trouble, and found he had insufficient funds with which to have the car repaired. His special concern, he revealed, was that he had brought a young lady with him for whose safe return he felt highly responsible. After learning that the extent of the young man's need was only three dollars, the writer, in a fit of chivalrous generosity, advanced the cash, bid the visitor a hearty adieu, and returned to his room with the solace of having been a good Samaritan. Later it was learned that the recipient was a well known beggar-swindler who had secured hundreds of loans on similar pretexts. The debt in this instance is still outstanding.

A begging swindler somewhat akin to the borrowing beggar is the beggar who purports to solicit funds not for himself but for some worthy cause. It is not his own needs which he portrays, but the needs of the cause which he represents. Sometimes these beggars are self-appointed representatives of legitimate and well-known organizations or movements. In other cases, the institution which they pretend to represent is purely fictitious. In any case, of course, they use the funds for themselves.

In St. Louis two crafty beggars appointed themselves collectors for the "Rummage Sale Charities." They made their headquarters in an old residence which had seen better days. By means of a house-to-house telephone directory arranged for them by schoolboys in odd hours, they would call all the residents on a selected street, and inquire if they would be willing to donate old clothes, cradles, furniture, magazines, and other debris which accumulates around the home to the "Rummage Sale Charities" for the relief of the needy. Having secured the resident's assent, arrangements would be made for a

wagon to call on a certain day when the articles would
be ready. The articles thus collected were assorted and
put into bins according to kind. They were then sold to
used furniture dealers, old clothes dealers, and other
buyers interested in the various wares. The proceeds went
to the two "needy" beggars.[3]

Beggars also collect alms under the guise of tips, and here
the beggar is sometimes hard to distinguish from the minister,
the evangelist, and other philanthropically supported public
servants. Posing as traveling evangelists, entertainers, or actors,
they, of their own accord, perform some service to incur the
obligation of the audience. Unsolicited, they make the audience their debtor. Then they pass the cup to square the account. In form, the beggar volunteers to give the audience
entertainment, and the audience volunteers to give the beggar
an undetermined sum in return. In this manner, the beggars
of some countries have a monopoly on the whole business of
entertaining.

> "The business of entertaining [in Mogador] is closely al-
> lied to mendicancy. There is no theatrical 'profession.' The
> amusement artists do not draw regular pay. As they are
> dependent on what people will give them, they have been
> shrewd enough to sanctify their calling to share in the
> bounty of alms." [4]

In modern America, such procedure is to be classed with
begging, probably on the basis of an assumption which, in our
conventions, underlies tipping, namely, that tipping assumes
a status of superiority in the giver and of inferiority in the
recipient. One of the oldest and best-known begging devices
of this kind is the traditional organ-grinder with his trained
monkey. Today organ-grinders have not disappeared but they
are less common than in days of yore. Traveling evangelists
who assemble crowds on street corners, in Salvation Army

[3] See "Putting Fake Beggars to Work," *Literary Digest*, XLVIII
(1914), 509-12.
[4] Albert Edwards, "The Beggars of Mogador," *Outlook*, CI (1912),
932.

style, are frequently encountered, and volunteer entertainers are seen occasionally.

Recently, on a boat which runs from Manhattan to Coney Island, a group of begging musicians were observed. A trio, apparently of Italian descent and dressed rather neatly, they were the only entertainers on board. Moving on the decks from one crowd of vacationers to another, they would play a few pieces for each gathering and then pass a cup for tips.

Begging, like acting, appeals essentially to the emotions. Indeed, it might well be thought of as the most natural form of the dramatic art. And since modern begging appeals primarily to pity, it might be classed as tragedy.

Since begging is a growing and a changing art, not conventionalized into definite schools, its devices are legion and of a wide variety. To completely catalogue them would require a volume of encyclopedic proportions, and such a volume would be obsolete before it could be published. These devices do fall into general categories, however, and it is possible to give a representative portrait of the art without giving a complete description of each device. This chapter will include, therefore, only a few interesting and selected samples from the beggar's repertoire.

The beggar's first principle is to depict to his audience a tale of woe in the quickest time possible. Without any scenery, except such as the street corner or the office affords, he must seize the attention of a transient and uninterested audience and in a single moment portray a story of tragedy, and do it forcefully enough to gain the sympathy of his audience and bring forth gifts against their intentions. True he leaves details to the imagination, but that is art. Even so, his task is not so simple or so easy as one might think.

Perhaps the beggar's highest attainments are in the class of devices which might be termed one-act plays. The most clever of these are designed for a public weary of pauperism and philosophically opposed to almsgiving. They catch the giver unawares, attract his attention before he knows it, and arouse a pulsating sympathy before his deliberate judgment has time to assert itself. Many such plays require a cast of two or more. A mother, father, and child, dressed in all semblance of humble country people and laden with suitcases, trudge along the sidewalks of a busy street. Having scrutinized the pedestrians carefully, they stop some kindly gentleman and inquire where they can get beds for ten cents each. Tactfully they reveal that they have just arrived in town and have had their money stolen by a pickpocket. Or, some night on a shadowy street in a business section, a woman, appearing to be in a well-advanced state of pregnancy and having a small child with her, begins to light matches and look along the gutter. The unusual procedure brings to her aid curious and well-meaning persons who offer their assistance. Upon inquiry she reveals that she has lost her purse containing all of her money and her return ticket. She lives, so she says, in a distant suburb. Such are the one-act plays which fall in this class. Perhaps one of the most clever, though not so frequently used, devices of this nature is the "drowning act," which requires a cast of three.

For the "drowning act," a river, a canal, or some other body of water located close to a business street is a necessary setting. One beggar, dressed as an impoverished and discouraged member of the "white collar class," leaps into the water as if to drown himself. A second beggar swims out and rescues the would-be suicide. By the time the rescuer has reached shore with the "drowning man" a crowd has inevitably gathered. Among the gathering is a third beggar, well dressed and apparently of comfortable means, who steps forward and asks the man why he attempted to take his life. The latter replies that he has been out of work for over a year, has met failure wherever he turned, and has had nothing to eat for the past two days. Thereupon, the well-dressed beggar takes a hat, places a five dollar bill in it, and suggests to the crowd that they join him in helping to give the man a new lease on life. The response is usually most generous.

Beggars do not always work in groups, however. They often work individually, and there are very effective one-act plays which a single beggar may execute. Like many other arts, begging can best be studied abroad. It is in Paulian's interesting little book, *The Beggars of Paris*, that one finds a classic example of a begging drama for one actor.

"One Sunday, in the place Victor-Hugo, at the time when many ladies troop out of the church, Saint-Honoré d'Eylau, a woman dressed in black fell into the basin of the fountain which is in the middle of the square. There was a rush to her rescue and whilst a gentleman pulled her out of the water, a lady picked up a Prayer-book, and chaplet which the poor lady had let tumble to the ground in her fall. A crowd gathers, several ladies offer their services, and they conduct the victim of the accident into a porter's lodge, where they made her drink some cordial.

"While dry clothes are being procured for the poor woman they question her, and ask if she has hurt herself—if she wishes them to take her to her home. The woman in the wet clothes does not answer; she is hunting for some object which she seems to care very much about.

" 'What are you looking for, madam?'

" 'My Prayer-book and chaplet.'

" 'Here they are.'

" 'Oh, thank Heaven! I thought I had lost them. I value them so much!' And the unhappy woman states that she is a widow; that she was going to church to give the last piece of twenty sous she possessed to have mass said, that her son, her only son, a soldier in Tonkin, might be speedily restored to her.

"You can easily guess the effect produced by this story upon the hearts of all, and especially on the purses of all of the ladies coming out of church. Soon a collection is made; they hand about fifteen francs to the poor woman; they give her clothing, and have her taken back to her home in a carriage.

"A week later the same accident occurred in the ornamental water in the Champs Elysées. . . .

"The following week the fountain Saint-Michel becomes the theatre for an accident of the same kind, and at last the *préfet* of the police discovers that a woman, called Louise Buffet, always the same, has found this ingenious way of making a small income for herself." [5]

Somewhat similar to these one-act plays is a sort of combination entertainment drama. In this form of appeal, the beggar does not disguise the fact that he is appealing for alms, nor does he carry out a dialogue which works up to an impressive conclusion. Rather, he uses a physical handicap or a make-up to tell his story, and he uses music to attract attention and to appeal to sentiment in the heart of the giver. Real artists with a device of this kind were the Hampstone family.

The Hampstone family consisted of a blind father, a blind mother, and three normal children. For several years they begged regularly in front of an old church in a downtown business section. This church was located in the heart of the business district and had a lawn some sixty feet in depth which bordered on one of the busiest sidewalks. The Hampstones had a small folding organ which they placed on the church lawn adjacent to the sidewalk, and on the organ they placed a cup. The mother and father, dressed very shabbily, sat behind the organ, and the children grouped around them in the manner of an old-fashioned family singing. Thus posed, the mother would play while they all sang such songs as "The Old Rugged Cross." In spite of the daily recurrence of this spectacle, the response was, to say the least, generous.

Even more closely related to the one-act play than the entertainment drama is the plain pantomime. In this the beggar says nothing at all, but through his actions portrays his need. The classical example of this type of appeal is what is known as "the crust-throwing act," which is supposed to have been invented by a German beggar named Lang and was

[5] Louis M. Paulian, *The Beggars of Paris,* trans. Lady Herschell (New York, 1897), pp. 85-86.

passed on to modern beggars through a French disciple, Lemaire.[6]

The author encountered one of these crust-throwing artists about two o'clock one afternoon while stopping in a small restaurant for a late lunch. Being an off hour, there were no other customers but himself when he entered. Just as his order had been filled, however, a decently dressed man of some thirty years came in, seated himself beside the author at the counter, and ordered a cup of coffee. While the waiter was getting the coffee, this gentleman gazed longingly at the author's plate as if to have some day such a meal (very unpretentious at that) was the sole dream and ambition in his life. Having heard of the crust-throwing act, the author watched the newcomer as carefully as possible without appearing too obvious in his intentions. At a propitious moment the man looked down on the floor, saw a piece of dry bread, seized it, and began eating it as if totally famished. Not a word was said, no request was made. For an observer not acquainted with the trick, none would have been needed. Without a doubt, the man, as all such beggars do, had unobtrusively placed the bread there when he came in.

Perhaps the most common of the begging devices is the still scene or tableau. The word beggar, to most people, probably brings to mind a picture of an old man dressed in tattered clothes sitting on a sidewalk, wearing a "Help the Blind" placard, and holding in his hand a tin cup or a box of pencils. It is this type of device which may be classed as the still scene or tableau. Through a skillful combination of old clothes, facial expression, and real or faked physical defect, the beggar presents a picture of distress which portrays to each person a different, but always similar, tale of woe. The pictures thus depicted by beggars are as numerous and as varied as the works of sculptors. They always, however, dwell on one of two themes. They either portray a physical handicap—blind, crip-

[6] T. Waters, "Six Weeks in Beggardom," *Everybody's Magazine*, XII (1905), 75.

pled, or deformed—or they depict a state of mental distress—pain, discomfort, dejection, poverty, or worry. A "high-powered" scene will embody both a physical handicap and mental distress. The still scene is often altered to the extent of a spoken solicitation to "help the blind," and after the gift comes a benediction of "God bless you." The latter is doubtless a carry-over from past centuries when almsgiving was a religious act.

In the one-act play, the entertainment drama, the pantomime, and the tableau, the beggar's appeal is in part or in whole to the sight of the giver. His personal appearance, therefore, accounts for much of the success which he attains. The art of make-up and of impersonation have long been integral parts of the mendicant's art. Many a poor wretch who is maimed or deformed needs no further exaggeration of his appearance than careless dress will give. Those not naturally "blessed" with such repulsive features, however, have to alter their appearance to simulate a more pitiful condition. To do this, they put acid on their arms to make "jiggers" (sores resembling insect bites), collodion in their eyes to make "blindmen"; they make liberal use of crutches, bandages, and false legs, partially throw joints out of place, and do other things to fake physical handicaps; and they use tattered or scanty clothes to simulate poverty and misery. The art is a very old one, and it was perhaps more highly developed in the Middle Ages, when there was more freedom from human consideration, than it is today. However,

"there is an extraordinary similarity between the practices of the beggars and vagrants at home and abroad in the Middle Ages. Skin diseases, inflammation and ulcers were counterfeited by the juice of plants, a mixture of lard and blood, and other nasty devices; they disguised themselves with patches, bandages, plasters and crutches so as not to be known from day to day in the same place; they paraded as maimed soldiers from the wars; they showed forged certificates of having been bitten by wolves or dogs or having escaped from prisons or galleys of the infidel

Turks; they posed as dropsical or otherwise diseased, women padded themselves to appear as with child, or begged with a child at breast and another carried at back or side; they counterfeited the demoniac or epileptic by feigned fits and soap in the mouth to create froth, inflicting wounds as proof of sincerity, others stood almost naked in public places pretending extreme want and starvation like the Shivering Jimmies of a later time, and so through a long list." [7]

While the above description is of mendicants of the Middle Ages, many of the devices mentioned sound strikingly familiar even to the lay giver. And when the inside story is known, the similarity is still more striking. It is doubtful, however, that any beggars of today break the arms, legs, or backs of their children or put out their eyes, as some claim was a mendicant practice in the Middle Ages.

Beggars by no means confine themselves to the use of a pitiful scene to portray their appeal; they also make use of the oral narrative. The so-called "hard luck story" is extensively used by the amateur and by the studied professional. Hundreds of such stories have been invented by beggars of the past, and are as common knowledge among beggars today as Mother Goose rhymes are among children. Others are formulated daily to suit the fancy of imaginative beggars.

The hard luck story is a tale of woe in which the beggar is the suffering hero. Supposedly it relates the chain of events which produced the beggar's present misery, usually events over which the beggar had no control and for which he was in no way responsible. He is the innocent and pitiful victim of unfortunate circumstances. The story is carefully planned, well rounded, and leads up to a fitting climax. Instead of the hero "getting married and living happily ever after," the poor innocent beggar has the hand of ill fate crush down upon him and lives in misery ever afterward, or will live in misery unless the donor sets the world rosy by proffering a gift.

[7] J. Cooke, "Vagrants, Beggars, and Tramps," *Quarterly Review*, CCIX (1908), 395.

"The very completeness, the perfect art of the professional tale of woe should be its undoing. Like the well rounded excuse of the culprit, it is all thought out beforehand, and the public should know that so many perfect 'plots' are without the bounds of probability. The professional is well aware of this, but he is also aware that the public likes its morsel of woe served well done. Does not the whole theatre-going public pay nightly to applaud just such well-rounded plots in spite of the knowledge that in the drama of real life the dialogue and the incidents are seldom in sequence?" [8]

To distinguish the story of a professional from that of a real unfortunate is sometimes difficult, and for the layman, often impossible. However, in addition to the well-rounded plot of the professional, there are other characteristic marks which may be recognized with practice. There is a striking similarity among the incidents embodied in the various stories, and certain diseases occur with unwarranted frequency. Also, when one hears the stories of numerous beggars, some of the more common stereotyped tales become familiar. Thus, when within two or three days a half dozen beggars profess to have been the victim of identical misfortunes, one may well question the veracity of the mendicants. With sufficient practice, therefore, it is possible to become a connoisseur of professional tales.

"A curious lack of inventive ability and a scantiness of versatility are shown in the way these details are rehearsed repeatedly verbatim. I have heard that identical story as many as seven times in one day. Even the very forms of disease from which they had suffered in the hospital are all stereotyped; the favorites are pleurisy, heart disease, or others which show no symptoms." [9]

[8] Waters, "Six Weeks in Beggardom," *Everybody's Magazine*, XII (1905), 76.
[9] "A Clergyman's Study of the Stranded," *World's Work*, IV (1902), 2513.

From the standpoint of art, it is a far cry from the stereotyped tale of a panhandler or a petty salesman to the persuasive tactics of a polished professional who approaches a
businessman in the quiet of his office and asks for a substantial
gift or for a loan. It is no stereotyped tale which the real professional tells to his wealthy prospect. With consummate care,
the beggar gathers facts about the businessman's past and
present, his friends and schoolmates, and his likes and dislikes.
Thus armed, he frames his tale to fit this particular client.
Posing as a "friend of a friend," the beggar approaches the
businessman as an equal who has met reverses or is in a temporary predicament. Just how beggars get all this information
on prospective givers is not easy to determine. Some of it
they get from newspapers; other bits they get from people
who are acquainted with the man or know about him, the
remainder may come from numerous more or less accidental
sources. When a beggar has once used such information, it is
no longer of any value to him, and he may exchange it with
another beggar for similar information on some other man. To
expedite the transfer of information, the beggars of Paris devised directories of donors, which were known as the "little
game" and the "big game."

> "The 'little game' costs three francs; it gives you the
> names and addresses of some hundreds of charitable peo-
> ple. The 'big game' costs six francs; naturally it is more
> complete. Not only does it contain a larger number of
> addresses, but to each name is added a small biography.
> The name and address of the charitable person, the hour
> at which one may call, his religion, political opinions, hab-
> its—nothing is forgotten.   .
> "Thanks to this valuable book, the beggar's part is much
> simplified; for he can ascertain even the small peculiarities
> of the person at whose door he is going to knock, and
> how he should present himself." [10]

[10] Paulian, *The Beggars of Paris*, p. 26. A similar publication was found
by New York authorities. For a description of it, see John D. Godfrey,
"A Capable Beggar Makes from $15 to $500 a Day," *American Magazine*,
XCIV (1922), 11.

Beggars have a fertile imagination for devising temporary predicaments or causes for permanent distress, and it would be an arduous task to list all of the plots around which their stories are built. Some form of unemployment or sickness is most common, with widowhood among women ranking a close second. Other common roles are the "respectable" person who has been robbed, the commuter who has lost his purse, the confessor who makes his confession the basis of a plea for help, and former "aristocrats" who have met reverses.

Another form of appeal which is used both by clever and by mediocre beggars is the begging letter. Like the hard luck story, some begging letters are strictly stereotyped while others are not. Some begging letter forms have been used for decades, and exactly the same form may be used for years by the same beggar.

Like any other form of written or printed communication, the begging letter has many advantages from the standpoint of the beggar. Through the begging letter, the mendicant may sit in the quiet comfort of his home or office and present his appeal to numerous prospects without suffering any of the discomforts of street begging or without expending the energy needed to call on men or women in the home or office. Furthermore, except in rare instances of an interested person who looks him up, he need not come face to face with the giving public. Thus, it is not necessary for him to put on old clothes, false legs, or other make-up to impress the public. With all of the comforts of an office worker and with a paid stenographer if he desires one, he may carry on his work in ease and at the same time address his appeal to a larger audience than he could reach with face to face contacts.

The simplest form of begging letter, a form which hardly deserves the name, is the begging note which is presented personally by the beggar to the prospect. Some such beggars are deaf and dumb, others play the role of a deaf-mute, while still others simply refuse to talk. Such notes contain in a brief form hard luck stories similar to those used by beggars in their oral appeal. The beggar has been in a hospital and is convalescing

from a serious illness, he has an incurable disease and is unable
to work, he is a World War veteran who received incapacitat-
ing injuries in action, or he is a tubercular trying to get to
Arizona. Some of these notes appear to have been, and sometimes are, written by the beggar's physician, or minister, others
purport to have been written by a friend or by the beggar
himself. A careful observation of such notes reveals that not a
few are stained by the touch of many hands, and many of
them are so worn from repeated foldings and unfoldings that
they are hardly legible. A date occasionally reveals that the
letter is several years old. This type of begging is, on the
whole, decidedly crude and unimaginative. Many such beggars are less than mediocre in their ability and some are actually feeble-minded. Nearly any giver could easily find grounds
for suspicion in such notes, yet no beggar using one has been
known to starve.

Probably the most common form of begging letter in America a few years back was the chain letter. Doubtless most
persons of middle age or past can recall having received one
of these letters. Such letters usually told the hard luck story
and gave the name and address of some supposedly unfortunate person, and contained the promise that, if you would
send this person a quarter and would send copies of this letter
to seven of your friends, some good fortune would come your
way. The appeal was both to pity and superstition. So long as
the device worked, it worked well. With an adequate supply
of superstitious people, such a letter, once started, might continue to circulate and bring in returns for years. Indeed, with
a willing public, a beggar whose address was in a chain, might
have a lucrative and indefinite pension. Though experiencing
great popularity a few years back, the chain letter seems at
present to be decidedly on the wane. It is giving way to other
forms of begging letters.

The begging letter which probably has experienced most
rapid growth in recent times is the newspaper letter. The publication of a begging letter in a newspaper not only reaches
many prospective givers, but it also gives the letter more cred-

ibility than an individual letter might have. Though the reading public has lost much of its unquestioning reverence for
newspapers, the printed line still carries considerable weight.
Many readers have a feeling, however vague, that the case
must be deserving or the paper would not publish the story.
Many of the smaller papers do not make a regular practice of
publishing begging letters but do make exceptions to their
rule in special cases. When such a policy is known to the
readers, the letters which are published carry the sanction of
the publication and are accepted without question by most
of the subscribers.

The Thames family lived in a small city and secured
their livelihood principally from begging letters. The
father pretended to be a carpenter and worked some, but
in comparison with the family's expenditures his earnings
were insignificant. They owned their home and drove a
car. The two daily papers in the city did not make a practice of publishing begging letters and had repeatedly refused to accept letters sent in by the family. Finally,
however, by accident or intention, the home was burned.
The following day both papers carried a write-up of the
fire and included an appeal for help written by the family
itself. The response to the publication of these appeals was
so generous that there were secured not only sufficient
funds to rebuild the house, but a substantial amount in
addition.

The daily papers in large cities receive so many requests
to publish begging letters that some of them have established
a special column for such solicitations. The intention of the
papers in establishing such columns is doubtless perfectly
laudable. When a paper establishes such a column, however,
many readers make inferences which are in no way justified
by the claims of the publication. Numerous subscribers assume
that, if a paper has such a column, it also has a staff for investigating the cases and selecting for publication only the deserving. Unfortunately, such is not generally true. An adequate
investigation is seldom made. Any sort of fake, therefore, can

publish an appeal, and the public is more gullible than it might otherwise be. An investigation made by Freund of begging letters published in the "Sally Joy Brown Column" of the *Chicago Tribune* indicates that there is widespread abuse of such columns.

"In January 1924 fifty-three appeals appeared in the column. Sources of information were interviewed and twenty-nine of the applicants were visited by the investigators. These twenty-nine were the ones whose needs, according to the news articles, appeared greatest. Other requests were insignificant or the applicant not to be located. Thirteen cases where the regular income exceeded the budget allowance arrived at by scientific principles for use by the United Charities as a standard above which a family of given size is expected to live in comfortable independence, and two cases where relatives stood ready, able and willing to meet the needs rather than have the applicants receive alms were responsible for the conclusion that the use of the Sally Joy Brown Column is sometimes, apparently often, a refined form of begging." [11]

The begging letter which most truly justifies the name is that which is sent directly from a beggar to a giver. In general these letters are of two types, circular and personal. Some beggars, employing "mass production," prefer making a casual contact with many prospects rather than working a few more carefully. By securing addresses from telephone directories and other sources, they are able to send out letters in such large numbers that only a partial response will mean a substantial income. The heart of the letter is, of course, a hard luck story. Frequently the begging is vaguely concealed by a selling device. With the letter is enclosed a package of seeds, an envelope of moth powders, a key ring label, or some other trivial object. The letter notifies the prospect that the sender is a poverty-stricken man of sixty-three, has been blind for

[11] R. H. Freund, "Begging in Chicago," unpublished Master's thesis, University of Chicago, 1925, p. 31.

twenty years, has an invalid wife and two orphan grandchildren depending on him, and that the income from his seeds is his sole source of support. In exchange for the package of seeds, the customer is asked to remit ten, fifteen, or twenty-five cents.

Not all begging letter writers are content to fish for dime gifts; many of them labor in terms of ten- to one-hundred-dollar donations. For such gifts the skillfully devised personal letter is required. It is in these appeals that the art of writing begging letters has real expression. Of course, not all people who write personal begging letters are artists, many of them are crude and unimaginative and abuse unmercifully the English language. Many who attempt the practice are failures, and others would be were their letters not such pitiful failures as to inspire sympathy. There are a few artists, however, who have tact and literary ability and whose letters are masterpieces of pathetic appeal. Such ability is well rewarded.

The artistic begging letter usually contains four parts; an apology, a tale of woe, a request for aid, and a promise. The beggar begins his letter by expressing his deep regret at having to burden the reader with such unpleasant matters, but he states that he is in such desperate straits that he must call on someone. Then comes the hard luck story which may be built around any one of a hundred unfortunate circumstances. This story leads up to the beggar's needs. Perhaps he is about to be evicted and must have at once $22.50 for rent, $11.00 for groceries, $7.50 for coal, and $9.30 for clothes, a total of $50.30. The real artist always states his needs in terms of a definite amount. Then follows the request, hope, or prayer that the reader can help out to the extent of a third, a half, or all of the amount required. In closing, the beggar swears by all the powers that be that if the donors will help him this one time he will never appeal again, or at least not until after a certain date. To give practical proof of the claims which they make, such beggars frequently attach to their letters eviction papers, pawn shop tickets, bills, and other evidence of financial distress. A man beggar and a woman beggar are even reported

to have gotten married just so they could get in the "eviction
paper racket." Whether enclosed with the letter or not, a wise
beggar will be armed with such evidence in case he is called
on by a solicitous giver or is investigated by the police. He
may intentionally let his rent go unpaid and even let eviction
papers be served, or he may pawn clothing and other belong-
ings whether he needs money or not.

Some writers of personal begging letters confine their appeals to past or present friends, acquaintances, or employers
with whom they have had some contact. These beggars are
professional only in the sense that their letter writing is a
habitual practice. Their claims usually have a basis in fact,
but their difficulties frequently are unconsciously magnified
by their imagination or are purposely exaggerated in the
account which they give. This type of begging, from one
point of view, is little more than an abuse of the privileges
of friendship. Wilson secures a livelihood through this sort of
exaggeration and abuse.

Wilson is a man forty-two years of age, is married and
has four children. He is the descendant of a fairly well-to-
do family and has near relatives of the comfortably situated middle class. Being the youngest child in the family,
he was not only spoiled to the extent of developing irre-
sponsibility but he also developed offensive personality
traits which have been a handicap to him, both economically and socially. He is stubborn, quarrelsome, and
cannot under any circumstance take orders from others.
He has had a number of jobs, but in each case has lost it
through difficulties with his employer. Therefore, he has
always been an economic failure. His relatives in years
past have helped him some but have had such difficulty
in getting along with him that they have more or less discarded any responsibility. His principal income for some
years has been derived from begging letters which he
writes to former friends of the family and to his acquaintances. Beginning with a distrust of his former employers,
he has gradually developed a paranoia complex. He now
believes that the Masons and the Catholics, in addition to

several individuals, are on his trail, and he lives in absolute mental agony. While he lives in perfect horror of the next day, at the same time, he entertains the hope that sooner or later his day will come and he will get his just dues. His begging letters reflect his present mental agony, his fear of the morrow, and his distant hope. He does not purposely misrepresent his condition, therefore, when he appeals for help, but his chronic state of mind greatly colors the facts.

The real letter writing artist does not limit himself to friends and acquaintances. In fact, he usually does not beg from friends at all. He does not wish to have his opportunities limited to the income of his acquaintances, nor does he wish to have his imagination fettered by being confined to facts. The beggar knows that as distance lends enchantment, so the misery of the distant poor appears more pitiable than the misery of those at closer range. He also knows that the tragedies of real life can be made more tragic in a well-rounded fiction. He prefers, therefore, to play on the sympathy of donors who know nothing of his past or present and who are in a financial position to give. With the free play of his imagination he can write for such a prospect stories worth reading, and can make of himself a hero deserving of aid.

The conquests of large gifts usually cannot be carried through in one letter and may envolve a correspondence covering a number of years. The sympathies of the donor must be aroused and he must be convinced of the validity of the claims made. In addition, real success, like a continued story, often depends on getting his interest so aroused that he is determined to see the drama through to the end. Then he may stop counting costs and start handing out gifts of unbelievable size. In such a process, the first letter and the first gift are just the beginning; the follow-up letters are the really important part of the art.

In the following case study, the begging letter writer succeeded in getting quite large gifts over a considerable period of time. Her technique of keeping givers interested once they started giving is good. The case also reveals how the stories of skilled beggars are often built on half-truths.

CASE STUDY

"Mrs. 'T' was a daughter of what appears to have been a highly respectable Chicago family. She was educated in an Eastern school and married at the age of 17. In 1920, at the age of 38 she had divorced 'T,' her third husband, and returned to the family estate and luxurious home on the South Side, Chicago, where her recently widowed mother lived alone. The father had been a man of some means, but after his death in 1918 it was revealed that all of his wealth had been placed in Colorado mining stock which during the War depreciated to practically no value. He left no insurance and the homestead was heavily mortgaged.

"The mother, aged 79, had suffered the amputation of both legs and in 1920 was a helpless dependent on her daughter. The mortgages on the homestead were foreclosed during the summer and bankruptcy was declared. Furniture and a share in the unsettled estate were all that remained. In the fall, Mrs. T. and her mother moved into an 'humble' apartment, rent $85 per month, and from there Mrs. T. sent out the following letter:

'Chicago, Illinois
September 21, 1920

Mr. B. N.
Jackson Boulevard
Kind sir:

A copy of this letter I'm mailing to the following ten influential business men. (Following a list of Chicago's wealthiest business men.)

Mr. B. B. C.	Mr. K. U. G.
Mr. S. U. D.	Mr. B. S. S.
Mr. K. W. G.	Mr. N. B. S.
Mr. D. G. N.	Mr. B. N.
Mr. K. N. D.	Mr. P. G. T.

As each and every one of you are men of broad business standing, the writer feels the request herewith made will meet with response. Without details, only where cared for, the writer begs to state she is at present a shut-in with a mother of 80 years who has recently been obliged to have both limbs amputated. We are at present without funds for current monthly expenses. If each of the ten gentlemen appealed to will kindly donate the tenth part —that I may raise $100.00, we shall manage to get along thereafter in a meager fashion. My mother's condition and the handicap to me is my excuse for needing and asking for sincere aid. This $100.00 I need to defray September rent, long overdue, plus two gas and electric light bills, groceries, etc. I have no one to whom to turn. So I ask *you* who I believe will help me over this hurdle. Know that it is a *dire* necessity that forces me to apply at large for aid. It is the eleventh hour for us. Out of our last dollar I will buy the stamps for these ten letters. But surely it will not be in vain. I feel it is not necessary to burden you with my whole story, for if you are inclined to help me I am sure my appeal will be sufficient. However, I am at home to any inquiry. Trusting my call awakens your sympathy, I will thank you after such time.

Conscientiously,

M. T.'

"Six of the gentlemen receiving this letter sent copies of it to an organized agency of relief, asking investigation. A seventh sent his own investigator. The visitor found the situation essentially as stated. Bills were presented and the seven-room, well-furnished apartment explained by the intent of renting out the three rooms as a means of support. Other work would also be attempted by Mrs. T. The report of the visitors was therefore very favorable to the refined Mrs. T. and before three weeks had expired she had received from $10 to $25 from each of nine of the gentlemen applied to, one hundred and thirty dollars in all.

"Attempts on the part of the visitors used by these generous men to aid Mrs. T. in carrying out her plan to place the crippled mother in a suitable home and find work for herself were frustrated at every turn by that lady herself. Further investigation, however, showed that her three rooms had been rented out. The record of the father's estate showed it to be still unsettled due to the fact that no buyer could be found for the mining stock at any price. The court record of bankruptcy showed that between June, 1918, and February, 1920, Mrs. T. had borrowed in cash $4,228 and bills covering household expenditures amounting to $2,166. Evidently all this money had been used up in the year and eight months period.

"The next letter which called for another investigation appeared in July, 1921:

'Dear sir:

I asked Mr. K. U. G. to loan me $200.00 in order that I might meet the demands of $215.00 for taxes and assessments against my late father's unsettled estate. Mr. G. said he would contribute $25.00 and thought the other nine gentlemen who assisted me last fall would be likely to do the same. So, here I am making my second appeal to all who so kindly helped me over the rent pressure last October. Mother and I are located in a more suitable flat this year, and my mother stands the heat quite well, considering. We could manage to pull through until next May when the time for final settlement of my father's estate is set, but to meet this call for taxes, and assessments on unpatented mining claims, was beyond me to handle. However I am naturally anxious to conserve our interests and to do so was obliged to look beyond my personal efforts for this $215.00. I deplore seeking "charity" a second time but as Mr. G. says, I should not be so concerned, for anyone is liable to need a lift. I shall consider all favors, as before, as debts to be squared when I am in position to do so. It was unfortunate my father's death at an abnormal national period and his assets being principally mining stocks—same has been held in abeyance until conditions were more favorable to an adjustment. Had the estate been closed this year we would have prospered little, but now with tariff bill favorable to Tungsten we anticipate the Tungsten industry will take on new life, and the estate,

when closed next May, be a matter of just returns. And I
long to return all favors extended me. We have pulled
along with all the handicaps, my mother's great affliction,
high prices, etc., for three and one half years, so of course,
I am anxious to conserve our interests the rest of the few
months intervening between now and next May.

If you and the other eight gentlemen consider to do as
Mr. G. has agreed and suggested, this matter of $215.00
will be cared for as it must by the end of July. I expect
Mr. G.'s check tomorrow as advised by phone today. Last
fall I received $25.00 as a "final" on the request I made.
It came from Mr. N. S. or from you for I had already
heard from eight. I never learned who was the kind person, so must at present thank both.

Grateful for your consideration,
M. T.'

"Investigation following the receipt of this letter revealed that the new address was a 'commodious, well
furnished apartment in the University neighborhood where
apartments are very expensive.' She had married a Mr.
A. A. who had formerly roomed with her. She was in-
censed at this investigation, declaring she was only seeking a loan. She refused to show any bills for taxes and her
lawyer, greatly surprised to learn of Mrs. T.'s request,
declared there were no assessments on the estate while
pending settlement. This information deterred some of the
gentlemen from giving again but others were loath to
believe her dishonest. Those who assisted her continued
to get appeals throughout 1922 and 1923. Excerpts from
a letter dated May 13, 1923, are as follows:

'Being most grateful for having been brought through
the months since last November when last I appealed to
you, it is in great part against my conscience that I now
relate to you some present circumstances.... I rejoice that
I have had shelter and food and other necessities.... In
January I stated to Mr. P. G. T. that I felt sure the time
was past.... Mr. T. considered me to a marked degree
at that time.... This storage expense of $25 a month [ref-

erence to which appears in some of former correspond-
ence] ... Mr. G. most kindly sent me $25 last week with
the suggestion that I refer the situation to others who had
formerly assisted me. I follow his advice by writing to
three gentlemen who may see fit to further favor my
cause.... My mother is comfortably sheltered. She is now
81½ years of age and today, Mothers Day, I can spend the
afternoon with her.... Please indulge this tendency to
drift into lengthy recital. No one can give, even *meagerly*
without retaining some interest in the progress of the
beneficiary. Hoping the months have dealt kindly with
you.

Most sincerely,
M. T.'

"Following this, the record of Mrs. T.'s life, past and
present, was more carefully investigated. It was learned
that for years she had kept up membership in various
women's clubs and made friends there only to beg and
borrow of them later. Business men other than the ten
were discovered who showed stacks of letters from Mrs.
M. T., asking from $5 to $50 each appeal. Mrs. T. had
separated from Mr. A. A. a few months after their marriage and it was learned that at the time of their marriage,
Mr. A. A., a gentleman of foreign nobility, had held a very
good position in a language and music school but that
Mrs. T. had made such use of his relation with the school
in her begging from its patrons that he had been dis-
charged. The marriage had taken place in May, 1920,
prior to the first reported letters that led to investigation.
For several months they lived at the Trenier Hotel, occu-
pying a $35 a week suite. A check of $90, quarterly pension paid by the government to Mrs. T.'s mother, as wife
of a Civil War veteran, and another check from the presi-
dent of a leading Chicago bank were offered as part
payment. When the unpaid bill rose to $410 the couple
was evicted and nothing ever collected on the account.
It was learned that Mrs. T. had a twenty-eight year old
son whose record since his army discharge contains shady
transactions and trouble with his second wife. Mrs. T.

denied any present knowledge or correspondence with him.

"The last known of Mrs. T. was September, 1923, when she was known to be living alone working as an addresser of envelopes at piece rate, continuing to write her letters to explain her desperate need of a definite amount for a specific purpose. Twelve of her letters to different persons are on file. Mrs. T. states in one of them that one gracious lady responded in 1923 with a check for $500.00 and the secretary of Mr. G. declares the latter sent her over $200.00 in small amounts during the three years. The last letters continued to refer to the shortly anticipated sale of Tungsten stocks. From all reports and information from Colorado these stocks are now valueless and without hope of recovery. The information that Mrs. T. has work, is able bodied, is unencumbered with dependents, and has a husband in the city who may be expected to support her was reported to all who were known to be receiving letters. The probability is that Mrs. T. has replenished her mailing list and continues the practice of writing her begging letters." [12]

[12] Freund, "Begging in Chicago," pp. 41-48.

~~~~~~~~~~~~~~~~~~

CHAPTER III

TYPES OF BEGGING

E MPLOYING the various devices and tricks composing their art, beggars do a number of different kinds of begging in sundry places. In the modern world the hotbed of begging is the central business section of large cities. The beggar caters to a great extent to the same customers as other forms of business do. Just as the business section is the center of business and of legitimate professions, so it is the center of begging.

The peculiar nature of the central business section makes it an ideal place for the beggar to ply his trade. The daytime scene is characterized by crowded streets and busy thoroughfares. Movement is intensified by the hordes of workers who invade the zone in the morning, swell the throngs at noon, and retreat to their abodes in the residential section in the evening. During the heart of the day the crowds are made up of shoppers from outlying residential and suburban districts who visit the retail and professional areas. These are further supplemented by numerous out-of-town buyers who patronize the wholesale and financial districts. In addition to these classes, the business districts of large market centers attract ranchmen and farmers who have brought their cattle and farm produce to market and who come to the "loop" for a few days of glamour. All of these are potential patrons of the beggar.

At nightfall business ceases and pleasure begins. The loop is transformed into a pleasure resort by the bright lights, brilliant show windows, theaters, cabarets, and dance halls, which cater to the recreation and play interests of the city dwellers. For a participation in this downtown night life, employees and shoppers remain in town, residents pour into the loop, and "small towners" commute to the city. To these are added numerous travelers, casual visitors, and out-of-town buyers who patronize the hotels and spend their evenings at theaters and amusement houses. Among these also are traveling salesmen who crave relaxation and pleasure after strenuous days on the road. The carefree holiday spirit which characterizes the night life makes the evening an opportune time for the beggar.

The whole nature of the loop is such as to develop in these crowds of pedestrians, both by day and by night, a mood for giving. Everything is done to make them feel opulent. Magnificent buildings, gorgeous clothes, expensive jewelry displayed in beautiful show windows, and flashing electric signs tend to make the pedestrians forget their financial worries. All of this elegance only places in sharper contrast the beggar's picture of woe. Amid this splendor the beggar sits on the walk in tattered clothes, one leg missing, and apparently in dire misery. The opulent-feeling pedestrian cannot escape the pathos and often cannot escape giving. These pedestrians who crowd the business section at various hours of the day are the gold mine of the beggar, and he has many methods of coaxing coins from their pockets. It is the street beggar appealing to these throngs who is probably the most familiar of all the begging types.

The stationary beggar, typified by the seated blind beggar who selects a "stand" and stays in one place, is the type of beggar who most commonly appeals to crowds of pedestrians. Since he gets gifts from only a small per cent of those who pass, he usually picks the busiest streets, where the sidewalks have many pedestrians most of the time. Unless prevented by law, therefore, the busiest streets of the central business section of a city will be dotted with numerous street beggars holding cups for the alms of all who pass.

In this area of crowded streets, some places are much better for a beggar's stand than others. Since what the street beggar wants is crowds of pedestrians, it might be supposed that the corner of two busy streets would be an admirable place for a stand. It is a good place for a drug store, but not for a beggar. People are too much engaged when passing a busy corner. They are watching traffic lights, looking for a break in traffic, and dodging other people. The scene of the poor beggar sitting on the sidewalk may never come before their eyes. In fact, he will be fortunate if he does not get run over by some engrossed pedestrian. The beggar who knows, therefore, will not choose a corner. He will choose the middle of a block for a stand, for here there are not so many distracting sights. But even here some places are better than others. A spot where there are no attractive show windows is favorable. During the hours for women shoppers a place where show windows display women's clothes is bad. If perchance a beggar can sit directly in front of one of these windows he may do well, but again he may get trampled. On the busiest streets the entrance to large stores or buildings and similar places of severe congestion are similarly distracting to pedestrians and unfruitful for beggars.

In addition to these "middle of the block" locations, a stand close to theater entrances is favorable during the evening hours. Here many people in a holiday mood are passing, and here are many young swains trying to impress their lady friends with their opulence and generosity. Here also the crowds may be moving at a more leisurely pace.

On the less crowded streets, the stationary beggar may pick his stands at spots similar to those he shuns in the more congested areas. Thus, on less crowded streets where pedestrians are not too plentiful, the beggar may safely and profitably station himself at a corner, at the entrance to a building or a store, or at any other place where numerous people pass. And immediately before or after a service is held, the entrance to a church is an extremely favorable place.

The beggars who work these throngs have to make their appeal in what might be called a billboard fashion. Their appeal is to people who are in a hurry and they cannot hope to stop individuals for an extended interview. Hard luck stories or written manuscripts, therefore, cannot be successfully used.

If printed in large poster-like letters, a brief request, such as "help the blind" may be used. Usually, however, such beggars simply set their scene of woe and let their outstretched palm tell the rest. If need be, they may use some music, usually hideous, to attract attention, and return a "God bless you" when a gift is bestowed.

Though it is usually the stationary beggars who work these crowded streets, the ambulatory beggar may be successful if he uses the right appeal. If he is to be successful, like the stationary beggar, he must use the billboard appeal, for he must appeal to people "on the run" and he must depend on one glance from the prospective giver to create the effect.

An ambulatory beggar was recently observed working the crowds in a busy downtown business section. He wore dark glasses and supposedly was blind. He was accompanied by a seeing woman who led him at a snail's pace down the middle of the walk while the pedestrians passed on both sides. As he crept along he played remarkably beautiful music on an accordion, and the woman held a cup. The exceptional music attracted much attention and produced a generous flow of coins.

Toward such ambulatory beggars the public has a curious attitude which is hard to explain. While a stationary beggar may sit at a stand for hours at a time and for day after day, the ambulatory beggar very quickly irritates the public. The pedestrian may be interested if he meets such a beggar once, but is likely to be annoyed at a second meeting, and repeated meetings are liable to bring a protest to the police. The ambulatory beggar, therefore, cannot work long in the same place.

On the less congested streets just off the central business section, beggars may work in a different fashion than they do on the more crowded streets. Unless the streets are too deserted, the stationary beggar may choose a stand to suit his convenience. Thus somewhere along a fairly busy sidewalk he may find a window ledge which makes a comfortable seat or he may bring a chair and sit in an unused doorway. In addition, since there is less noise, he may supplement his "billboard" appeal with a brief spoken solicitation to the people passing.

A Negro woman had a regular stand for almost a year at a point about a hundred feet from the entrance to a hotel which was located in the edge of a central business district. There was a large slab of concrete by the side of the walk which made a very comfortable seat and she sat on this for hours at a time. She was very shabbily dressed and held a box containing some pencils and a few small coins. To each pedestrian who passed she would hold out the box and say "Mister, buy a pencil, help me to get something to eat." If the victim hesitated, she would begin a story of being a widow with lots of children, and she would continue to talk until he either walked away or gave her a coin.

The type of begging most typical of these side streets, however, is panhandling. The panhandlers approach pedestrians individually and ask for help. Usually they do not detain their patron long enough to tell a hard luck story. They simply inquire, "Could you spare a nickel for a cup of coffee?" "Could you give a hungry veteran a dime?" or make some such brief request. Such beggars, however, always have a story in reserve in case it is requested. If a conscientious pedestrian wishes to stop and inquire into the beggar's misfortune, he will not find the panhandler unprepared.

The panhandler is not always content, however, to make a brief request and let the pedestrian pass on; he often works by attaching himself to a pedestrian and attempting to worry the victim out of a gift. Instead of "Could you spare a dime?" such a panhandler says "Could you help a fellow?" or something of the sort. This is the beginning of a harangue of indefinite length. A brief hard luck story follows the salute, and then persuasion of any kind which the panhandler thinks will bring results. The barrage continues until either the victim gives in or the beggar gives out. Usually the beggar does not ask the pedestrian to stop and listen to his discourse. Instead he obligingly walks along with the prospective giver. Sometimes the more bold and crafty of these panhandlers will try to assume familiarity with the pedestrian and to pass as a former acquaintance. The hope is that the victim will feel complimented in being remembered and will feel, at the same time, embarrassment at having forgotten the other person. Rather than acknowledge his embarrassment, it is hoped, he will make the gift. Usually, in such a case, however, the beggar does not ask for a gift, which would likely be small; rather, he asks for a loan of some size.

I had an interesting five blocks with one of these panhandlers sometime ago. While walking down State Street just out of the edge of the main Loop in Chicago, a man who looked to be about forty years of age, in excellent health, and who was reasonably well dressed, approached me with a hearty "Hello, there," extending his hand to shake hands. I obligingly shook hands, inquired how he felt, and curiously awaited the next move. He then asked why I happened to be downtown at that time of day. Careful to give him no clues to my identity or occupation, I asked him what was so curious about being downtown. He said he thought I would be at work, and to that I replied that perhaps I was at work. Thereupon he took a new tack and said he did not believe I remembered him. I told him that I expected I remembered him as well as he remembered me. He said he remembered me perfectly. I asked him, therefore, who I was and where he had known me. He assured me that I was a "soda jerker" in a drug store out in a certain suburb of Chicago. In turn I assured him that he had made a bad guess, that I had never "jerked soda" in my life and I had never been in the suburb he mentioned. He then said that if I was not that fellow I certainly did look like him. And he went on to say that he had just gotten into town, was dirty, and hated to go out to his home in such a condition. He needed fifty cents to put him up in tip-top shape, and he hoped to borrow it from me, his friend. When informed that I could not make the "loan," he began to insist that he was "on the square" and would repay me. To this I only gave a doubtful smile. This spurred him on to more persuasion. All of the time this dialogue was in progress we were walking. Finally, tiring of his jabber, I turned in a direction where I saw an officer standing, and my friend immediately staged a retreat. By that time we had walked a good five blocks.

As might be expected, panhandling is primarily a man's profession. Most panhandlers are able-bodied men and many are young men. Correspondingly, the victims of panhandlers are mostly men. It is rather risky for panhandlers to approach women, and they seldom do it. Even a carefully worded appeal may be mistaken for an insult or a threatened attack, and the strapping panhandler may find himself in the grip of the law with serious charges lodged against him. Wise panhandlers, therefore, work early in the morning, late in the afternoon, and in the evening, since these are the periods of the day when the most men are coming into or leaving the business sections.

While, as has been said, the central business section is the chief gold mine for street beggars, it is not by any means the only place in the city that is favorable for plying their trade. The smaller business sections scattered out over the city are quite suitable places for street begging, and most of these attract types of beggars similar to those found on the side streets of the central business section. In addition, city transportation systems provide numerous begging points. The entrance to elevated or subway stations and prominent streetcar transfer points have numerous pedestrians and perhaps people waiting, and such places afford favorable stands for beggars. At other points in the transportation system automobiles have to stop and the beggar can appeal to those waiting in them. Even a stop light can be used to advantage by a clever panhandler. And a place such as a ferry landing where cars may have to wait for some time is an excellent place for an entertainment mendicant.

At a certain ferry landing in New Orleans an entertainment beggar has a regular stand. He is a middle-aged man with no glaring physical defects, and he is usually dressed passably well. While cars wait for a boat, he sits on an iron railing by the side of the road and sings doleful "old time" dirges, playing his own accompaniment on a guitar. Then he passes a hat to those waiting in the cars. If necessary, he supplements his entertainment with a spoken appeal for help.

Somewhat similar to the subway entrance as a location for a beggar's stand is the gate to a factory, railroad yard, or the entrance to any plant where many people are employed. Any such place has many pedestrians coming and going and can be used to advantage by beggars. The entrance to a large movie studio is such a place.

"It's getting so a person has to have a Southern California football player accompany him in order to break through the line of cadgers that surrounds each studio front door in Hollywood.

"Almost imperceptibly a certain sort of racketeer has taken over the studios' front doors. Any one going toward the movie plants suddenly finds himself accompanied, one on each side, by two soft treading gentry. The first hint is a wheedling voice from the right, asking for 'a little change, because I haven't eaten for two days.'

"At this point the shadow of a big glum looking fellow crosses the accosted one's path from the left shoulder. For those who don't shell out, there are a couple of truculent looks, and maybe a nudge before the pair disappears to await the next comer.

"An investigation of the racket, started by those who must visit Hollywood studios nearly every day in the week, discloses that the studio front gate panhandlers have been working in teams of two and three, each pair working one studio for two or three days, and then moving to another studio, to be replaced by another team." [1]

For street beggars, a Saturday afternoon in the business section of a small city or a country town has all of the advantages

[1] *Chicago Daily Tribune,* November 26, 1931, p. 32.

afforded by the various regular stands in the city and some additional ones. In most parts of the country, Saturday afternoon is the weekly shopping period for rural people and they swarm the streets of the smaller cities and country towns. Here, therefore, the street beggar can find crowds of people, people who are not in a hurry to get somewhere and can take plenty of time to inspect his scene of poverty.

These rural people provide a very responsive audience for the skillful street beggar. They do not see beggars every day. In fact, they only see these wretched-looking street beggars once a week, and they are not "fed up" with the beggar's appeals. Indeed, these "believe it or not" beggar monstrosities are a part of the attractions which make coming to town worthwhile. Furthermore, the rural person knows little of the humbuggery of beggars and he is not liable to be so doubtful of the genuineness of the wretches he sees on the street. He does not necessarily believe, but he does not seriously doubt; the city is full of mysteries for the rural person and the beggar is one of those mysteries. The rural person, therefore, looks on the beggar with intense curiosity and with some bewilderment. Since old religious beliefs and old methods of giving help are stronger in rural people than in urban, the rural person is very liable to drop his coin into the beggar's cup. This is especially probable since he has usually brought a little spending money to town with him for his weekly holiday. Beggars, therefore, have learned to cater to these Saturday afternoon clients, and many of the street beggars in large cities desert the streets to visit rural outposts on Saturday afternoon.

Early one Saturday afternoon a pair of ambulatory beggars were observed in the business section of a city of about 35,000 population. The two men, apparently blind, very shabbily dressed, unshaven, no glasses, and looking enough alike to be twins, were a striking scene. Arm in arm and in perfect step they walked with a slow and hesitating step down the center of the walk, singing a mournful dirge. The effect was terrific. Not even a calloused observer could escape the drama. It reminded one of prisoners from dungeons taking their last walk to the guillotine, or of the ghosts of lost souls wandering among the tombs. As may be surmised, everyone looked and most gave.

Later in the same afternoon the same pair were encountered on the streets of a small town about thirty miles from the city in which they had first been observed. This time a seeing young man seemed to be keeping watch over them and giving directions as to where to turn. When engaged in conversation, the young man revealed that he was their chauffeur, and he frankly gave their itinerary for the afternoon. This, as he disclosed, included practically all of the small towns in a radius of forty miles of the central city.

Combining practically all of the advantages of other types of begging places, fairs and circuses probably provide the richest field for street beggars known in modern America. Here are crowds of people strolling leisurely, and among the crowd are numerous rural people. Everyone is in gala spirits, and everyone has some spending money in his pocket which he must get rid of before he leaves. Most are prepared to pay for a good side show whether it be Tarzan, a fat woman, or a well-done beggar scene. Beggars, therefore, swarm to such places. Most any enterprising street beggar will desert his regular post and travel forty or fifty miles to attend a fair or a circus; numerous beggars make a specialty of working such public occasions. These "camp followers" are known as "trailers."

"Trailers are men who follow circuses or anything else that draws a crowd. They live by preying upon the people. Among the trailers with this circus were legless men called crawlers who traveled with their bodies strapped to small wheeled platforms. They propelled themselves with stirrups held in each hand. They literally walked with their hands. Each time they struck the ground with a stirrup the wheels rolled under them. There were, too, trailers born double-jointed who twisted their bodies in every conceivable and grotesque manner. Hard faces they had, and they moaned with pain when anyone drew near who might give them money. Other trailers there were who could play the part of blind men. Yet others knew how to twist their hands.

"One trailer carried a hard slice of bread with him. He would drop it on the sidewalk at a convenient place. When he saw a person approaching he would dive madly for the bread. This trick seldom failed to reap its reward. Another old trailer was a particular pet of the lion-tamer's. I soon became attached to him also. He walked about—playing blind—tapping a crooked gnarled cane on the pavement. He would tap three times every ten or twelve feet. He wore a long tobacco-stained beard that reached to his belt. The whiskers hid all of his face but the eyes, over which his brows projected at least an inch. He belonged to the great body of men who write. As may be supposed, he was not always tolerant of other literati. Since his doggerel rhymed, he had a special scorn for writers of blank verse." [2]

A type of begging somewhat akin to those already mentioned is what might be called transport begging. This type of begging may be done anywhere there is a crowd, preferably seated. If the public and the law allowed, such beggars would infest church services and all sorts of public gatherings, and they do in some parts of the world. In America, however, such mendicancy is not usually allowed. In spite of efforts to keep them out, though, this type of beggar frequently sneaks into streetcars, ferryboats, and trains, and they are quite common around railway stations.

The technique of transport begging differs considerably from both panhandling and ordinary street begging. Especially in America where there is so much opposition to such begging, this kind of beggar usually works as quietly as possible and tries to avoid creating a scene. To do this he commonly uses a written or printed appeal which is often put in some semblance of poetic form. Most such "poems" contrast the condition of the giver with that of the beggar. And many of them

[2] Jim Tully, "The Lion Tamer," *American Mercury*, VI (1925), 143.

contain a touch of superstition, or a quotation from the Bible, or both. Following is a typical sample of this kind of poem.

Good Luck to the Purchaser of This Card

I once was happy the same as you,
But now I am a cripple with nothing to do.
I'm compelled to ask strangers some assistance to give
So please give me something—Live and Let Live.
I pray God will reward you, my wants you will relieve,
And remember it is more blessed to give than receive.

Another type of transport beggar is the one who puts on an act for the benefit of a crowd in a streetcar, ferryboat, or bus. Women are particularly adept at this racket. They may make up to appear with child and while on the streetcar suddenly feign labor pains, they may suddenly find that they have lost their purse, they may simply "faint," or they may play any of numerous tricks. At any rate, they get the interest and sympathy of the crowd, and upon proper encouragement they tell a hard luck story which often sounds so plausible that it is never suspected.

"The 'high-heeler' is a throw-out (usually a woman) who adds to her equipment an iron framework some three inches high on one of her feet. Obviously this 'heel,' which is set askew, forces the wearer to walk with the knee bent at a most uncomfortable angle. The high-heeler also works the street railways, but in a manner differing from that of the throw-out.

"One of the best high-heelers I ever saw was called Toledo Annie. She was not more than thirty years old, with a pleasant smiling expression and a well-bred appearance. She was always neatly dressed and kept her dark hair, which was very fine and abundant, done up in a plain but becoming knot. She wore gold rimmed spectacles and looked like a school teacher. She possessed the faculty of throwing her hip joint partly out of the socket, which greatly exaggerated her apparent deformity. No one, watching her painful progress down a sidewalk or the aisle of a street car, would have doubted that she was the victim of congenital hip disease.

"She used to stop a street car and get herself hoisted aboard by the conductor and hobble painfully down the aisle to a seat. The passengers, their attention drawn to her misfortune, watched breathlessly until she was safely seated; and were attracted by her neat appearance and her cheerful smile. They gave her credit for a great deal of pluck, which indeed, she had!

"When the conductor came to collect her fare she would plunge her hand into her skirt pocket and after fumbling about for a minute, withdraw it empty. At the same time she would stop smiling and begin to fly distress signals. Tears would come to her eyes.

" 'You will have to let me off,' she would say, trying to muster up the smile again. 'I'm afraid someone has stolen my pocketbook, and I can't pay my fare.'

"It would be an ungallant conductor who would not insist on her riding to her destination free, probably adding a few indignant words about the character of any thief who would rob a woman—and a cripple at that! Some of the passengers would not be slow to inquire more minutely into the affair, and would be touched to learn that the poor woman had lost her little all.

"Don't think that Annie would pour forth her story readily to the first-comer. She was too much of an artist for that. Four or five charitable and well-meaning souls cross examining in concert were not too many to drag the story piecemeal out of her. The end of the act would find Annie leaving the car full of smiles and tearful gratitude, and richer by anywhere from ten to a hundred dollars. The smallest takings in a day was eighteen dollars and her largest one hundred and twenty dollars." [3]

While the various forms of street begging constitute the type of begging most familiar to the majority of people and while such beggars are, to say the least, numerous enough, this is by

[3] Godfrey, "A Capable Beggar Makes from $15 to $500 a Day," *American Magazine*, XCIV (1922), 119.

no means the only type of begging. A kind of begging very different in a way from street begging is store begging. Every city has quantities of beggars who visit stores and shops all over the city asking for alms. Almost any day during shopping hours these mendicants may be encountered in stores or making their way from store to store.

From the standpoint of begging art these store beggars are among the crudest of the begging profession. They do not dress carefully for the part, they have no clever hard luck stories, and they do not skillfully fake or play up real physical defects. In fact, about all they do is walk into a store and hold out a cup. They use none of the subtle appeals of cleverer mendicants. Yet with all their stupidity and amateurishness they garner a fair harvest. The reason is that, in a way, they are not really begging; actually they are playing a mild game of blackmail on the storekeeper.

The store beggar's game, insofar as there is a game, is to get the sympathy of shoppers who are in the store and to put the merchant in an awkward situation. Here is the merchant with his shelves stacked with groceries or other wares; he must have plenty. All the beggar asks is a loaf of bread, a little meat, or anything that the merchant is willing to give. If the merchant refuses, a tenderhearted customer may think him stingy and hardhearted and he may lose trade; rather than run this risk, he usually gives. The beggar may then pass his cup to the shoppers, but this is only a gesture to assure them that he is in need and does not want to slight anyone who wishes to help.

Most merchants know why they give to such beggars and they know that a small gift will serve the purpose as well as a large one. The usual merchant, therefore, gives cash, and he has his gift standardized to a small coin. The beggar by experience has learned of this standardization and he has learned that he will get the standard gift whether he makes much of an appeal or not. He also knows that in most cases he will not get more than the standard gift even if he makes a carefully studied appeal. As a result he becomes slovenly in his dress and careless in depicting pathos. It is in this way that the art of store beggars has fallen to such a low ebb.

In America the blackmail nature of store begging is kept pretty well under cover. It is recognized by many merchants and by the more intelligent beggars, but it is little known to the general public. In China, however, it is an open game and at times it is carried to its logical conclusions. There the beggars are definitely organized into a guild, and the guild makes stringent demands on storekeepers. When a new store is to be opened the merchant must pay a bounty to the beggars' guild. If he refuses, the beggars will virtually blockade the front of his store. So many blind, crippled, and deformed monstrosities will drape themselves on the walk and around the entrance that customers will find it almost impossible to get into the store. But, aside from this opening ceremony, the store beggars make themselves such a nuisance that in some towns agreements have been made between the merchants and the beggars' guild whereby a stipulated sum is paid periodically to the guild members.[4]

The chain store and the large department store in America have been quite a blow to store begging. Such places are usually owned by absentee capitalists and are run by hired employees. These employees are popularly thought to be underpaid, and customers do not expect them to give liberally to beggars. The absentee owner cannot be expected to know about the beggar. Thus beggars can be refused gifts in such places with very little danger that customers will become offended. While, therefore, the store beggar preys upon the small merchant, the two may well join hands to oppose the growth of chain stores.

Closely akin to store begging is restaurant begging. Many beggars make a regular practice of begging meals from restaurants. Such beggars usually declare themselves to be broke and hungry, they often tell a hard luck story, and occasionally they offer to wash dishes to pay for their meal. The more

---

[4] See Sidney D. Gamble, *Peking, A Social Survey* (New York, 1921), pp. 274-75.

racketeering of them will go into a restaurant and ask that a meal be sold to them on a promise of future payment, and some will order a meal and eat it and then declare that they have just discovered that they have lost their money. Success in this kind of begging requires not only tact in making the appeal but also skill in selecting the restaurant, rather in selecting the right proprietor. Company-owned eating places are as hopeless as chain stores. Much more skill is required, therefore, to do restaurant begging than to do store begging. And, since money is seldom given, the returns are pretty definitely limited by the capacity of the beggar's stomach.

Another type of begging which is very common is office begging. There are many types of beggars who would visit business and professional men in their offices if they could. Transport beggars, panhandlers, and "shoestring salesmen" would be willing to visit offices if they dared and if the results obtained were sufficient to pay them for their trouble. The precautions against beggars commonly taken by the staff of a large office building and the resistance of the phalanx of stenographers and secretaries who barricade the entrance to most offices rather effectively discourage the efforts of small change beggars. The only beggars, therefore, really worthy to be called office beggars are the pseudo-gentlemen mendicants who are skilled in the art of telling hard luck stories.

These pseudo-gentlemen dress very respectably and pose as members of the middle and upper classes who have met "temporary reverses" or are in an embarrassing predicament. Because of their appearance they are able to get past the elevator operators and other building employees who might be on the lookout for beggars, and on some plausible but fabricated pretext they evade the vigilance of the staff in the "outer office." Having once gained entree to his victim, the beggar tells a more or less carefully planned hard luck story. The burden of the story is that he is in urgent need of a certain amount of money, usually between one and ten dollars. And as has already been said, these stories may have personal touches designed to appeal to this particular victim.

The activities of these beggars are often so similar to those of the petty swindler that the distinction between the two is almost imperceptible. To them a gift and a "loan" mean the same thing, and they often fail to state clearly which they are requesting. Such terms as "could you spare?" or "could you let me have?" are used with great frequency by such mendicants and to the uninitiated victim they might mean either a loan or a gift. Rather than miss a dollar almost any office beggar would insist that his gift was a "loan." In most cases, of course, whether it is taken by the beggar or the petty swindler it is a gift.

Doubtless the class of persons most harassed by these office callers are ministers, Y.M.C.A. secretaries, and other representatives of organized religion. By virtue of the position which they hold they are supposed to receive all who come to see them. They are supposed also to have a special responsibility for and an interest in the woes of other people. The beggar is not ignorant of the defenseless position of such people and he is not above taking advantage of it.

"Few persons have any conception of the number of total strangers who visit rectories and parsonages of city clergymen to ask assistance. It has become a sheer necessity for every clergyman of a city parish to appoint an office-hour when he will see them, and to see them at no other time. Partly for my own amusement, partly for the purpose of composing this article, I have kept for a year a careful record of the number, names, peculiarities and errands of persons who have called upon me in my 'pastor's office hour.'

"For one year there were just six hundred entries. In every case the request was either for advice or for money." [5]

While women are found to some extent in most types of begging, there is a kind of begging which is to a high degree their own special domain. This is residence begging. A typi-

[5] "A Clergyman's Study of the Stranded," *World's Work*, IV (1902), 2510.

cally skilled residence beggar appeals to the housewife. She calls at homes during those hours of the day when the man is liable to be away and seeks an audience with the lady of the house. If successful, she pours out her troubles, usually imaginary, as one woman to another. Almost invariably her story is a tale of domestic woe. She is a widow with numerous children to support, she has sickness in the family, and there is no money to buy food, let alone medicine. Or perhaps she has a husband, but he is a regular demon. He is unemployed, drinks, abuses her, and is cruel to the children. Not infrequently she is about to be evicted and may even display eviction notices. To strengthen her story she often has with her a small, preferably anemic, child, or perhaps a "babe in arms." Often she will say that she does not want gifts, she wants to earn her living. She has used her few spare moments to make paper flowers, little aprons, or some other handwork which she offers for sale. She is willing to sell them for anything which the lady is willing to give.

Lily, a widow with one child, has been doing residence begging regularly for many years. She usually carries some small articles along with her to "sell" and tells a story of being a widow in ill health with a sickly daughter to support. This "sickly daughter" is not sickly but she is undersize and is far from robust in appearance. Lily always takes a child on her begging trips, either her own or one borrowed from relations.

In addition to these female artists of the doorbell, there are a great many men who do residence begging. In the city, however, this masculine house-to-house begging is, for the most part, of a very low sort. It more or less corresponds to the back-door handout begging done by tramps in small towns and rural areas. These men usually do not attempt to get inside the house to deliver an extended hard luck story. Generally they make a very brief request for help, and complacently take what is given. Often they call around mealtime, particularly in the evening, saying that they have been out hunting work all day, have been unable to find any, that they have a house full of children with no food, and that they cannot face going home without taking something. On such a plea they frequently ask for food instead of money.

The bane of all residence beggars are the bill collectors, the salesmen, the advertising agents, the research investigators, the delivery boys, and all the multifarious persons who go from house to house. This horde of doorbell pushers so bedevil residents that the poor beggar gets a cold welcome when she arrives. In fact she may begin to suspect that maids are hired solely on their ability to barricade the front door, and she may exhaust her wits and her patience trying to get her plea before the head of the house. Some of them may even suspect that the better residences have a secret entrance for relatives and friends. As a matter of fact, many families do have a special ring of the doorbell which is known only to themselves and their acquaintances.

It is, to a considerable extent, this resistance which city people have to seeing strangers at home, in the office, or on the street which gives such an impetus to the begging by letter which was discussed in the preceding chapter. Some people who cannot be reached by the beggar through personal contact can be reached by mail. Even in this medium, however, the beggar has much the same competition which he has at the front door. Bills, circulars, philanthropic requests, and numerous other unwelcome communications litter the mails, and the beggar's letter may be cast into the wastepaper basket along with the rest.

A final type of begging which has experienced a great growth in modern cities is what may be called "organization begging." The city is filled with civic clubs, lodges, women's clubs, churches, and organizations of various sorts which do not give relief regularly but can be touched by a particularly pathetic case. There are numerous beggars in the city, therefore, who make a specialty of working these organizations. If he manages properly, such a beggar may gain a rich harvest. Since there is little co-ordination between the activities of such organizations, the beggar may have three or four of them giving him help at one time.[6] In fact, if he is a bona fide dependent, he may be getting help from a regular relief agency while he is getting aid from these other organizations. When he has worn out his welcome in one part of the city, or when his game is discovered, he may move to another part of the city and start all over again. If necessary he may change his name to conceal his identity. By such moving and by changing names he may be able to dupe the same community every few years without being recognized. If, however, he does become too well known in one city, he can easily move to another. Without much travel, therefore, an organization beggar may work his racket for years, and can often do it for a lifetime in the same city.

Sampson has been getting a livelihood from churches and other organizations in one city for about fifteen years. On the proceeds of his begging he has taken care of a family of seven children. Some of his children have married young, and he has often had his in-laws and grandchildren to care for as well as his own family. Frequently he has as many as five churches giving him help at one time. When one neighborhood gets too "hot" for him he moves to another. By this process he covers the city once every few years. Even though the city in which he lives is rather small, he seems to be no nearer the end of his resources than he was ten years ago.

All told, thus, there are a number of different types of begging. The begging fraternity practices its art almost anywhere people can be found from whom to beg. The street beggar besets pedestrians as they pass along the sidewalk, enter and leave stores, office buildings, churches, railway and subway stations, attend theaters, and celebrate at fairs and circuses. He plants himself almost anywhere that pedestrians can be

---

[6] Such duplication of relief would be prevented for the most part if all organizations cleared their cases through some confidential exchange. Many of these pseudo-relief organizations, however, fail to take such precautions.

found in sufficient numbers to make begging profitable. The store beggar browbeats the puzzled merchant as he pulls at the two horns of his dilemma, the office beggar haunts offices, and the residence beggar harasses servants and housewives with her pushing of doorbells. And the begging letter writer swamps the mails with mournful epistles. The organization beggar, on the other hand, is always seeking to attach himself, like a leech, to some organization for succor.

These various forms of begging probably constitute the most universal and the most characteristic types of begging. The begging techniques change from time to time and the almsgiving motives to which the beggar appeals change, but, in practically all countries, certainly in all cities, and at all periods virtually all of these types of begging will be found.

CHAPTER IV

~~~~~~~~~~~~~~~~~~~~

BEGGARS OF THE OPEN ROAD

SO far as popular fancy is concerned, the hero of the begging fraternity, throughout the ages, has been the hobo, the tramp, the migratory beggar. They are to be described here in the past tense, referring primarily to the postwar period. It is not to be inferred, however, that any part of this nomadic element is today extinct—quite the contrary. The war, postwar, and depression periods have, however, effected significant changes, in the transient world as well as in the rest of society. And the trends of change can best be understood if we understand the condition of this group as it was before these changes began.

Traveling by foot, horse, or automobile, these vagrants have traversed continents, crossed national boundaries, and visited isolated farmhouses, small towns, and large cities. For food and clothing he has traded hard luck stories, poems, and jokes, and if these were of no avail, he has either worked or stolen. He has slept in barns, on haystacks, on improvised beds in his jungles, and in city missions and "flops." Like a mysterious shadow he has moved in and out of villages, gaining a livelihood from them but becoming in no way a part of them.

"In all countries there are these strange beings, living in the midst of the people but not of them: the weary tramp of England, the nonchalant hobo of America, the bronzed sundowner of Australia, the sad-visaged Gorioun of Russia, no less than the more intimate associates of the peasantry, as the tramp usually is, in pastoral countries such as Ireland. But each in his own way carries on the tradition

76

of freedom, if only the almost lost tradition of freedom from the tyranny of owning things." [1]

Wherever the tramp has gone he has always aroused a quiet and often a vocal admiration. He has been the symbol of the unfulfilled dreams, the inward longings, of those in sedentary life. To the partially enslaved, he was a person without a boss; to those bored with living on one patch of land, he was one free to travel where he pleased; to those tired of the routine of organized society, he was a person without a program; to those who were financially harassed, he had neither liability nor asset, nor did he strive; and to those who were burdened with dependents and unruly offspring, he had neither kith nor kin. He was the embodiment of freedom from all the worries that beset men in the toil and struggle of daily living. He was free of care. Thus people have admired and envied him, have talked of him, and written about him. But, most of all, people have given generously to extend to him the freedom which they themselves were denied.

His, however, has not been an unmixed blessing. While he was carefree, he was poor, secretive, peculiar, mysterious, annoying, and sometimes dangerous. For these traits he was disliked, even despised. The public, therefore, has responded to him with a most ludicrous mixture of approach and withdrawal. It has loved and hated him in the same moment, praised and ridiculed him in the same breath, and has pampered and punished him at the same time.

"He is always with us, yet we never locate him. No one wants him, yet we always send him to someone else. We make laws to get rid of him but succeed only in keeping him a little longer in custody at our own expense. Most of us laugh at him, and some of us cry over him. We draw funny pictures of him in our newspapers and in our billboard advertisements, but we are really afraid of him. We blame the police for not keeping him off the streets, or at least out of sight, and yet we feed him at our own doors.

[1] Holbrook Jackson, *All Manner of Folk* (London, 1912), p. 59.

We fear to meet him after dark, and nevertheless give him a nickel or a dime to keep him in town over night. He is an object of charity, or a criminal, just as we happen to feel. He is sometimes the hero of our melodrama at the theater, and gets our tearful applause. At the same time he stands for all that we brand as mean and vile. We spend money lavishly to support him without work by charity, or we imprison him in idleness by law. Yet we keep on raising his kind. Like murder, he cannot be hid, he 'will out,' like the 'spot' on Lady Macbeth's hand, he will not 'out.' We treat him sometimes as though he were all our own, to do with as we please. At others we refuse to regard him as belonging to anyone but himself, or to permit him to be anywhere or do anything at his own not altogether sweet will. We facetiously call him by such pet or pettish names as 'vag,' 'bum,' 'tramp,' 'hobo,' 'Weary Willie,' yet exhaust the sternest language of the law in defining him so as to deal with him as severely as we can. We curse him at his worst and coddle him at his best. He is interchangeably both vicious and a victim. So we find it unjust to be strict and yet cruel to be kind. We know him so well that we do not want to know him better, and yet we know so little of him that we really do not know what to do with him. We seem to be as elusive in our treatment of the vagrant as he is himself in his dealings with us." [2]

To the general public, for the most part, vagrants have been vagrants. Little distinction has been made on a basis of age, looks, or race. Hoboes, bums, and tramps were all in the same category.

Perhaps the most important distinction which the public has failed to make was that between the hobo [3] and the tramp. The hobo was not essentially a beggar though he did beg at times. Fundamentally, he was a migratory worker and as such he was an important adjunct of our national economy until

[2] Graham Taylor, "On the Vagrant 'Elusive,'" *Charities*, XVIII (1907), 575-76.
[3] For a study of the hobo as a sociological phenomenon, see Nels Anderson, *The Hobo* (Chicago, 1923).

very recent years. When a continent is in the process of settlement and development, each locality tends to operate on a
minimum labor supply and, when other than routine work is
to be done, labor must be imported. There is thus a demand
for an army of foot-loose laborers who can be shunted from
one locality to another as extraordinary demands arise. The
hobo was the answer to this demand. He furnished labor for
the building of railroads, the construction of towns and cities,
the development of oil fields, the building of dams and levees,
and he helped harvest the vast wheat crops on the sparsely
settled western prairies.

Although the hobo was fundamentally a laborer, he did not
always succeed in making a livelihood by working. The construction industry has always operated by booms and lulls, and
during these lulls the hobo often found himself stranded. Furthermore, the winter months were usually a lean period for
him. The construction industry was usually at a low ebb at
this time of year, and the seasonal farm labor demand was
entirely lacking. The hobo, therefore, attempted to save up a
"stake" during the warm months which would be sufficient
to tide him over the winter months, but this "stake" was frequently gone before he found another job. Thus the hobo often
found himself without money and unable to get work. At these
times he resorted to begging. If he was in the open country
he often got handouts from back doors, but in the city he either
did panhandling or received help from missions.

Just how many of these laborer-beggars America has had is
difficult to say. It seems quite certain, however, that at any
given time during the last quarter century their numbers
amounted to hundreds of thousands. Most of these were regu-
lars who depended on this mode of life entirely for their livelihood. Their ranks during the summer months, however, were
customarily augmented by a large "in and out group" attracted
by high wages or the lure of travel, or both. College boys,
temporarily unemployed men, and foot-loose youths joined
these migratory hordes. Up to the development of the combine, the wheat fields were invaded annually by an army of

males ranging all the way from the most hardened hobo to the precocious youngster.

The tramp was a sharp contrast to the hobo. The hobo begged when he could not work, the tramp worked when he could not beg. The tramp was typically a defeated man in the most absolute sense. At some time in his life, perhaps, he had tried both work and crime and had found each too strenuous to suit his proclivities, and he did not fit into settled life or organized society. Even unnecessary begging was a task to him. He seldom begged, therefore, except for what he needed at the moment—food or clothing. For a tramp to build up a fortune, as some beggars have done, is, so far as the author knows, totally unheard of.

The tramp's outstanding trait was his endless travel. Where he went made very little difference so long as he went somewhere. Like legitimate tourists, he frequently went to warm sections in the winter and to cool areas in the summer. Unlike the hobo he tended to travel away from places where work was plentiful. But on the whole, he had no more reason to go one place than he had to go to another. As someone has put it, "He came from where he started and was going where he went."

In an earlier day, the railroads were the chief highways for the tramp's aimless wandering. With a stick and a small bundle he trudged over the crossties, sometimes riding freight trains, but often walking for long distances. He begged food and clothing from back doors as he needed them, and with a few tin cans and some fuel he pitched camp whenever he wished to stop. On the outskirts of virtually every town he and his kind maintained more or less permanent camps which have been called "jungles." These usually had some sort of facilities for washing clothes, cooking accommodations for a group, and often some kind of shelter with improvised beds. But this jungle was more than a service center, it was a social center. Here tramps met and talked, exchanged travel notes, told of towns that were easy and those that were hard, told of railroads that had special "bulls" and those that did not, and sometimes even managed to brag a little. Only one thing was forbidden: no tramp inquired regarding another tramp's past or allowed others to inquire about his.

The real tramp was a rather drab character. He was free of responsibility, but he was not proud of his freedom. His clothes were worn and dirty, he was noncommunicative, and he wore the hangdog look of a defeated man. Frequently he was either mentally or physically deficient. In all, the price which he paid for his freedom is too evident to make him colorful. He had, however, numerous camp followers who, while in the minority, were more colorful and were probably responsible for most of the glamour which was accorded his fraternity. These camp followers were such a diverse assortment that no attempt will be made here to completely classify them. Only a few of the more common types will be given attention.

One of the most interesting of these semi-tramps was the philosopher. He was in a way mentally alert, sometimes fairly well educated, and often surprisingly well read. Usually social philosophizing was a sort of a mental hobby quite divorced from his everyday life. He had certain theories regarding the ailments of society and he liked to discuss them with others of his kind. The most interesting of these philosophers, however, were the ones who had a living philosophy regarding the tramp life. They knew all the drawbacks to settled social life and were sincerely glad to be rid of them. They abhorred the routine, responsibilities, and struggles of organized society, and they both pitied and looked down on those who accepted such responsibilities. They were therefore proud, self-assured, and even bold, for they were wanderers by choice. Some of these philosophers did writing on the side and a few produced very presentable works. Through their writings at least two, William Davies and Jim Tully, became very well known.

Another "sport" of the begging nomads was the speed demon or so-called "passenger stiff." All migrants have some of that mystical trait known as wanderlust, but the passenger stiff was decidedly overdosed with it. He loved to shuttle back and forth across the continent in the shortest time possible. He was not in a contest except with himself, and he did not have any reason for wanting to reach the destination on any of his hurried trips. Speed was an end in itself; he spent his life racing with time, and he only begged for what he needed to sustain himself in transit.

"In Frisco I met a passenger stiff who was getting old. His joints were stiffening, and it was no longer easy for him to take the jumps. Perhaps that is the reason why he was so friendly. His mania for speed was as great as ever. I joined him on a trip to New York. Roy Malkins was his name.

"Until we got past Cedar Rapids, Iowa, good luck was with us. We made every connection and were lucky in panhandling. The Los Angeles Limited, which we rode, stopped for thirty-five minutes in Salt Lake City, and in that time I collected five dollars, bought a supply of food, and had leisure to stroll back to the yards. . . .

"Just after Cedar Rapids, in the early hours of the morning, we were in the blind of the American Railway Express car, when we heard a fumbling at the lock of the end door. Quickly each of us slipped around to the outside of the blind. I stayed there perhaps twenty minutes, my foot desperately lodged on the two inch ledge on the end of the car, while the train thundered on. It is a hazardous place to ride and only the continued rapid movements of the train, pressing you against the folds of the blind, can prevent you from losing your balance.

"When at last I judged that the coast was clear, and crept carefully around inside again, Roy was not there. I looked around to his side of the blind, but he was not there either. That's the way a passenger stiff finishes." [4]

Another interesting member of the migratory brotherhood was the pseudo-gentleman, who as a rule circulated chiefly among the larger towns and cities. He usually did not beg in the open country or small towns but was versatile in begging in large cities. Somewhat similar to the passenger stiff, his primary interest was travel and his begging was a means to

[4] H. Tascheraud, "Passenger Stiff," *American Mercury*, V (1925), 371.

that end. Seldom did he try for large returns in begging. Some of these "gentlemen" begged from individuals, others were petty swindlers, and others were highly skilled at working charitable organizations. Brown was one of the latter.

"Brown had not been in Chicago an hour until he had located the chief organizations to which he might go for help. He knew that he could check his bag at the Y.M.C.A. He learned where to go for a bath, where to get clean clothes, how to get a shave and haircut and actually succeeded in getting some money from the United Charities. He was able to 'flop' in a bed even though he had come to town without money late in the afternoon; whereas many other men in the same position would have been forced to 'carry the banner.' . . . After his case was traced it was learned that he told about the same story wherever he went and that he was known in organizations in all the cities to which he referred. He is twenty-seven years old and has been living for the most part in institutions or at the expense of organizations since he was thirteen." [5]

While begging has been the chief support of the migratory element, excepting the hobo, the anonymity of the transient life furnished a strong shield for those criminally inclined. The tramp world, therefore, has always had its criminal hangers-on. Some of these confined themselves to petty thefts of food and clothing which they preferred to steal rather than beg; others, however, were criminals who centered their efforts on more serious jobs and used begging and the tramp life as a shield from the law.

"I was initiated into the mysteries of 'yegg' make-up methods, when I saw a roommate in a Bowery Lodging House remove from a normal hand what appeared to be the stump of an amputated wrist. It was made of muslin and paper and admirably served the purpose for which it was intended, for several months later I saw the same gentleman industriously displaying his handless arm and

[5] Anderson, *The Hobo,* p. 48.

selling small cakes cut from bars of cheap laundry soap, for anywhere from five cents to a quarter, as the crippled arm happened to move the sympathy of the guileless purchaser. A day or two after, I saw him seated on a tie pile in friendly converse with a bunch of 'yeggs,' one of whom I knew to be a 'peterman,' or safe blower. As a matter of fact, these men were then planning the robbery of a small bank in a suburban town. They had rented an old house near the place and furnished it with a second-hand cook stove, cooking utensils, dishes and bunks, and were biding their time when a large deposit for the payment of railroad employes should be made. They were regarded by the people of the community as a 'harmless' lot of vagrants, and maintained themselves for several months by selling soap, shoestrings, pencils, and begging, pure and simple. They were only partially successful in their attack upon the bank, but got safely away, the local authorities never having suspected their character. Three months later, two of them were arrested for 'blowing' a post office safe in eastern Pennsylvania, and sentenced to five years in the penitentiary. Later on another of the gang got two years for shooting a bartender, and at the same time was indicted for shooting the chief of police in a small town, while on a prowl job." [6]

In addition to these elements, the tramp life always attracted a number of drug addicts, mentally diseased persons, and eccentrics. The use of drugs and alcohol and perverted sex practices were so common among the transient element that it was often difficult to tell whether these habits had caused the person to become a migrant or whether they were a by-product of his roving life. Some mentally diseased persons, however, were evidently on the move primarily because of their mental twist. Persons roving the country in search of a "lost relative," persons fleeing the "persecution" of some person or organization, and persons in search of some "golden grail" were rather common.

[6] J. N. Tillard, "The Criminal Mendicant," *Charities*, XVIII (1907), 747-48.

As has been inferred, the migratory world was primarily a world of homeless men; it was populated mostly by adult males. There were always some women in it, however. These usually traveled disguised as men and often attached themselves to a sturdy male for protection. A more interesting element was the boys who took to the road. Up until rather recent years these boys were decidedly in the minority in the tramp group, but they were an important minority. Sometimes they traveled in gangs, but, in riding freight trains, keeping a gang together is no small task. The gang, ordinarily, therefore, soon found itself broken up and individual members often found themselves entirely separated from their pals. Such stragglers were often taken under the wing of a seasoned tramp and gradually forced into the role of a "jocker." James Forbes describes the lot of a "jocker," a boy enslaved by a tramp for immoral purposes:

"As he becomes exhausted by excesses he comes to know more and more the peril and hollowness and misery of the life he leads, and can see no possible way to escape from it. He is able to achieve momentary forgetfulness only by the use of stimulants. When liquor fails to produce the effect, he often resorts to the hypodermic syringe. Possibly five years after the commencement of this career he will appear in the streets of a great city, a complete wreck, morally and physically." [7]

More or less in a class by themselves among these migratory hordes were the roving college boys. They have usually been considered irresponsible and often a bit crazy, and hence have been allowed to do many things which were not proper for other people of their station in life. Thus, along with hazing, taking cows into the college chapel, and riding in dilapidated cars, college students have usually been given a license to roam the countryside and even to beg. They have bummed their way to and from college, and during vacation they have gone to the wheat harvest or on pleasure jaunts. Sometimes

[7] "Jockers and the Schools They Keep," *Charities*, XI (1903), 622.

these pleasure jaunts have been quite extended travel tours in this country and sometimes even abroad. Usually the college student traveled "on a shoe string," that is, with very little money. As such he rode freight trains or got free rides in automobiles. For meals and lodging he sometimes worked, but, more frequently than his parents knew, he got them by begging or stealing. Usually, also, he was merciless in sponging on relatives and friends who might live on his route.

"College-bred 'bummers,' round the world hoboes from the upper classes, are lately appearing in increasing numbers, according to reports from overseas; and a perfect flood of them is expected shortly after the various colleges close for the summer. These gentlemen hoboes—there appear to be few lady hoboes among them so far—make it a point to travel without spending anything. They 'work their way,' as they commonly put it. They sponge, borrow, and bully their way more often, however, reports a man who has met a good many of them on the other side of the globe. They use letters of introduction, they brazenly sponge on distant acquaintances and friends of friends—and the friends of friends especially in the far East are reported to be getting 'good and sick of such poor sports.' " [8]

Thus the migratory hordes, as we have seen, consisted of hoboes, tramps, roving criminals, drug addicts, alcoholics, sex perverts, insane persons, eccentrics—mostly men, with a sprinkling of women and young boys. They gained their livelihood by begging, stealing, and working.

The World War dealt what seemed for a time to be a death blow to the transient society. The demand for labor was so great, the patriotic fervor was so intense, and in many cases the hand of the law was so relentless that the migrant found "going on the road" very difficult. With jobs plentiful he found begging met a poor response, and he was constantly in danger of being termed a "slacker" and being thrown into jail or put

[8] "Cheerful Dead-beats Who Go Around the World Without a Cent," *Literary Digest*, LXXXIV (1925), 59.

to work on a rock pile. He was virtually forced, therefore, to simulate doing some useful activity, and this was not entirely an unmixed evil. With the high wages which were paid and the slothful work which was tolerated, he could work a few days without too much misery and then could travel in comfort to a job in some other part of the country. The begging migrant, therefore, practically disappeared, but it is generally conceded that as a worker he was still primarily a migrant.

The end of the war brought a quick restoration of the nomad world, very much as it had been before except that it thrived under the prosperity of the "gay twenties." The begging fraternity discarded hand-me-down civilian clothes, donned dilapidated army uniforms, and sailed peacefully under the banner of unemployed veterans. The hobo found jobs plentiful and wages high in the harvests and in the construction of buildings and highways. As the "gay twenties" became more gay, however, the lot of the hobo became less flowery. As the combine for harvesting wheat came into use some two hundred thousand of his group had their source of livelihood taken away. The hobo had to turn almost entirely to the then thriving construction industry for employment, and when the depression stilled the concrete mixer, he was left completely stranded. The depression thus virtually forced the hobo to become a tramp.

The plight of the hobo, however, was only the beginning of the depression story. The seasoned "bum" must have stood aghast as he saw his world changing before his eyes. The number of young boys on the road increased by leaps and bounds until by 1932 they were declared a national menace and a national disgrace. The tramp further found his jungles swarming with unemployed of all sorts, persons of all degrees of education and of all walks of life. Even women flocked onto the road in surprising numbers. How strange it must have seemed to the aged tramp to suddenly find his freight trains crowded, his jungles filled, and even his highways lined with foot-loose humanity wandering as aimlessly as himself. As these wandering hordes increased in numbers, towns and localities became both puzzled and alarmed, and the arm of the law became diligent. Trains were met by officers, and "bums" were ordered not to set foot on the ground, vagrants were ordered out of town, and everything conceivable was done to keep the transient on the move. Thus the transient found himself almost literally shoved from coast to coast and back again without a chance for food and rest. The boxcar was his prison.

While the world of migratory individuals was undergoing a metamorphosis, another type of transient was becoming a national problem. Migratory families had appeared on the road many years before the depression. In a sense, the migratory family had two predecessors, the migratory social agency family and the hobo family. For years there had been families who managed in some way to get social agencies to ship them from one city to another, and thus they traveled and lived continually at the public's expense. Until nationwide agreements between social agencies were formulated, such "shipping" was fairly easy to secure and there were many families who availed themselves of it.

The hobo family was a somewhat different phenomenon. This family lived primarily by temporary work and spent much time and most of its surplus earnings traveling from one job to another. Some of these families earned their livelihood in the construction industry, but perhaps most of them depended on seasonal harvest work for their income. Wheat, sugar beets, potatoes, fruits, and even cotton demanded extra labor for the harvest. The small fruits were particularly popular with large families because all but babes in arms could be employed. These casual laboring families usually lived reasonably well during the summer, but the winter season was always a problem. There was little labor available and their reserve was seldom sufficient to tide them over. As long ago as the early postwar period, many of these families started in the early summer with the wheat harvest in Texas or Oklahoma and worked their way to the northwest by means of the successive harvests of wheat, sugar beets, Irish potatoes, and fruit. Often as winter came on they found themselves stranded on the north

Pacific coast with no mode of livelihood for the winter and no way to get back to their original starting point for the next summer's harvests.

As the automobile developed, both the social agency and the hobo families took to the highways in large numbers. By some method they managed to get a dilapidated car and usually some semblance of camping equipment. Thus travel was facilitated, for they could secure gasoline easier than they could get railroad tickets.

As the twenties went by, the hobo family saw its mode of livelihood wrecked by the same forces which destroyed the labor market for the homeless hobo. During the same time an increasingly precarious common labor situation was forcing more and more families onto the road in search of work. Consequently, even before the rumblings of the big crash were at all distinct, social agencies everywhere were driven to distraction by the numerous "automobile families" which applied to them for help. These families usually drove into town and pitched camp on any spot that was available. They then applied to some relief agency for assistance, giving people in distant cities or out-of-the-way places as references. The usual practice was for the agency to give relief pending investigation which often required several days. And as a rule by the time the investigation was completed the family had disappeared, having gone to some other city to go through the whole process again. The amount such families cost social agencies for telegrams alone would doubtless be a staggering sum. The history of one of these families is very revealing.

The Thetal family came to Nashville from Texas in a dilapidated car of the cheaper class. Apparently their purpose in coming was to file suit against the parents of Mrs. Thetal's first husband for money which they asserted was due them as back support for a child by this first marriage. Soon after arriving in the city their money ran out and they went to a relief agency for aid. During the three months they were in the city they were on the relief rolls of this organization almost constantly.

The family at this time consisted of the father, the mother, three daughters, ten, six, and five years old, respectively, and one son, eight years of age. The two oldest children were placed in school, and it was found that the ten-year-old girl was only prepared for grade 2-C and that the boy was only prepared to handle the work in grade 1-B. A physical examination showed that Mr. Thetal had a very severe heart disease which made it necessary for him to stay in bed most of the time and made it impossible for him to do any work. Mrs. Thetal's physical condition was not an unsurmountable problem, although she was ill occasionally and had to have hospital care once. Her diagnosis was: obesity, high blood pressure, and congenital deformity of the spine. However, she was able to work most of the time. Employment was secured for her in a laundry where her work was very satisfactory.

In addition to the work which this first agency did for this family, they solicited and secured aid from three other organizations and from numerous individuals. Mrs. Thetal especially was apt at securing help from individuals and from stores.

After the family had been in this city about three months, Mr. Thetal left for parts unknown, and a week later Mrs. Thetal left without warning. Confidential information showed that her baggage was shipped to a point in Texas and several days after she left wires were received from Mr. Thetal in Georgia asking the whereabouts of Mrs. Thetal.

Data gathered from various sources by the Nashville relief agency revealed that the family had a complicated but interesting history. Mrs. Thetal was born in Oregon of very mediocre parents. Little is known of her father, but her mother was still living at the time the study was made and was characterized by the Red Cross worker of that place as "a good woman of weak mentality who has brought up several children, none of whom are a credit to her." Mrs. Thetal, however, had in her possession papers which seemed to indicate that she had finished high school and had later taken some work in a normal school.

At the age of sixteen, Mrs. Thetal was married to a man

who was working in the lumber camps in Oregon. For a time they lived in one lumber camp and then another in that section of the country. Later they moved to Florida, but soon afterward settled on a farm in North Carolina. She soon got restless on this farm and got to going into town and spending several days and sometimes weeks at a time. During this time she was a client of the charitable organizations and seems to have received help from quite a number of philanthropic sources. Finally, the tension between her and her husband became so great that at her request he sent her back to her mother. He later secured a divorce in North Carolina, and she claimed to have secured one in Oregon. There was one child, a girl, born to this union, and she took this child with her to Oregon.

About eighteen months after Mrs. Thetal returned to Oregon she was married to Mr. Thetal. His history previous to this time is mostly unknown. He refused to give much information about this period of his life, and no other records were found which gave much light on this point. His account, however, was that he was born in Haywood, Wisconsin, and that his father deserted his mother when he was about four years of age. They lived in hotels until he was about thirteen years of age, when they began to travel back and forth from the West. He later settled in Oregon in a lumber camp. He was still working in the lumber camps when he met Mrs. Thetal and married her.

For a time after Mr. and Mrs. Thetal were married, Mr. Thetal continued to work in the lumber camps. Some of the time Mrs. Thetal stayed in the camps with him and part of the time she lived in towns nearby. In several of these towns they are known to have received aid from the social service organizations and are reported to have had quite a bad reputation. It seems that at this time they had quite a moving disposition, and frequently moved away from a city suddenly, leaving unpaid bills behind.

In 1925, they were residing in the same city in which Mrs. Thetal's mother lived when Mrs. Thetal had an attack of influenza which left her considerably weakened. At that time Mr. Thetal was working as a lineman for the telephone company, and their records show that he was considered a very poor and undependable worker. Because of Mrs. Thetal's condition, they decided to move to Salt Lake City, and when they left for Salt Lake City they stole everything they could get from Mrs. Thetal's mother and fraudulently secured compensation money due Mrs. Thetal's invalid brother. Soon after arriving in Salt Lake City, Mr. Thetal had influenza, and it left his heart in such a serious condition that he was unable to pass the physical examination for re-employment with the telephone company.

After staying a time in Salt Lake City, the family left for California, and from then until the time they reached Nashville they apparently moved from one city to another almost constantly. They were known to the social agencies in a number of these cities, and were almost invariably described by these agencies as being "beggars" and being "entirely unprincipled and undependable." In most cases they left the city suddenly and left unpaid bills behind. The study disclosed that they were known to social agencies in three cities in Oregon, two in Idaho, one in Wyoming, one in Utah, four in Washington, two in California, four in Texas, and one each in Florida and Tennessee. Even this array is probably only a partial list of the cities which they visited.

In addition to its social agency record, the study revealed that the family had had a number of "run-ins" with the law. In California they were arrested for illegal possession of a car, and on this charge both Mr. and Mrs. Thetal were thrown into jail at different times. While they were in Texas a letter written by them was intercepted, which showed that they were connected with parties who were engaged in the stealing of various things. Specifically, it showed that one member of the group had been sent to jail for stealing bonds and that, if he had not been caught, the Thetals would have received a portion of the bonds. At the time the study was made they were wanted on stealing charges in a certain Texas county.

In addition to these outward conflicts with society, there was evidence of internal tensions in the family. The apparent separation of Mr. and Mrs. Thetal while in Nashville has already been mentioned. Previous to this Mr. Thetal had deserted for a short time while the family was in California. Dora, the daughter of Mrs. Thetal by her first marriage, was also a center of difficulties. Evidence indicated that she had been grossly mistreated, and for a time she was removed from the family by social agencies in California. Finally, shortly before the family went to Nashville, she ran away and married an automobile salesman who was thought to have another wife elsewhere. Her family claimed to have not heard from her since her marriage.

When the depression broke there were already thousands of homeless individuals and migratory families roving the country by railroad or highway. And most of them were economically dependent, garnering a livelihood from social agencies, individual begging, or stealing. To these were quickly added other thousands, as economic bedlam spread across the nation and the unemployed weighed anchor in the hope of finding work elsewhere.

This was the situation into which the federal government stepped with its far-famed Transient Bureau. Being the first national attempt in the United States to deal with the migrant, it worked practically without precedent. Knowing that transients come from all over the country but tend to congregate in certain centers, such as Chicago, New Orleans, Denver, and the Florida and Pacific Coast cities, which cannot be expected to shoulder the full responsibility, many have considered the problem the proper responsibility of the federal government. Therefore, the establishment of the Transient Bureau was hailed with high hopes by those who knew the field.

The Transient Bureau experiment, however, was in general a disappointment. During most of its existence it seemed to work on the theory that the transients under its care were almost entirely normal persons traveling in search of work. Thus it devoted its efforts primarily to giving food, clothing, and lodging with some aid in finding employment to those under its care. Fundamentally its method was to provide "shelters" in the different cities and through the shelters provide these necessities. Usually it had a workhouse program and a recreation program in each city. There was little special service provided for individual or abnormal cases and almost no apparent effort was made to cope with the old-fashioned chronic tramps and beggars mixed in among the migratory laborers. Poor co-ordination with local ERA units tended to blur still further the demarcation between the transient and the unemployed. Families in localities where ERA relief scales were low went to other places and as "transients" received higher relief apportionments, persons finding local relief agencies overworked and behind schedule went to other cities and secured immediate care from the Transient Bureau, and youths in families of the unemployed went "on the road" to relieve the economic pressure in their family and were cared for by the bureau. Some of these persons thus set loose traveled much but others traveled little. At any rate the program of the bureau seemed to confuse rather than clarify the transient scene.

With the establishment of the WPA in 1936 the Transient Bureau was discontinued. The transients were supposed to be returned to their respective places of legal residence and there cared for like other local residents by the WPA work program. In many localities the WPA quotas were not sufficient to care for all, and part of these semidetached transients found themselves excluded. In addition we found what England had found centuries earlier, that many of these people were unable to establish legal residence anywhere. With births never recorded or birth records lost or destroyed and with the background of a semi-migratory life for many years, thousands of them were in no position to establish legal claim to any locality as their residence. Consequently numbers of them were left in the same position they were in before the Transient Bureau was established. Federal programs could not help them, such local agencies as were open to them had niggardly support, and each locality tried to solve its problem by pushing the transients on to other localities.

The effects of transiency on the individual are most easily seen in the life and culture of those groups which are habitually and continuously transient. So far as effects on the individual are concerned, there are three types of transients: the transient individual, the transient family, and the transient clan, typified by the gypsy. Of the three, the life of the transient individual has the greatest tendency to create permanent maladjustment to settled society. This tendency to maladjustment arises both from what the person gets and from what he fails to get in the migratory life. The culture of the transient world is more or less the opposite of that of settled society. Most of the things which settled society approves the transient world belittles, and most of the things which settled society taboos the transient world condones. The transient world has a very scant conception of private property rights, almost no standards of personal morality, and dependence is accepted as a matter of course.

To the extent to which a person accepts the culture of the transient world, he is ill-equipped to adjust to the opposing culture of organized society. Equally significant, however, are the by-products of the transient's existence. Settled society is organized, and the individual to adjust to it must belong to and participate in groups and institutions of a wide variety, and the migratory individual gets practically no training for such participation. The transient's own world is a highly individualized affair with few groups or institutions which he can call his own, and the institutions of settled society he sees as a recipient or as an observer but not as a participant. He sees family life as he gets a backdoor handout, but as a transient individual he does not participate in the experiences of family life. He receives help from social agencies, but he neither administers them nor supports them. He sees church buildings, but he does not sit on a board of deacons or teach a Sunday school class. So long as he is a transient, therefore, he gets virtually no experience which would help him to participate in society's institutions.

Another by-product of the transient individual's mode of

life is the effect that it has on his ability to react to other persons. As has been noted, the world of transient individuals is mostly a one-sex affair and there are very few children in it. Having to associate almost entirely with men, the migrant tends to lose his ability to react to the other sex and age components of settled society. But perhaps of even greater significance is the fact that typically the individual transient does not have any continuous or intimate contacts with individuals even of his own kind. His contacts are very transitory and very casual. Even when he dies there is usually no one to mourn his fate, and as a rule no one can even identify him. Everything about his life tends to make him very self-centered, very much of a shut-in personality. He does not love, nor is he loved; he does not receive sympathy, nor does he give it; and he has no conception of working and sacrificing for others. In brief, he fails to develop any of the finer virtues to which settled humanity aspires.

In contrast to the transient individual, the person in a migratory family does experience participation in family life, which seems to be the primary institution of society, and this participation gives him enduring and presumably intimate contacts with a few individuals. He is likely, therefore, to be more human than the transient individual. With respect to the secondary institutions of society, however, he is at the same disadvantage as the migratory individual: children cannot attend school or church and adults do not stay in one place long enough to identify themselves with local institutions. In addition, the values found in the culture of the transient family world are very similar to those in the "world of homeless men."

The gypsy has evolved a mode of life which alleviates many of the disadvantages of the life, both of the transient individual and of the migratory family. Though a transient and a parasite, the gypsy usually does not beg. The chief innovation of the gypsy in comparison to other migrants is that he carries his "neighborhood" with him. Ordinarily he does not travel as a "lone soldier" or by single families. He travels in groups of families. Thus, in addition to the family, the individual lives in a society, a society which has definite standards and regulations. His society distinguishes clearly between relations within the gypsy group and those with the outside world. Stealing within the group is one thing, stealing from the outside world is something entirely different. The gypsy consequently knows how to respond to and participate in group and institutional life. The gypsy life, of all the forms of transiency, therefore, would seem best suited to train the individual for participation in settled society. It cannot be said in truth, however, that it has had that effect. The gypsy, in fact, has a cultural and racial continuity older than that of any other transient element known, and these cultural and racial traits have made his world so different from that of the societies through which he travels that few have ever crossed in either direction the chasm which separates them.

While the price which the individual and society have to pay for habitual transiency is very great, as long as there are crops to be harvested and construction work to be done, mobile laborers will be required. There are areas which deplete their resources and have to be vacated and others in which the population increases so rapidly as to make movement desirable. So transiency is still both desirable and undesirable, or, as others view it, it is neither desirable nor undesirable.

That something more should be done about the problem than has yet been done seems to be generally accepted. Just what should be done is not so clear, but perhaps the general nature of wise action is best indicated by a recent statement of the objectives of the Council on Interstate Migration, one of the best informed organizations in this field.

"Early in 1938 the Committee's examination of its position, accomplishments, and objectives resulted in the determination that a change in emphasis was necessary. It had become increasingly apparent that concentration upon meeting relief needs for transient and homeless persons was not enough. These needs are only manifestations of wider and deeper problems which should be attacked.

The whole question of migration within the United States was seen to be basic. Migration in the past, it was noted, had made possible the unprecedented development of the country; and much migration is still called for if that development is to continue. Some areas are over-populated in relation to their resources; others require a larger population to speed their progress; seasonal industries and agriculture depend upon a mobile labor supply. Problems affecting health, education, employment, and social conditions arise when this necessary migration conflicts with the traditional theory and underlying principle of our institutions that people are born, live, and die in one community. The barriers to migration established by the various states and their local communities make it a hazardous venture for the individual or family who would move in the quest for opportunity. These same barriers give rise to the social philosophy that everyone has a "home community" to which he should be returned if he happens to be in need of assistance. The larger objective now envisioned calls for such adjustment of our social, economic, health, legislative, and employment structure as to provide for the necessary migration of individuals and families." [9]

[9] "Memorandum on Organization of the Council on Interstate Migration," p. 4.

~~~~~~~~~~~~~~~~~~~~~~~~~~~~~~~~

CHAPTER V

URBAN BEGGARDOM

IT IS a rare and unusual person who is not accosted by beggars from once to many times daily in the modern city, but in spite of this continual contact with beggars, few people have any comprehensive knowledge of the begging world as it lives and operates in the present-day metropolis. To picture local beggardom, it must be differentiated from the world of transient beggars, as typified by the tramp, hobo, and bum. Though it is impossible to classify all people as either transient or nontransient, most people do fall into one of the two classes, and there are essential differences between them. Beggars, likewise, fall more or less naturally into transient and non-transient groups. The local beggar differs from the transient in much the same way as the settled merchant and the settled mill worker differ from the traveling salesman and the migratory laborer.

Contrary to popular belief, most of the beggars in the usual city are not transient but local. Of the beggars who may be found on the streets or who visit the stores, offices, and residences of the ordinary city, the majority are generally permanently attached to that city. A record of their current and past wanderings would not be radically different from that of the ordinary citizens. An investigation would reveal that some of them are native to the community and have traveled little outside of it; others were born and reared in other places. Some of these would be found to have lived in the city for a short time only, while others would have been there many years.

The current travel of such beggars is strikingly similar to that of other people. Some have a regular stand at which they beg continuously year in and year out. Others beg in almost all parts of the city. Still others have their home in the city and use the city as a base from which to beg in the surrounding country. In other words, they supplement whatever they may do in the city with excursions to adjacent towns and cities. Especially do they frequent smaller agricultural towns on Saturday afternoons, and they always attend all of the fairs and public celebrations held within a radius of from fifty to seventy-five miles of their home base city.

But who are all these beggars and what are they like as human beings? That is a query which the average almsgiver never gets answered. The answer is that they are about as heterogenous a collection as the general population.

The marital status of the local beggar is virtually the same as that of other people. Every possible type of marital status will be found among them. Many are the heads of families. A considerable number are widowed, divorced, or deserted, but have their children with them. Others have had families in the past but for one reason or another no longer have immediate family connections. And some are single persons who have never had a family of their own.

To understand the majority of local beggars, it is necessary to understand that if the beggar has an immediate family, begging with him is not an individual occupation; it is a family affair. Because of the fact that begging is an outlawed and socially outcast occupation, the family status is almost wholly determined by the beggar or beggars in it. Begging is seldom practiced, therefore, by one member of a family while other members of the family work at respectable occupations. Some members of a beggar's family may work at common labor or as hucksters, but they will hardly ever be found in skilled labor groups, the white-collar occupations, or the professions. They may be employed in some of the other outlawed occupations, but often the more "aristocratic" of underworld professions will not tolerate begging by members of their family.

This integral relationship of the beggar's profession to his family connections is due not only to the status of begging but also to the peculiar philosophy which underlies the profession. This philosophy entails an acceptance of the fact that the family or individual cannot or should not earn a livelihood by means of socially approved occupations. Furthermore, having deserted the field of socially approved occupations, the beggar, in contrast to members of the other underworld occupations, does not go to war with society. Rather, in reality or in form, he throws himself at the feet of society and appeals for help. The beggar's philosophy, therefore, while it has some elements in common with that of other outlaw occupations, has some elements peculiar to itself. Because of this peculiarity in the beggar's philosophy it is seldom possible for one member of a family to hold it if the rest of the members do not. This, coupled with the fact that the whole family status suffers from the begging of one individual, makes it almost inevitable that the whole family concur in the beggar's philosophy or that the begging member separate himself from his family.

The fact that begging is usually a family rather than an individual phenomenon does not imply that for a family to be classified as a begging family all members must beg. As we shall see later, any or all members may participate in the actual begging. But however that may be, the essential factors are that all members of the family share in the proceeds from the begging, have the beggar's philosophy, and bear his social status.

In studying begging families, it is frequently difficult to draw the line between the merely dependent families and the begging families. There are many families which do some begging but do not beg regularly and do not depend entirely on begging for their support. Some of these families are in the process of developing the begging pattern, and they may at a later date become habitual beggars. Some, however, while they may continue their limited begging, will probably never materially increase their activities.

From the standpoint of numbers, probably the most prevalent type of marginal begging family is the social agency family. A large number of families in the lower ranks of the economic scale are temporarily forced into dependency at one time or another in their history. During these periods of dependency, the family must have aid from some source, and in the city it is these families which normally comprise the major case load of the family social service agencies. At such times they, of necessity, learn the technique of securing aid from organizations, and in the future they have a tendency to call for help in crises which they formerly would have come through by themselves. In other words, they tend to develop a dependency or begging attitude. Symptomatic of the development of such an attitude is the tendency of the family to manufacture excuses why it should have relief instead of applying for aid only as a last resort. The tendency for families to develop such an attitude constitutes one of the most difficult case work problems which relief agencies have to face. To prevent the complete pauperization of such families, the agency frequently has to bring pressure to bear on the family or to refuse it aid entirely. The Herrick family is typical of such cases.

Mr. Herrick is about thirty-five years of age and is apparently in good physical condition. He has a high school education, is generally neat in appearance, and has a pleasing personality. In addition to his wife, there are four children in his family. Mr. Herrick is a carpenter by profession and is reported to do reasonably good work. For years he has applied periodically to local social agencies for relief. Sometimes he has been given aid, at other times refused. Every time that an agency has started giving relief he has remained "unemployed" until the agency stopped giving help. Then he usually succeeded in finding a job.

Frequently families who have begun to develop the dependency attitude turn to other forms of begging when the social agencies begin to put pressure on them to earn their livelihood. In many cases this results in the development of

professional beggars. The Kutz family has reacted in this way
to pressure from social agencies.

The Kutz family consists of the father, the mother, and
a daughter. The mother was married once before her
present marriage, but neither of the two children born to
this marriage lived. The father was left an orphan at an
early age and was reared by an older brother.

The mother lost her sight upon the birth of the daughter, and the father has been in poor health for a considerable time. The family now lives in a small city. For several
years before coming to this city they lived in small towns,
and in these places help came easily because of the blindness of the mother. Finally, a postmaster in one of these
towns gave them money to come to the city "because that
county is good to its poor." They fell into the hands of a
relief agency soon after reaching the city and have been
almost constant charges for twelve years.

Mr. Kutz has been pronounced incurable, but he is
able to work at times. He has developed such a dependent attitude, however, that when his health does im-
prove so he can work he almost invariably has to be
arrested for vagrancy before he will take a job. In addition
to begging from social agencies, he frequently begs from
other organizations and from individuals. Once he even
got so bold as to make a special visit to the governor's wife.
He puts up a pitiful story of being broken in health and of
having a blind wife and a child to support, and the story
usually brings results.

Another type of the marginal begging family is that which
does casual or part-time begging. Such families have a definite
begging technique, but only resort to it in times of crises. They
are not radically different from hundreds of other families who
are on the verge of dependency. In normal times and under
normal circumstances they are able to make a living for themselves, and they have enough pride to do so. But when some
calamity befalls the principal wage earner in the family, some
help is imperative, and the begging technique is resorted to,

much as other families appeal to the social service agencies for help. The Hankton family is of this type.

Mr. Hankton is a semi-paralytic and has been in this condition for many years. His left arm is drawn considerably, and his left leg is drawn sufficiently to give him a pronounced limp when he walks. He has had very little schooling but he has a reputation of being honest and morally straight. He is also reputed to be a good worker on such jobs as he is able to do, and for a number of years he was a regular employee of the city railway company. For the past ten years he has been selling fruit and candy around the business section and has acquired a large number of friends and patrons. Although many of his patrons buy his goods because of sympathy, his business can hardly be classed with the begging-street-trades because he keeps his goods clean and most of his customers take goods in exchange for their money.

Mrs. Hankton is a most repulsive woman in appearance. She weighs about two hundred and fifty pounds, has a coarse shrieky voice, and has a rather heavy growth of beard. Her clothing is always untidy, and her carriage is extremely awkward. She never attempts to do any work except care for the house and is apparently unemployable or nearly so. When Mr. Hankton is unable to work because of illness, as is frequently the case, she sends out begging letters to his friends and to citizens in the community and usually secures sufficient help to tide them over until he can return to his work.

In addition to these numerous marginal begging families, there are many families who beg regularly and who usually depend entirely on begging returns for their livelihood. Occasionally one of these families will be found in which some of the members beg and others work at socially recognized occupations, but such is the exception rather than the rule. The Hillard family has such a dual source of income.

Mr. Hillard is a man in his late forties, and he is normal physically. He appears, however, to have a very low mentality, and is completely docile and entirely lacking in resourcefulness. His wife is blind and is very domineering, aggressive, and irritable. In addition to the parents, there are five children in the family. Mr. Hillard works at a lumber yard where he is reported to be dependable but incapable of doing anything but the most simple tasks. His wages, of course, are very small. The major part of the family income is derived from Mrs. Hillard's begging. She begs regularly from house to house, using one of her children to lead her, and usually she is very successful.

In considering the full-time begging family, the division of labor is an important factor. In other words, who does the begging? Unlike most other professions, the practice of begging is not confined to any age or to either sex. Any or all of the members of the family, therefore, may engage in the practice. It is not to be inferred, however, that the family has no plan or organization to its begging. Usually the family specializes to some extent in one type of begging, and one or two members of the family have skill in the techniques requisite to its practice. Just which members the responsibility falls on may in the beginning be a matter of accident, but it is frequently determined by the suitability of the individual for the task. If the father is able-bodied or looks to be so, he will have difficulty in making much of an appeal to the public, and the begging task will likely fall to some other member of the family. If, however, he is crippled, blind, or sickly looking, he will probably do part or all of the begging. On the other hand, the wife even if she looks strong and healthy can always make a forceful appeal if she is apt at telling hard luck stories of how her husband fails to support her or is cruel to her, and if she does not fail to stress the fact that she has a large family of children to support. Children, as we shall see later, have a natural appeal to givers, and in some cases the task of begging falls on them. Perhaps more frequently, however, they accompany some adult either as aides or to furnish atmosphere. While it is difficult to predict in any given case just who will do the begging, it is generally true that the blind, crippled, or deformed person, if the family has such a person, will bear most of the begging burden. If there is no physically handicapped person in the family, the work of begging tends to fall on the wife, the children, or the aged, and not on the husband. The Hibbs family is a more or less typical chronic begging family.

The Hibbs family has lived in one city almost continually for about thirty years, and has supported itself by begging during most of that time. Mr. Hibbs, the father, is about sixty-five years of age and is blind, but otherwise he is a perfect physical specimen. He is about six feet in height, weighs some two hundred pounds, and is well-proportioned. Mrs. Hibbs is about the same age as her husband, is a good match for him physically, and has a semblance of Irish features. She has good eyesight. There have been four children born to the couple, two boys and two girls. One of the boys was drowned a few years ago. The other boy is married and lives in the same city as the parents. In addition to his wife, he has one child. He is partially blind and depends for support on work furnished him by an agency for the blind. One of the daughters has been married, but her husband deserted her, leaving her with a child. She and this child now live with her parents. The other daughter is technically married at present, but her husband is serving a life sentence for murder. She and her two young children, therefore, are also living with her parents. The household therefore consists of Mr. and Mrs. Hibbs, their two daughters, who for all practical purposes are widowed, and three young grandchildren.

The chief income of the family is derived from the store begging done by Mr. and Mrs. Hibbs. Both of them dress in very shabby clothes, and Mrs. Hibbs leads Mr. Hibbs to the door of a store where he stands and plays a hand organ while she passes a cup on the inside. Except during very bad weather they beg regularly every morning, and occasionally in the afternoon. They shed their begging togs as soon as they get home and dress in very neat and comfortable clothes. The daughter whose husband de-

serted her is the housekeeper for the family and takes
full responsibility for that work. The other daughter
divides her efforts between helping with the housework
and doing residence begging. When, before the depression, an investigator told Mr. Hibbs that these two daughters could nearly support the family if they would go to
work, he became very indignant and said, "I do not want
them to work. I cover every inch of the ground that I
stand on and I am going to take care of my family."

Apparently the Hibbses have made a fair but modest living from their begging. They own their home, a reasonably nice four-room house located in a poor residential
section. They claim, however, that this is not completely
paid for. They seem to have all of the essentials for quiet
living, but they do not possess any luxuries such as an
automobile. And so far as could be determined they have
not accumulated any appreciable savings.

The attitudes and philosophy of the Hibbses are more
or less typical of their kind. Characteristically, they call
their begging "work" and see nothing wrong with it. Mrs.
Hibbs probably told the truth when she said, "Some people say I ought to be ashamed to beg, but I am not
ashamed of it. I am proud of it. Lazarus was a beggar and
he went to Heaven, but the rich man didn't." And as a
manifestation of their pride they can easily grow eloquent
in bewailing social agencies and the police for meddling
with begging.

Somewhat similar to these begging families are the aged,
single beggars of the city. With the lower economic classes,
particularly in the city, old age is in many cases a period of
dependency. The city laborer seldom is able to accumulate
savings or pay for insurance to care for him in old age, industry no longer wants these worn-out wheel horses, their
relatives are weighted down with family problems of their
own, and social agencies have not made adequate provision
for caring for them in their own homes. If, therefore, the city
worker lives to a "ripe old age," he in many cases has to choose
between the "poor house" and begging, and often he chooses

the latter. Every city, therefore, has a considerable group of these old persons who turn to begging as an old age pension. In their day they may have worked at anything from regular labor to a nondescript assortment of odd jobs. Many of them have been married but have lost their mate through death, divorce, or desertion. Likewise many of them have grown children who are married but unable to care for them, and some of them have never been married at all. Some of these old characters are as lovable as they are pathetic.

Henderson was a well-known old bachelor beggar in his city. For many years he begged regularly at a stand on one of the main streets. He usually sat at the opening of a stairway with a cup on the walk in front of him and played his violin. He was what is known as an "old time fiddler" and many enjoyed his music.

Henderson was born and reared in a rural section not far from the city in which he spent most of his life. He left home at the age of twenty-five to work in a pencil factory near his home. After working in this factory for two years, he became restless and moved into the city. At various times in the city he worked at a number of different jobs, all of which were common labor. He never married, and while in the city lived for the most part in boarding houses.

Henderson had two sisters, but he outlived the last surviving one by ten years. After her death he had no near relative living.

Henderson did not have many intimate friends but there were many people who liked him and enjoyed talking to him. Even well-known business men would walk by his stand, listen to his music, chat a little with him, and drop a coin in his cup. When he died at the age of sixty-three, the local papers made prominent mention of his passing.

Sometimes these aged, single beggars make life more tolerable by setting up a co-operative relationship. Some of these arrangements resemble common law marriages, while others are almost purely economic.

Wells, an aged widower beggar, lives in an upstairs room of a cheap tenant house. An adjoining room is occupied by Ethel, a widow beggar of some sixty years. She lives with a son twenty-five years of age who is a chronic drunkard and spends most of his time in jail. Wells furnishes most of the groceries for Ethel and she in turn prepares his food and cleans his room. On cold winter days they frequently economize on fuel by keeping a fire in only one room.

Another interesting group of local beggars are what might be termed "vice beggars." Prostitutes or criminals are usually as unfortunate in old age as the laborer and many of them have to turn to begging. Frequently, by the time they have reached this stage they have become victims either of "dope" or of "booze." Whether old or young, however, most drug slaves are physical, moral, and economic wrecks and they have to beg or steal for a living. These various vice victims, regardless of age or past history, tend to hang together, and they blend begging, sex, intoxication, and the use and sale of drugs into a "mess" of the worst order.

Emma and May were born in the city in which they now live and have lived there all of their lives. Their father was a laborer in a cotton mill, and the family was always in very poor circumstances. There were six children, and all of them had to go to work in the mills at an early age to help support the home.

Emma, who is the older of the two sisters, was forced by her parents to marry when she was thirteen years of age because of the financial condition of the family. She only stayed with the man one night, however, and returned to her parents who made no further attempt to make her live with him.

When she was three years of age, May had a stroke of infantile paralysis which left her lame and her left arm and hand drawn. Like the other children, she attended school very little. When she was fourteen she married a boy eighteen, who worked in a factory and was a neighbor. They established a home to themselves, but after two

weeks he lost his job, and they moved back to her parents.
Her husband proved to be a very poor provider and, in
addition, he had a disreputable character. Considerable
friction developed between them, and they separated frequently. All this time they continued to live with May's
parents.

A few years after May's marriage, her mother became
an invalid. All of her brothers and sisters, except Emma
who was working in the cotton mills, had gotten married,
and so May was left to care for her mother during the day.
At times, Emma was forced to stay away from work to
help. This continued twelve years before the mother's
death.

Upon the mother's death, the two girls were left alone
with the father. May's husband was in the home some, but
he was not a substantial contributor to the support of the
household. Shortly after this, May became pregnant. She
suffered so much pain from this that she began using
dope, at first buying it in powdered form and touching it
to her tongue with her finger. From this beginning, the
habit grew rapidly. The child was born perfectly normal,
however, but only lived eleven months. It died from an
illness contracted during the teething period. About a year
later, May and her husband separated for good.

By this time the father was getting old and was unable
to contribute much to the support of the family. Emma
and May worked in the hosiery mills, but even then they
had to have help from the social service organizations frequently. Emma gradually took up the dope habit from
May, and it soon had such a grip on them that they were
unable to handle their work in the mills. May, making use
of her physical deformities, started begging on the streets,
and Emma stayed around home doing nothing except
making occasional excursions out along the railroad to
pick up coal or to the dump pile to find articles that might
be of use to them. They were tossed around from one
place to another because of their inability to pay rent.
For twelve years they lived this way. Several times they
were placed in the county asylum to be cured of the dope
habit, but each time they returned to their old ways

shortly after being released. Gradually they fell into other delinquencies. Several times they were arrested for drunkenness and were often suspected of immoral conduct. Finally they drifted into an old, condemned house known as the "Free Brick." No rent was charged in this house, and it was a settling basin for dope fiends and worn-out prostitutes of the poorest sort. Eleven addicts were taken from here at one time by federal narcotic officers.

Beggardom in the local urban community at any given time contains another element which is not strictly local; this consists of a semi-transient and in a way highly professional element. The members of this group are in general more intelligent and better educated than the local beggars, and before the depression it contained more able-bodied young men. In its culture and social contacts this group is in many respects very cosmopolitan. Its members know beggars of similar type in all parts of the country, and members are constantly coming and going from the local aggregation. Each one keeps posted, therefore, as to begging conditions in other cities and as to where conventions, races, or fairs are to be held. In general, they are better begging artists than the local beggar; they have a more studied appeal, use a better make-up, and are more practiced in their simulation of physical ailments. Since they can pay a fine and move on to another city if they get caught, they can use false claims and faked physical defects which might prove disastrous to the local beggar. In addition to the usual desire for new scenery, therefore, their travels are prompted by the prospects of more fertile fields for forage elsewhere and by the danger of arrest for using a fake appeal too long in the same place. In each of these cities which they visit, there are certain cheap hotels and lodging houses which are known to the fraternity and at which they stay. In fact, there are cliques in this larger grouping, drawn together by common interests and often practicing the same begging techniques, and there is a tendency for each of these cliques to have a favorite lodging place in each city. Many of these semi-transients live a very care-free, modest existence, but others work for larger returns and live in luxury.

Mr. and Mrs. Heter are beggars of professional rank. He is able-bodied, but he is also a real artist at faking palsy. She has had both hands amputated above the wrists and uses her stubs very effectively in begging. Both do begging, but they work separately.

Both Mr. and Mrs. Heter are about fifty-five years of age, and they live a life which many couples their age would envy. They own an eight-room home in a northern city where they live and beg during the summer. As winter approaches they close their house, get in their Lincoln car, and start south. Usually they make their way by begging to Hot Springs, Arkansas, where they take a round of baths; then they go to other southern cities for the winter tourist and racing season.

A characterization of the local mendicant world would not be complete without mention of the relation of the beggar to his giving public. This relationship is a most curious and a most interesting one; for even though the beggar lives in the same city for a lifetime and gets a livelihood given to him, supposedly because of his needs, few givers have any knowledge of his personal life or of his real needs. In the case of some beggars this anonymity is solely due to the lack of public interest. Other beggars, however, take extensive precautions to shield their private life from the public gaze. The faker who tells a fabricated hard luck story or simulates a physical defect must make his appeal to an unknown public. Likewise, the beggars who make a practice of working social agencies, churches, and civic organizations are severely handicapped if their identity becomes too well known. Ordinarily, they cannot secure aid from those sources if they are known to be beggars; they must always appeal on the basis of temporary difficulties. Such beggars, therefore, take every precaution to prevent becoming familiar figures. They do not call on the same agency or organization too often, they move from one section of the city to another, and they pass under different names. Because of the aliases which they assume, it is often difficult or impossible to check them through agency records or through confidential exchanges. The professional social worker, therefore, frequently has to learn to know by sight the worst charity rogues. A new worker, a new staff, or a new organization is at a distinct disadvantage and is liable to be duped by the professionals.

During the recent Mississippi River flood, a refugee camp was established at Memphis, Tennessee. As the flood waters receded the refugees returned to their homes, and the time came for closing the camp. By means of private and public efforts all of the refugees were disposed of except one woman. Through no means could the authorities locate a relative, friend, or acquaintance of this woman. Finally, in despair, they made arrangements with the local Salvation Army to take care of her for a time. She was taken over to the Army headquarters by one of the camp officials and one of the Army workers immediately recognized her as a local beggar, and called her by name. Realizing that her game was up, the woman made a hasty get-away.[1]

In contrast to these beggars who make such strenuous attempts to keep their identity concealed, other local beggars become quite familiar figures and may even acquire a certain status and reputation. Even so, few givers will know much about the individual or his family. The public will infer more than it actually knows. If a person knows that a beggar has been begging for ten years, he will assume that the beggar needs the money. Likewise, if a beggar tells the same hard luck story to the same giver a dozen times, the giver may accept the truth of the story and certainly will not wish to hear it rehearsed again. The local beggar, therefore, sometimes loses his begging art because his giving public accepts his needs and there is no longer any necessity for a special appeal.

Among the most interesting of these "familiar" mendicants is the street beggar who acquires a squatter's claim to a given

[1] From an interview with a camp official.

corner by begging regularly on it for a number of years. His regular appearance at his stand makes him an integral part of the architecture. The corner does not look right without him. He is missed when he is absent. Any other beggar on this corner looks like an impostor, and local property owners and police frequently help to reserve the stand for its "rightful owner."

Willie is a deformed Negro about thirty years of age. Both legs and one arm are pitiably misshapen. For a number of years he has begged regularly in front of a bank in a certain city. In spite of the fact that the city has an ordinance prohibiting begging, he is never molested. The officers of the bank, even though they cannot tell you his home address or his name, wish the stand preserved for him and the policemen on that beat respect their wishes even to the extent of keeping other beggars away.

Occasionally one of these local beggars becomes a community joke and is supported by the sense of humor of the citizens.

Jim, for example, is a well-known character in a certain city. He is variously characterized as feebleminded, crazy, and queer. To say the least, he is eccentric. He is a white man some sixty years of age, about five feet and six inches in height, and of slight build. The eccentricity which gains him most favor is his love for gaudy, overdone dress. It would not be considered unusual for him to appear on one of the main streets at any hour of the day dressed in a "stove pipe" hat, a swallow tail coat, white trousers, a brilliant red tie, a corsage of flowers on his lapel, and carrying a parasol. Indeed, the variety of ridiculous clothes combinations which he conceives might put to shame the best comedian.

So comical is his usual appearance that local business men support him as a community joke. A florist gives him a large corsage of flowers daily, clothing stores give him articles designed to suit his taste, and numerous gifts come from other sources. He gets many things through pranks of which he is the butt. For example, some time ago it became known to some business men that he had a "crush" on Clara Bow. Though it was then midsummer and very hot, they sent him on consecutive days packages, with a note in each signed "Clara," containing blue woolen underwear, a red flannel golf shirt and hose and cap to match, gaudy checked knickers, and a pair of black and white sport shoes. Then, after getting him to tell them about receiving these articles, the men urged him to wear them as a token of appreciation to "Clara." Finally, one hot afternoon when the temperature was a few degrees past the hundred mark, he appeared on the street dressed in this gaudy woolen golf attire, plus his usual corsage and parasol.

In cities having anti-begging ordinances these local beggars often get a preferential rating by the police. The police know many of the local beggars by sight if not by name and often tolerate them while strictly enforcing the law against transients. Sometimes this tolerance or protection is bought by the beggars through one form or another of political corruption. In many cases, however, the police tolerate these local beggars purely from sentiment and tradition.

Jack is a Negro about thirty years of age. His only deformity is one peg leg. He is a well-known character in his community because, though he uses his peg as his main begging appeal, he has the reputation of being able to outrun any policeman on the force when cornered.

One week while the community chest campaign was in progress, the police department gave orders to keep the business district clear of beggars. An investigator walking over the section one afternoon found no beggars at all on the busiest streets. Off on a side street, however, he found Jack begging. Knowing that he usually begged on the busier streets, the investigator asked him why he was begging there. Jack said that the police had told him that he would have to stay off the main streets for a few days, but that it would be all right for him to work on the side streets.

As is apparent, the begging fraternity in a city is in some respects a very heterogeneous lot. It includes people of all ages and many types, and in its activities covers the whole city and often the countryside as well. With this diversity added to the social and legal opposition, the profession in American cities is very poorly organized. There are many small cliques and groups, but these are more likely to be "social clubs" than "trade associations." Occasionally, however, an effective beggars' organization is found; it usually controls only a small part of the city. Because of the difficulty of controlling begging over a whole city, these organizations are likely to concentrate on the central business section, which is most lucrative, small in area, and reasonably easy to control.

There are in general two types of beggar's organizations found in America. In one, an entrepreneur goes into the business of hiring and managing beggars. Having employed a group of likely beggars, he provides them with whatever make-up and equipment they need. From his stock of supplies, he provides old clothes, false legs, hand organs, monkeys, and he may even supply the "widows" with children; if necessary, he may even teach them the art of begging. Then he selects stands for the beggars and designates the working schedule. In other words, he furnishes the equipment and the brains and the beggars furnish the physical handicaps. In addition, he may provide lodging to his employees. In financial settlement, he may charge the beggar so much a day for his services as manager and let the beggar keep all collected over this amount, or he may take all the money and pay the beggar a stipulated salary.

The other type of organization is confined to cities which attempt to exert legal control over begging. Here the chief purpose of organization is to secure protection from police interference. Such an organization may be similar to that described above, except that the manager buys from the political machine a begging franchise on a certain area. On the other hand, political bosses may become the managers and levy a bounty on the beggars' earnings. Such an organization is reported to have had a monopoly on begging in the central business section of one of our largest cities.

An organization of beggars formerly had their headquarters in the rear end of a saloon run by Joe Thomas on a side street just off the central business section. In this back room the beggars kept a supply of old clothes, crutches, false legs, collodion to put in the eyes to make "blind men," acid to make "jiggers" on the arms, and other articles needed in their make-up. They would come here in the morning dressed in their regular street clothes and would change to their "begging togs." At the end of the day, they would return to headquarters and change back to their street clothes. There were usually about seventy members of this gang, including ten or twelve women. They were in charge of a precinct captain for an alderman who was a political friend of a state senator. For protection each paid $1.50 to $4.00 per day depending on his "stand." This protection consisted of security from police interference and assurance that other beggars would not be allowed in the loop area.[2]

In some respects it is a bit remarkable that American racketeers and politicians have not taken in hand more generally the begging profession. Knowing the general tendency of American entrepreneurs to capitalize on the weakness and stupidities of mankind it is somewhat surprising that some ambitious gentleman has not recognized the profit to be gained by an efficient organization. For there are decided advantages of organization.

Givers are of many different types and give for many different reasons. No single beggar can touch the hearts of all givers, and no beggar can meet the needs of all who desire to give for their own good. Beggars and begging devices, however, are of as great variety as the moods of givers. In the total repertoire of beggardom, there is some appeal to complement the mood of every giver. It seems, therefore, that an organization with

[2] From an interview with Eddy Jackson, "the Immune," famous pickpocket of a past generation.

an efficient system for bringing the proper beggar in contact with the proper giver might be of profit to both.

"There is, doubtless, every morning in the pockets of four million New Yorkers a pretty definite sum which can be coaxed out of them by the right sort of pathetic appeal. There are almost a dozen different types of beggars, each one's misfortune calculated to touch a different class of hearts. If anything like the maximum possible return is to be secured every day, sound economic principles demand that the mendicants be distributed so as to appeal to the largest number of citizens, and that each be assigned to a district where his peculiar talent may be most effectively employed." [8]

In addition to systemizing the distribution of beggars, an efficient organization might restore the respectability of begging. Many people "simply love" to give to beggars. With the begging profession degraded as it is, however, and with promiscuous almsgiving in such disrepute, many of these would-be givers cannot peacefully drop a coin into the beggar's cup without having at least a slight prick of the conscience. An organization, therefore, which could calm the conscience of givers might render these poor souls a great favor and at the same time greatly increase the flow of alms.

To allay the conscience of givers, an organization would doubtlessly have to employ twentieth-century methods. It could not copy the patterns of the Oriental guilds or the methods used by the orders of friars during the Middle Ages. So far as the author knows, the most notable attempt of this kind is the Blind Beggars Guild in London which was organized by the late Lord Pellington (then plain Mr. Paruki) following the World War. Ostensibly, the purpose of the guild was to protect the public from mendicant impostors feigning blindness or other physical handicaps. Through arguments to this effect and through other methods Lord Pellington convinced the legal authorities and the public of the need of such

---

[8] "Begging as a Fine Art," *The Nation*, LXXIX (1904), 516.

a safeguard. To assure this protection, admissions to the guild were restricted, the members wore uniforms, and the beggars' earnings were carefully audited. That the venture proved to be a financial success may be deduced from Belloc's summary of its activities in 1924.

"As is always with success, the last efforts of the enterprise were the greatest, and we have remarked within the last twenty-four months the great new central offices in Holborn and the District Offices in the various parts of London, which have sprung up, with their characteristic Grecian architecture, almost before our eyes. Today, apart from the Grand Masters, the Wardens, the District Inspectors, the Local Inspectors, Checkers, Accountants, and the rest, no less than 7532 members of the Blind Beggars Guild now stand upon the rolls, and there has recently been added, standing between the magnificent Enquiry wing of the Central Office and the Employers' Lounge, a department which occupies itself with all the legitimate branches of banking, including as a special feature, operations in the foreign exchanges." [4]

[4] H. Belloc, "The Blind Beggars Guild," *New Statesman,* XXIII (1924), 409-10.

~~~~~~~~~~~~~~~~~~~~~~~~~~~~

CHAPTER VI

CHILD BEGGARS

IT is impossible to give a complete picture of the world of beggars without giving prominent mention to the begging child, for children have been prominent in the ranks of beggars. They were used by the fake friars of the Middle Ages and by the beggars' guild of China; they were rented by the professional beggars in Europe during the past century; and they are common on the streets of our modern cities.

This prevalence of children in begging is doubtless accounted for by the fact that by nature and training the child is admirably suited both to beg and to arouse sympathy. One of the first things the child learns after he is born is to beg. By virtue of his helplessness he has to ask his mother, his nurse, his father, or his brothers and sisters for things and services from the beginning of his life. At first, of course, he is not conscious that he is crying for his mother to give him food, but as time goes on he becomes conscious of what he wants and he learns how to beg for the things that will satisfy his wants. The first use the child has for language, for crying, or for having a tantrum is to secure what he wishes from others. His months and years of utter or partial dependency bring a continued development of the art of begging. And as is usual with dependent persons, the longer the child is dependent the more skilled he is likely to become in the art of begging. By the time the boy or girl has entered college, therefore, he knows not only how to do face to face begging from his parents and other relatives, but he also knows how to write begging letters, so well, in fact, that the distracted father finds himself sending money to his college offspring far beyond the amount which he had planned to spend.

Such begging of children from parents and other relatives is an integral part of their period of dependency and is considered normal by society. What is considered abnormal is for the child to extend his begging activities to persons other than the members of his family. This is a distinction made by society, however, and is not made by the child unless and until he is taught to make it. What mother has not been embarrassed by her child's hinting or asking outright for a nickel from some visitor? From the child's point of view, it is natural for him to do so. It is the way he has always secured things, and he at first does not easily distinguish between uncles or aunts and mere friends of the family. From whom it is proper for him to beg and from whom it is improper are things which he must be taught through careful parental training. Many, unfortunately, do not get such training and they sometimes go through life begging continually from relatives, friends, and even from acquaintances.

The same factors which tend to make the child's early training prepare him for begging tend also to give him a strong appeal to the giver. In order for a person to be a successful beggar, he must identify himself by fair means or foul with some class of persons whom society considers legitimately dependent. Thus, he must appear to be crippled, blind, deformed, sick, aged, a war veteran, unemployed, or the like. And of all classes of dependent persons, the child has in all societies probably received first preference. The family itself probably had its origin in the fact that society at an early date recognized the child as a dependent and instituted the family as a device to provide for this dependency; and the money spent by the adult world on such things as education, orphanages, child care agencies, and health programs bear clear testimony to the fact that society today considers the child a legitimate dependent.

When the child begs, therefore, the mere fact that he is a child gives him the status of a legitimate dependent. The paternal giver thus does not question the fact that the child is a legitimate dependent; his only quandary is whether the child is rightfully a charge of his family or of the public. And since the answer to this question may be considerably involved, he frequently gives to the child without taking the trouble to secure an answer.

Because of this natural appeal which the child has for the giving public, children have long been an integral part of the begging profession. In fact, the use and abuse of children by adult beggars constitutes the most tragic and inhumane chapter in the history of begging. Thus the beggars of Europe have long been accused, and perhaps rightly, of making human monstrosities out of their children in order to give them the strongest possible appeal to the public.

"Some break the back and others some bone of their children, and go begging with them ever after.

'There are mo mes-shapen among such beggers
Than of meny other men that on this molde walken.'

"The maiming and injuring of children for the purpose of appealing to the pity of the public, giving them as it was shockingly called: 'The arms and legs of the Almighty,' is a custom that has been practiced for centuries, and is not unknown in our own day. Barclay's *Ship of Fools* (1508) tells the same tale as Piers Plowman:

'Manglynge their facys, brekynge theyr bonys
To skere the people to pety that passe by.'

"Spiders and beetles were often enclosed in a cockleshell which was placed to the eye of the child and held in position by a bandage. The child suffered torture and was often blinded by this cruel process. Reynolds describes this abomination in the *Mysteries of London,* as occurring in his day; and it is but a few years ago that a woman was sentenced in Paris for this crime." [1]

[1] Cooke, "Vagrants, Beggars, and Tramps," *Quarterly Review*, CCIX (1908), 392.

Similar practices are reported among the beggars of China.

"Occasionally a man whose own powers of exhibitionism or cajolery are insufficient, will steal a child from a country district and bring it into the city to aid him in begging. The muscles of the child's arms and legs are cut, the tiny, growing limbs encased in a harness so that they become misshapen. I once saw one of these children crawl toward me on all fours, dragging his naked, distended belly, scuttling sidewise in a horrible agility, so that he resembled a huge and loathsome spider. From that queer insistent cry of his, from the speed of his skeletonic limbs weaving so close to the earth, there is no escape, even in recollection. Here, one is squarely confronted by a condition of intolerable injustice that encompasses even the children." [2]

If such atrocities are ever practiced in America, they are not common. The use of children by adult beggars, however, is exceedingly common. Beggars recognize the natural appeal which children have and they do not hesitate to capitalize on it. The child gives "atmosphere" to the beggar's appeal and helps to substantiate his hard luck story. Children are therefore used to some extent in practically all types of begging. The use of children in residence begging and in organization begging is particularly common.

In the use of children for begging, the parents themselves are frequently the worst offenders. Parents show no more hesitation in taking their children along on begging trips than they do in having them hoe cotton or do any other kind of work. Sometimes a beggar begins by using his own children and ends up using the children of his relatives, neighbors, or friends. In residence begging this is particularly common. A mother may start begging when her children are young on the pretense of having a large family to support. As a result, she may develop her whole begging art around this theme and may have to have children with her, therefore, to make her begging appeal effective. Her children, however, will not stay

[2] J. W. Bennett, "China's Perennially Unemployed," Asia, XXXI (1931), 217.

young always, and when her own children grow up, she uses the children of her relatives—nieces, nephews, or grandchildren. In such cases the children are usually secured in the spirit of borrowing, but as a general rule the parents of the child are given part of the proceeds of the begging.

Sara has been a house-to-house beggar for many years. She began begging when her husband died and left her with three young children. All during the early years of her begging she took one or more of these children along on her begging expeditions. She told a story of being a poor widow with three children to support, and often she offered small articles for sale as well. All of her children are now married, but she still tells the same story, and she still takes children along with her, but they are not her own; they are her grandchildren.

Not all beggars, however, have children, and many have no relatives from whom children may be secured. Particularly, they may not have sickly, anemic, crippled, or undersized children who will produce the best results. It has been a common practice for centuries, therefore, for beggars to rent children. Even young babies are rented by such beggars.

"Babies a few months old are sometimes rented out to 'blackhoods' by their parents, who are themselves professional beggars or very poor people. A blackhood is an old lady who sits on a camp stool in some populous thoroughfare with a crying baby in her lap and a tin cup in her hand. She gets her name from the fact that she wears a hood of dark material, from under which peep out a few wisps of gray hair. These hoods if desired, with gray hair attached, can be purchased in certain shops well known to the fraternity.

"The life of an assistant to a blackhood is not an easy one. If you remember having given anything to that sort of beggar you will recollect that the baby was always crying. This flood of infantile tears works on the sympathy of the passer-by and he is more liberal than he would be if the baby were well-fed and smiling. But even little beggar babies do not cry all the time without some inducement. The blackhood, to make the child weep, uses methods more simple and more efficacious than the glycerine dodge of the movies: she either pricks it sharply with a pin, or drops it on the sidewalk, and like some well-wound-up musical instrument, the wretched youngster will cry for some time without any intermission at all." [3]

Instead of merely serving as atmosphere for the adult beggar, the child himself is often forced to beg. Not infrequently a parent, who may himself beg, teaches the child how to beg and then stations his offspring in one block while he begs in the next. If such an enterprising parent has numerous children, he may be able to "man" a whole street in this way.

The mendicancy investigator for a social agency recently found a child begging on a side street just off the central business section of a certain city. Engaging the child in conversation, the investigator found that he would give no information. It was observed, also, that he seemed afraid to move from the spot where he was standing. The investigator, therefore, suspected that the child might have a supervisor, and he started wandering around the area looking for a prospect. In another block he found a second child from whom he got the same reaction he had gotten from the first. Then in other blocks more children were located. Finally on one corner a woman was begging on one side of the street and a man on the other. And as it turned out, all were members of the same family. The two adults were the parents of six children who had been found stationed along the street.

Parents, however, do not always accompany their children on begging trips. Very often they send them out alone. So many cases in which parents have sent their children out to beg are on record and so frequently do such cases get into the press that the public is becoming fairly well acquainted with the practice. Often such parent-instigated begging is carried

[3] Godfrey, "A Capable Beggar Makes from $15 to $500 a Day," *American Magazine*, XCIV (1922), 119.

on in stores and shops, and here it is especially liable to become associated with stealing. If the child cannot get what he wants by asking for it, he may steal it, and thus gradually take to shoplifting.

"In Chicago we have the problem of wholesale market streets. Very often the children who beg for everything from meat to fruit in the market streets are given carfare by their parents to go and to return, and the food begged, salvaged from barrels of waste, or stolen, is used on the family table. We have records of children habitually begging on these streets from homes of which their parents are the owners. No man, or woman, could possibly extract from the market men week after week the quantities of food the children carry off in their sacks and baskets." [4]

If we were to get moralistic, we would probably class the parent who is too lazy even to go out and beg, and who sends his children out instead, as about the most worthless rascal in the begging fraternity. Of course, not all such parental action is due to laziness. In cases where an attempt is made to enforce anti-begging laws, the child is perhaps less likely to be arrested than the able-bodied parent. In other cases the parent may be employed in some occupation and sends the child out to supplement the family income. If the child is defective or abnormal the temptation for this is especially great. Indeed in such a case the parent may feel that he is starting the child in the calling which is inevitably to be his life's work. As Rhodes says, "There is a kind of sad grim humor in the fact that in the swarming families of the poor a little hunchback must be actually welcomed as having his own special chance in the world, as perhaps have also the maimed, the halt and the blind." [5]

Whatever reason the parent may have for forcing the child to beg, the practice frequently results in gross injustices and

[4] F. Z. Youmans, "Childhood, Inc.; Child Beggars," *Survey*, LII (1924), 462.

[5] Harrison Rhodes, "Business of Begging," *Harpers Weekly*, LVIII (1913), 14.

untold harm to the child himself. The exposure to inclement weather and to unwholesome street influences are enough to condemn the practice. The situation is made even worse, however, by the devices to which parents frequently resort in an attempt to make children produce results. One of these devices is the quota system. When the parent sends the child out he often specifies an amount which the child must secure before he can return home. If the public is not disposed to help the child, he may either go home without his money and take a beating or stay out on the streets begging until the early hours of the morning. On the other hand, if he secures his quota in a reasonable time, his parents will probably increase the amount required the next night, and he is again in trouble. As a result of such practices, it is not uncommon for even very young children, who have been unable to secure their quota, to be found almost frozen on the streets at all hours of the night.

Another way in which children are used by adult beggars is as guides and helpers. Blind beggars, in particular, almost invariably use children to lead them around. They may, depending on their technique, also have the child pass a cup while they themselves supply music. These "guides" in most cases are hired by the beggar. If the beggar or any close relative has a suitable child he will probably use it. But if such is not available, the blind person seldom has any difficulty in hiring a child to lead him. Neither the beggar, the child, nor its parents ordinarily see any harm in the child leading the blind person around on his begging tours. Occasionally one of the blind (or fake blind) beggars will engage from three to five boys to pass cups while he himself attracts and entertains the crowds by furnishing music.[6]

By no means, however, is all of the begging by children done for the benefit of adults. Much begging, like much delinquency, is carried on either because the child wants spending

[6] Most modern American cities have the legal machinery to prevent such exploitation of children, but because of public indifference and official negligence these practices continue in many places.

money which his parents cannot furnish or because he likes the sport of begging. Occasionally, as an extension of the period of dependency of the child, he may get into the spirit of the professional beggar and develop a veritable mania for the sport of begging.

Mary, a white girl twelve years of age, had an unsatiable desire to beg. Every time she could escape from home or from school she would go out on the street and beg. At school it eventually became necessary to have her sit continuously at the principal's desk, but even then she occasionally succeeded in escaping. And invariably when she escaped she was found begging on some nearby street corner. The begging techniques which she used might well have been the envy of any professional. She told most uncanny tales about the condition of her family, she posed as being blind, crippled or deaf, and invariably she played the role convincingly.

Though begging as a gang activity is not a common form of delinquency among juvenile groups, it occasionally constitutes the chief source of income for a juvenile gang. A crippled or deformed boy is especially likely to be used by a gang for begging purposes.

A rather extreme case of gang begging was recently discovered in one of our southern cities. John, aged thirteen, who was a member of the gang, was a semiparalytic, crippled in both legs. The gang would place John on the sidewalk where he would solicit from pedestrians. When a likely prospect would come along, John would accost him with a request for help. If the person showed any hesitancy about giving, the rest of the gang would gather around and lay down a barrage of "Mister, help the boy, he is crippled and deserves a break, etc." The combined appeal usually brought results. When a few dollars had been collected, the gang would take the money and either gamble with it or spend it for eats and shows. When more was needed, John would be placed out to beg again, and the procedure would be repeated.

Occasionally a professional begging manager will capitalize the tendency of children to beg and will hire a gang of his own. He will hire children and teach them a clever begging technique. And by providing them with a suitable makeup and placing them in a good location he may make a profit both for himself and the children.

"Another Chicago round-up of beggars was directed toward a gang of small boys and girls, all of whom were hardly old enough to be brought into court. These youngsters had been taught by a man who escaped the police net to stand in front of the theatres and hotels and beg. The exposure came about in an unusual manner. A man saw a nine-year-old lad begging before a motion picture theatre, thinly clad, eyes blackened, one sleeve empty. The man's heart gave a quick throb of sympathy but he could not stop to do any real good for the boy as he had to catch a train. So he went up to the first policeman, gave him a bill, and told him to see that the boy was given a meal, and that with the change from the bill he was sent to his home in a cab. The policeman did as he was asked, but in the clear light of the restaurant it seemed that the boy's eyes were too bright for one who was blind. His suspicions were aroused and he felt for the stump of the missing arm. Instead he found a perfectly good arm and hand strapped to the boy's body." [7]

Another type of child beggar, who is pathetic in the extreme and who is more frequently found than may be thought, is the drug addict. Children who are habituated to the smoking of marijuana cigarettes are found among the lower class, and children who use other drugs are not uncommon. Such child "dopies" have a decided tendency to beg and some of them beg as regularly as any adult. Their chief reason for begging, of course, is that they need the money to buy drugs. For them begging is a particularly desirable way of getting the money. Being physically and mentally below par as they usually are,

[7] Courtenay Savage, "Beggars Collect Fortunes from the Public," *Dearborn* (Michigan) *Independent,* October 11, 1924, p. 13.

stealing would be too strenuous and too hazardous. Further-more, having an escape through drug-induced dreams, they do not crave the thrill and excitement which often drive other delinquents to commit daring deeds. Begging, on the other hand, is not hard work, the returns are in cash which may be exchanged for drugs, and the risk of being arrested and locked up where no drugs can be secured is less than in the case of stealing. Such child addicts may operate alone or they may be members of a gang.

Frank, age fourteen, is the leader of a gang of six boys, all of whom are addicted to the use of drugs. All of the boys are proud of the number of capsules they can take, and Frank is proudest of them all because he claims to have the largest capacity. They get the money to buy their drugs by begging. Frank is only mildly proud of his beg-ging ability, but says that he can collect $1.50 in about two hours. And that is about what he needs at one time to buy drugs.

Frank's parents are very much disturbed over his habit, but as yet they have been unable to do anything about it.

In spite of the fairly common occurrence of outright beg-ging among children, perhaps the most common form of child mendicancy is the use of begging salesmanship in the street trades. In selling newspapers, magazines, flowers, firecrackers, and even Christmas trees, children frequently resort to the use of hard luck stories to increase their sales. Such practices may be instigated by the child's parents, but it has generally been found that most of the proceeds from the street trades go to the child himself. In other words, many of the children who sell on the streets do so because they want the money, and they use begging techniques in their selling because they can secure more money by doing so. They may even use begging devices in spite of stern parental opposition.

Henry, a white boy, fourteen years of age, is the son of a carpenter. The father is so extremely honest as to be almost puritanical in his views on personal morality. He has, however, met with many adversities during his married life. Among other things his wife died, leaving a large family of children which he finds it difficult to support. The finances of the family are continually, therefore, an open problem. Henry who is the oldest boy is very affable and affectionate and apparently almost worships his father. He is old enough to be conscious of the financial strain of the family, and he has apparently come to the conclusion that he should at least support himself. His only method of earning money is to sell papers, but he makes this very remunerative by using hard luck stories. The father strongly opposes the practice and frequently punishes the boy severely for using such methods. Sometimes he stops Henry from selling papers because of his begging, but the pressure of finances eventually forces him to let Henry return to the streets.

Quite similar in nature to begging salesmanship are the numerous rackets which have become prevalent among children, especially in cities. A common form with which most people are now acquainted is the practice of boys proposing to sell curb space or watch cars for people. Such child racketeers can be found in the vicinity of football fields just before a game is to be played, or in the vicinity of nearly any public gathering. Usually they attempt to appropriate a section of the street along the curb, to which they have no legal rights, and charge people to park there. They have no right to charge for the space, nor do they watch the cars as they usually propose to do. This is only one of a multitude of such rackets which have become too numerous to catalogue here.

Regarding child beggars in general it should be said that their begging skill is to be commended. There can be little doubt that starting young is an advantage in begging as it is in other skills. The child who starts young and is properly tutored, therefore, may develop a begging skill and a persuasive power that might well be the envy of any professional oldster. What adult panhandler could do a better job than the boy described below?

"A boy of eight, arguing earnestly that he should be given a small copper coin, first plead hunger. When this failed, he gave his imagination full swing. He asserted variously that the money would help to buy him a new cap, then new shoes, and finally that it was urgently needed, that with it—one cent was all that he asked—he could go to the dentista Americano and have a tooth filled. And if one cent could do it, that tooth is now filled. The dentist's address might be useful." [8]

While equaling adults in skill, child beggars often excel adults in good common sense. Unless coerced by some adult, they usually do not beg long hours. The motivation for their begging is in most cases some immediate desire. They want to go to a show or to do something else which they do not have the money to do, and as soon as they get enough money to do this they do not beg any longer. Children of their own volition do not drive themselves to long hours of begging and exposure in order to stack up large earnings as do some adults.

Among child beggars, boys are more prevalent than girls, doubtless for the same reason that boys are more prevalent than girls in most forms of juvenile delinquency. Even in the homes of the very poor some attempt is usually made to protect and restrain the girl, and while young she is much less likely to be turned loose on the street than is the boy. When she does get the opportunity to beg, however, apparently she can do just as effective begging as can the boy. She does tend to do a different type; her favorite is usually the sob game. As a rule, girls talk more fluently than boys and are better able to tell and act out a hard luck story. Like women, therefore, they may do well in residence begging, or even in street trades begging. Boys, on the other hand, frequently show unlimited persistence in attaching themselves to pedestrians and following them sometimes for blocks. They have a tendency, therefore, to practice panhandling or the street trades.

In conclusion, it should be said that the causation of child begging lies in deficiencies in the home and the community

[8] Rhodes, "Business of Begging," *Harpers Weekly*, LVIII (1913), 14.

background of the child. As was said in the beginning, the period of infant dependency tends to train the child for begging and he has to be taught not to beg. Unless, therefore, he is taught to beg from no one except members of his family, he will do at least some begging as a natural extension of his childhood prerogatives. As a consequence, the early years of the child's life are the danger years from the standpoint of the development of begging tendencies.

~~~~~~~~~~~~~~~~~~~~~~~~~~~~~~~~

CHAPTER VII

WHERE THE BEGGAR LIVES

THE nature of the beggar and his mode of life are so inseparably linked to his abode that it is impossible to understand him without knowing where he lives. The importance of the beggar's habitat, however, is not in the condition of his living quarters. These may be clean or dirty, shabby or neat, crowded or spacious; that is of little significance. What is important is the community in which he lives. And since the beggar is for the most part an urban dweller his habitat is a part of the whole urban residential scheme.

The residential structure of a city is a product of its history of growth. The town or city tends to be circular in shape, with the business section in the center and the residential areas surrounding it. As the city grows in size the new residences are almost invariably built by the wealthier class of people and are constructed on the periphery of the city. In a growing city, therefore, the more wealthy residents are building new residences for themselves farther and farther from the center of the city. The houses which this class discard in their retreat pass into the used-home market to be sold or rented to people of more moderate means. In the city, therefore, almost everyone except the wealthy class lives in a second-hand house.

As a result of this process of building, the age of a residence in a city is directly related to its distance from the central business section. The oldest houses are adjacent to the business district, the newer ones are farther out, and the newest ones are on the extreme periphery. Furthermore, with scant attention given to the repair and alteration of urban residences, the condition of the buildings is closely related to their age. The best residences in the city, therefore, are the new ones on the outskirts, and the most dilapidated ones are those aged structures located adjacent to the central business section.

This combination of age and deterioration of urban residences has a definite correlation with rental values. Naturally the most desirable residences are in general those farthest from the center of the city. From this extreme, rents graduate downward to the rent free houses which often can be found close to the center of the city. As a result of this uniform gradation of rents from the edge of the central business section to the outlying sections of the city, the population tends to be correspondingly distributed on an economic basis. Like rents, the income of the residents is lowest near the central business section and gradually increases out to the periphery of the city where the highest income groups live.

The areas along the main thoroughfares reaching from the central business section to suburban sections tend to be an exception to this general scheme. The central business section extends out along these thoroughfares for some distance. Farther out are middle-class rooming houses, efficiency apartments, and apartment hotels for semi-transient persons who are able to pay and who wish to be fairly close to the central business section. Then the middle- and upper-class residential areas usually are drawn more closely to the central business section along these thoroughfares than elsewhere. For much of the distance, therefore, the areas immediately along these thoroughfares are in sharp contrast to those immediately back of them.

In this scheme of things, the area immediately surrounding the central business section plays a unique part. Since the business district is usually surrounded by residential areas, if it grows it must either build up into the air or spread out onto the land formerly used for residential purposes. Usually it does both. Consequently, long before the land in these residential areas adjacent to the business section is actually taken over for business uses, it is bought by real estate speculators who hold it in the expectation of selling it for a profit to some business concern. When and if the land is used for business purposes, however, the residence must be razed. The speculator thus expects the residence to be torn down and spends little or nothing for repair. In addition, since he expects to make a profit on the eventual sale of the land, he is little interested in the present return from his investment. He is willing, therefore, to accept very low rents. Such buildings are deteriorated from age, dilapidated for want of repairs, and have phenomenally low rents.

Accordingly, this lowest rent area adjacent to the central business section is inhabited by the city's poor. People live there because they cannot live elsewhere. It is a settling basin for economic failures and for persons who make their livelihood by means which are outlawed and socially outcast. Among migrants to the city it is the place of first residence for persons ill-equipped to cope with life in the city and for persons who are temporarily stranded. In collecting these multitudes of failures and "undesirables" the area takes on an outward appearance which reflects the perverse elements who occupy it. In brief, it becomes the slum, the city's underworld.

The following description of the slum in Nashville, Tennessee, as it was several years ago, gives a bird's-eye view of the beggar's "home town."

> Church Street is the retail shopping center. Its clanking street cars, streaming traffic, and surging crowds all proclaim the typical downtown center. On the edge of the loop, to the north, is the State Capitol with its great dome. Farther east stands the ancient courthouse with its Grecian front.
>
> Still farther to the north under the shadow of the State Capitol is Sulphur Bottom, a sea of deteriorating buildings bisected by railroad tracks and crowded over against the factory-fringed river. The whole area is darkened by clouds of smoke pouring forth from the factories and the air is laden with fumes from the nearby packing plants. This is the city's slum, the beggar's habitat.

The whole area presents a scene of disorder. Here and there a large residence, blackened with smoke and deteriorating for want of repair, bears the marks of former colonial splendor. In its windows can be seen the familiar sign "rooms for rent." These old buildings have home-like fronts, but within they are as gloomy as the small frame buildings which are banked against each other and pushed out within a few feet of the walk. With their crude porchless fronts and weathered paint they skirt the street in striking monotony. The small front courts enclosed by board fences and littered with trash are the sole playgrounds of throngs of unwashed and shabbily dressed children. At intervals vacant lots are strewn with parts of old cars, discarded wagons, old bottles, and refuse of all descriptions. On some corners can be found the community grocery store with its vegetables and fruits displayed on the walks in front.

A narrow section of Sulphur Bottom immediately bordering the loop is inhabited by Negroes. This gradually changes into a white section which in turn evolves into the district of respectable working men's homes which borders the slum.

Towards the east end of the section is the great retreat for homeless men. Here are found a preponderance of cheap rooming houses with their gaudy fronts and gloomy interiors. Here also are the cheap hotels, the mission, the flaunting houses of prostitution, and the cheap restaurants. This is the city's settling basin. Here the dregs of humanity gather. In it the criminal seeks a place where he may be lost from the world. Here the "bootlegger" finds a cover under which he may ply his trade. And here the failure retreats with the bitterness of his disappointment.

On the other side of the loop to the south is Black Bottom. The residences, for the most part age-worn structures, might well be mistaken for the ruins of Pompeii. With doors missing, windows out, stepping stones hollowed, and floors marked with the indelible footprint of many generations, they stand by the hundred. They bear the marks of long exposure to the elements and have a uniform finish of smoke and grime. From windows, back porches, and before doors clothes are hung to dry. From side doors, and second story windows "sewing," "house painting," and numerous other signs tell the trade of the inhabitants. Here and there is a small grocery store with its dirty windows decorated with "hunks" of bacon and strings of "baloney." Such are the scenes among which the beggar spends his hours of sleep.

Lying about half way between Black Bottom and the loop is East Broad Street, the "West Madison Street" or main stem of the city. This is the beggar's social center. Here the pawn shops, one after another display their second-hand guns and used tools. Interspersed among them are the cheap clothing stores which bedeck their walks with "sample shoes" and used "army goods." Here too is the inevitable hot dog man with his wagon wedged in between two buildings and the odor of hamburgers pervading the air. Not to pass unnoticed are the cheap hotels, restaurants, and bakeries. Here too is the street faker with his collar buttons, and the medicine man with his magic pills.

To this street as night comes on and the sun's light is replaced by the lights of the white way, the unfortunates come forth from their abodes to mingle with the busy throngs or to make their way into the loop to ply their trades among the teeming crowds.

As is indicated in the foregoing description, the slum contains a number of different areas, each inhabited by a different element of the poverty class. There are racial areas for immigrant groups or Negroes, areas for transient single men, poor rooming house areas for single persons and childless married couples seeking an adjustment in the city, and residential areas for poor native whites. In addition there are smaller areas for artists, homosexuals, communists, and non-conformists of many types.

In each of these areas the living accommodations are adjusted to the elements which inhabit them. In the immigrant, the Negro, and the native white areas the population is made up for the most part of families. The tenement house with scanty family apartments, community toilet and water supply is the rule. Large families are commonly crowded into one or two small rooms which are poorly ventilated, repulsively unattractive, poorly kept, and decidedly unsanitary. There is usually little or no play space for children and no place for privacy either for adults or children. The rent is usually very low and is paid weekly. The following is a description of a tenement occupied by Negro families.

"In a crowded negro section of the city, there is a large tenement house. The main building is very dilapidated and is badly in need of repair. The tenants are fearful of falling when they use the stairway and the structure has not been painted for several years. The yard is devoid of anything green and creates a barren and desolate atmosphere. The many shacks in the rear of the yard are crowded to capacity with negro families, and their quarters are equally shabby.

"Lena Smith and her five children live in an upper section of the main house. They occupy one room which opens into the hall. There are two windows, one a southern exposure, and the other an eastern. The room is well ventilated and is fairly bright, but it is small and gives the appearance of being very crowded.

"Lena was happily married to John Smith in 1916. Her husband enjoyed a steady income and was able to support his family fairly well. Prior to his death, they were financially able to rent, and furnish adequately, a three-room dwelling for $12.00 a month. When Mr. Smith died, the furnishings were gradually disposed of, and their equipment now consists of an iron bed with a fairly good mattress, a small table, a dresser, two chairs and a furnace (charcoal burner). In addition, they use several small boxes for their clothing. As there are no lockers, they hang their other clothes on lines stretched across a corner of the room.

"The family group consists of Lena and her five children; three girls, aged thirteen, eight and five, and two boys aged ten and six. The boys are being treated at the Anti-Tubercular League for tuberculosis. They sleep on a pallet on the floor with their five-year-old sister. The family owns another bed but there is no room for it in their crowded quarters. The other two girls and their mother sleep in the bed. There is barely enough covering and Lena is always concerned about the possibility of the children contracting more severe colds.

"An oil lamp is used for lighting and a furnace (charcoal) is used for heat and cooking. There is a grate fireplace in the room, but it is really an ornamental structure, as coal is not available at the present time. There is no running water in the room and the family uses a stationary washstand at the end of the hall. Their toilet is also located in the hallway. It is filthy and apparently has not been cleaned in several years. Both of these are used by all members of the building. Lena and her children have been living in these quarters for the past three months. Their rent is $1.25 weekly and they have only paid the first week's charges." [1]

Each of these old houses tends to be occupied by people of a like sort. Some, such as the one just mentioned, will be inhabited by families with children, others by single young people, and others by broken-down old persons or married couples. In other words, members of the different types of unfortunate and maladjusted people gravitate toward others of the same type. "Birds of a feather flock together."

A large old tenement building just out of the business section of a certain city is occupied for the most part by old men and women and aged married couples. All of them get social agency help when they can, some of them work a little at times, most of them beg part or all the time, and at least one practices prostitution. Also in this house lives an "old widower" who begs for a living and claims to be a local preacher. He has organized a group of these old people into a "church" of which he is the "minister." Services are held in the crowded living quarters of one or the other of the members. In addition to persons in this tenement, a few from surrounding tenements attend.

[1] Unpublished manuscript by Louise Mullins.

Very similar to these old tenement houses and often difficult to distinguish from them is the rooming house. Scores of old residences are converted into rooming houses where furnished rooms are rented by the week, with rent paid in advance. These rooms are occupied mostly by single persons of the low white-collar class. Since no questions are asked of those seeking a room, some panhandlers and many pseudo-gentlemen beggars find these houses a suitable abode.

"The rooming-house is typically a large, old fashioned residence, though many apartments are converted into rooming-houses as well. And the population living in these rooming-houses is typically what the labor leader refers to as the 'white collar group'—men and women filling various clerical positions—accountants, stenographers, and the like, office workers of various sorts.... Most of them are living on a narrow margin, and here they can live cheaply, near enough to the loop to walk to and from their work if they wish.

"The constant comings and goings of its inhabitants is the most striking and significant characteristic of this world of furnished rooms. This whole population turns over every four months. There are always cards in the windows, advertising the fact that rooms are vacant, but these cards rarely have to stay up over a day, as people are constantly walking the street looking for rooms. The keepers of the rooming houses change almost as rapidly as the roomers themselves. At least half of the keepers of these houses have been at their present addresses six months or less." [2]

For the transients who stay for only a short time in these areas there are cheap hotels of a variety of sorts. Every city of any considerable size has many cheap hotels around the edge of the central business section. Some of these are quite small, others are fairly large. The smaller ones tend to be the headquarters of some type of underworld character. Some

[2] H. W. Zorbaugh, *The Gold Coast and the Slum* (Chicago, 1929), pp. 71-72.

are used primarily by prostitutes, others by crooks of certain kinds, and some are the headquarters of professional beggars. The larger ones often cater to "homeless men" and as such they attract men more according to what they are able to pay than according to their particular racket. Even so they get the atmosphere of those who inhabit them.

"Different types of hotels attract different types of men. The better class of workingmen who patronize the Mohawk, where the prices range from forty to seventy cents, wear collars and creased trousers. The hotel provides stationery and desks. Hotels where the prices range from twenty-five cents to forty cents are patronized by a shabbier group of men. Few of them are shaven. Some of them read, but most of them sit alone with their thoughts. In some second class places a man is employed to go the round and arouse the sleepers.

"In the twenty-five cent hotels, the patrons not only are content to sit unshaven, but they are often dirty. Many of them have the faces of beaten men; many of them are cripples and old men." [3]

Occasionally a small lodging house or "hotel" will be a sort of beggars' club, run in a way on a membership basis. It may be run by the club members and provide lodging and meals as well as being a social center for the members. These clubs usually sail under false colors.

There is a lodging house which used to be the headquarters of a chapter of a semi-radical labor organization. A group of intellectual young beggars joined this organization and gradually other members dropped out, leaving the chapter in their control. They still keep the organization charter and all of the members carry union cards for the legal and other protection which these afford. They are very selective in admitting new members and have been able to keep a very congenial group. The club facilities consist of a number of bedrooms, a dining room and kitchen, and a lounge which is used as a social room

[3] Anderson, *The Hobo*, p. 29.

and as a reading room. Most of the members read extensively books which they secure from the public library. They are very clever panhandlers but they only work two or three hours a day, preferring leisure to money.

Often one of these old buildings in the transition zone gets in such a bad condition that it becomes a rent free building. In some cases such buildings become rent free because they are so dilapidated that the owner cannot rent them for enough to pay the cost of collection. In other cases the buildings may be condemned as dangerous for habitation and the owner prohibited from collecting further rents. In either case persons may continue to live in them without paying any rent unless the owner makes an attempt to keep them out. Usually he does not go to this trouble. These free rent buildings are often taken over, therefore, by the dregs of humanity, and in such places all sorts of vice and crime are often found. The following description of one of these "dives" from which a number of drug addicts and peddlers were eventually taken is revealing.[4]

"Reference is made to your letter in which you request certain information regarding the premises located at 715 Seventh Avenue North.

"In this connection, please be advised that on several occasions during the early summer of this year, I visited the above premises accompanied by Narcotic Agent Frank C. Henderson. These visits were in line with our duty of investigating violations of the Harrison Narcotic Law.

"It was learned while on these visits that the premises publicly known to the drug addicts of this city as the 'FREE BRICK,' is occupied by May Hennesy and her sister, Emma Hennesy. Both of these women are addicted to the use of morphine, and they admitted having used morphine for some years past. May Hennesy is a well known character on the streets, and is known as a professional beggar to the officers in the city. Not so much is known of her

---

[4] Names and addresses given in this description have been changed, of course, to conceal identity.

sister, Emma Hennesy, other than she lives with her sister
at the above mentioned premises, and is addicted to the
use of morphine, and that when same cannot be had, both
of these women resort to the use of paregoric for the
opium contained therein. Both May Hennesy and her
sister Emma Hennesy stated to myself and Agent Henderson that neither of them were suffering from any physical ailment, and that if things got much tighter that they
intended going to some institution and be relieved of their
addiction to morphine.

"The building at 715 Seventh Avenue North, better
known as the 'FREE BRICK,' I understand has been condemned, and is in an untenantable condition—it is an old
ramshackle sort of affair, and impresses one as about to
tumble down without a moment's notice. The Hennesy
sisters occupy the back room on the first floor. In it is a
bed and bed springs upon which many pieces of cloth
are strewn. The condition of this room was vile, and the
air, at the time of our visits, was always very foul. While
myself and Agent Henderson were visiting the above
premises, men came to this room and seemed to be seeking certain women who congregated at this place, but did
not live there.

"The front room in this dilapidated building at the time
of our visits had recently been scrubbed, and was used by
a notorious prostitute, and drug addict, known as Lula
Cly. The only article of furniture in this room was a mattress upon the floor in the center of the room, and we were
advised that same had been taken from some dumping
ground by the occupants of this house, and used as a sort
of bed. Lula Cly admitted to us that she practiced prostitution in this room, and solicited men on the streets.
While on one of our visits, the particular date I cannot
remember, a sister of Lula Cly, who claimed to be seventeen years of age and married, was found by us asleep on
this mattress—when awakened, she advised us that she
was not feeling well and was not living at these premises,
but had come to visit her sister, Lula Cly, and was simply
resting at the time of our visit. We asked her if she was
there on the same mission as her sister, but she denied that

WHERE THE BEGGAR LIVES 145

she was practicing prostitution, although she admitted that
she was not living with her husband. She further stated
that she was not addicted to the use of morphine.

"On another occasion while both Agent Henderson and
myself were at these premises, a well developed young
girl, approximately nineteen years of age, came in, and
from her appearance she did not look like one who was
addicted to the use of narcotic drugs. However, upon being questioned she stated that she simply came to visit
the girls, but we learned from Lula Cly that she was a
married woman and practiced prostitution at this place.
Lula Cly further advised us that this woman lived in the
neighborhood, the exact address she did not know, but
that she was in very bad condition physically. Upon being
further questioned, she stated that this young woman was
at that time suffering from chancre, although she was
constantly soliciting men, and bringing them to this place
for money.

"The other rooms at this place were unoccupied, and
were in a very dilapidated condition. The various visitors
to these premises generally meet in the room of the Hennesy sisters, or the front room where Lula Cly holds forth
in the day time. This place is a rendezvous for drug addicts and drug peddlers who meet there daily for their
supply of narcotic drugs, and it is our opinion that our
presence was made known to the peddlers who visit this
place, and for that reason we were unable to apprehend
them." [5]

The most broken and disreputable beggars often have no
fixed abode. They sleep in boxes, in back alleys, or on door
steps, in fact any place where they can lie down or even
recline comfortably. Some of these bums attach themselves
to a nook and assume a squatter's claim.

Snead, a dope addict, slightly past middle age, has been
"living" for some time in the doorway of an unoccupied
building. This doorway consists of a sort of vestibule and

[5] From a letter written by an officer of the Bureau of Narcotics of the
United States Government.

has plenty of room for a person to lie down. His only furniture is a broom and a box of broken glass. When he
leaves he scatters the broken glass over the floor to keep
others away. And when he returns he uses the broom to
sweep up the glass.

In addition to living quarters, these deteriorated areas are
plentifully supplied with facilities to meet the other needs of
the beggar. There are numerous cheap restaurants where he
can get food for almost any price he is willing to pay; to satisfy
his sex cravings there are numerous prostitutes and houses of
prostitution; and to provide him recreation there are quantities
of cheap and gaudy shows, risqué night clubs, and gambling
places. A recent survey of one of these areas, which is a dozen
blocks long and half as wide, showed that there were 165
rooming houses and 11 hotels in addition to several hundred
tenement houses. Other facilities were in proportion. Even
though the survey was made in the daytime, there were 79
houses from which the boys making the survey were solicited
by women. In addition, there were 234 saloons in the area.
Many of these were also gambling places; in them were found
133 slot machines, 67 pin-ball machines, and 18 iron claw
machines. No count was made of other types of gambling
facilities which might be harder to locate.

Perhaps the favorite playhouse of these areas is a multi-
service type of "joint" which may call itself a beer parlor, a
restaurant, a bar, or a club. Often it is a combination eating
place, beer parlor, saloon, gambling resort, and house of prostitution. During an evening in one of these places, therefore, a
beggar may get almost anything he wishes. Many of these
resorts have their patronage primarily among some one class
in the underworld. It may be thieves, confidence men, or
beggars. Waters gives us a description of such resorts in New
York.

"In a lower bower near Chatham Square are perhaps a
dozen resorts, the bulk of whose trade is derived from the
revenue of New York's begging population. These places

are licensed bar-rooms, kept for the most part by ex-crooks, who have, as they say, 'made good,' or by scoun-drels as bad, who have managed to evade the law so entirely that they have never been convicted. You will never find an honest beggar in one of these places, that is, one of the genuinely unfortunate class. Every man and woman beggar in these places is a professional in the strictest sense of the word. . . .

"The habitues of the various places intermingle more or less, but there are certain individual characteristics to be observed among them. For instance one place seems to cater to a gang of fake sailors, clever rogues in uniform, who collect money from the passerby on the pretense of having been left behind by a newly departed battleship. Another place may be the nightly hangout of begging let-ter writers, those semi-educated imposters who ask money of the rich in all sorts of places. Still another place will be infested with sham paralytics, or floppers or regular strong arm men. And a fourth place may be the rendezvous of yeggs or 'pete' men: in other words, tramp safe-blowers, who hang out there and blow in their 'white money' after a big haul of 'stickers' from a country post office." [6]

As is apparent, the beggar's habitat is anything but pleasant. One may well wonder what attracts him to such a disreputable area. True it is a place of cheap rents, but often the beggar is not as poverty-stricken as he appears. Indeed, many beggars could afford to pay much higher rents than they are forced to pay in this area.

The beggar is attracted to these areas, in part, because the low rents and other advantages attract to these areas a popu-lation with which he is congenial. As we have seen, the beg-gar's home town is not inhabited by the beggar alone. It is also the rendezvous of members of most of the other outcast professions. Prostitutes, "dope peddlers," thieves, confidence men, and even "big time" gangsters make their headquarters here. Though differing from each other in many respects, these

[6] Waters, "Six Weeks in Beggardom," *Everybody's Magazine*, XII (1905), 72-73.

perverse elements have certain things in common; all are socially outcast and most of them are legally outlawed professions. As such, each has a certain sympathy for the other, and each aids the other in protecting itself from legal and social control. As a result of this mutual aid against organized society, therefore, the beggar can get better protection here than in any other part of the city.

Also it is within these mutual aid areas that the beggar is able to hide his private life so completely from the rest of society that he can tell with impunity all sorts of weird tales, fake all sorts of diseases and physical defects, and portray dire pictures of poverty to an unsuspecting public and be believed. It is this veil of secrecy that protects the beggar both from the police and from the skeptical giver.

The attractiveness of these deteriorated areas for the beggar is further enhanced by the fact that they are adjacent to the central business section. As has been said, the central business section is the happy hunting ground for beggars. At some periods of the day hunting is much better than at others, and the more or less lazy beggar, therefore, goes out at those times of the day when conditions for his kind of begging are most favorable and the rest of the time he takes life easy. To minimize the time and inconvenience of several trips from his home to his work, as well as for the other reasons, the beggar lives close to his stand, which usually means living in the transition zone.

CHAPTER VIII

~~~~~~~~~~~~~~~~~~~~~~~~~~~~

THE NATURAL HISTORY OF A
FAILURE

PERHAPS most people have wondered at one time or another who beggars are and where they come from. Few questions are more puzzling to the ordinary man than how so many people can bring themselves to accept alms, and many have doubtless wondered what can be the state of mind or philosophy of life of a person who accepts such help.

In itself, however, the accepting of help or gifts is not such a heinous sin or such a tax on one's peace of mind as many imagine. Few people have difficulty in accepting unearned money if it comes in the right form. The child experiences no compunctions in being dependent on its parents, the wife is not disturbed at having to receive a livelihood from her husband, the kin has no difficulty in accepting his inheritance, and the gambler or speculator has no qualms in accepting unearned increment on his investment. All of these forms of technically unearned support are socially approved and are accepted without disturbance.

The conscience of people, however, can be easily stretched much beyond these few socially approved channels of unearned money. With no apparent mental disturbance the World War veterans have accepted billions in gifts from the government and may crusade for more. And during the present depression nearly every trade and occupation has "held out the beggar's bowl" to the Federal Treasury. Even these do not exhaust the limits of man's conscience in accepting free money. An advertisement headed with "Free" in bold

149

type brings a storm of response from those who are naive enough to believe there is a Santa Claus in the business world. And we are told that Henry Ford receives ten thousand begging letters a week from people in all walks of life.

"The charity seekers are not all on the street corners of the world. They live in high and low places everywhere. They will not seek alms publicly, but they are not above begging in confidence, when their friends and neighbors may never know. They think there is a chance that Mr. Ford may do for them what they ought to do for themselves; and they write the letter, in the hope that their particular burden may touch his heart and thus find the way to his seemingly unlimited purse." [1]

Accepting alms, however, is thought of as being different from accepting other forms of gifts, and it is different because it is so considered. Accepting alms requires a special state of mind because of the social and legal status of the begging profession. The person who would beg and accept alms, therefore, cannot remain in organized society and maintain the philosophy of the workaday world. He must become a member of the underworld and adopt its philosophy.

The term "underworld" has been greatly misused in popular parlance and must be employed with caution by the scientific writer. The popular concept, however, does have a counterpart in reality. There is no unified and completely organized underworld, but there is a chasm of more or less complete social isolation which separates the socially outcast from the socially approved world. Each has its own philosophy or philosophies, its own interests, its own culture, and its own conceptions, which differ essentially from those of the other.

Both the socially approved world and the underworld are organized to a great extent around occupations. The socially approved world is held together by the common interests and

---

[1] E. A. Guest, "10,000 People a Week Ask Henry Ford for Gifts," *American Magazine*, XCVII (1924), 5.

the interdependence of its occupations. Farmers, industrial laborers, bankers, and the professions may be disturbed by competitive strife, but no one of the professions seeks the destruction of any other. Underneath their competitive strife there are common interests and a basic interdependence which holds them together in a co-operative unity. Over against the world of socially approved occupations is the world of socially disapproved occupations. Briefly they include prostitution, violation of property rights (such as robbery and stealing), illegal commerce (such as bootlegging and smuggling), and begging. These occupations and the persons engaged in them have been outlawed and outcast by organized society. As a group these occupations are in competition with the socially approved occupations, and they are essentially at war with organized society. Those engaged in this minority group have in a certain way a war consciousness. The members of organized society likewise have a degree of consciousness of being at war with the underworld, but being the majority group and having engaged a mercenary army of police and coast guards to wage their war, they do not have the personal interest in the conflict which the members of the underworld have.

Being in a state of conflict with the rest of society, the underworld has adopted a policy of isolating itself as far as possible from intimate and confidential outside contacts. Any information which may be pertinent to its conflicts against society is zealously guarded. Codes of ethics have grown up which entail great secrecy and these, if need be, are enforced with bloodshed. The criminal who squeals is often killed without mercy and everyone who has had dealings with the underworld knows what confidence must be gained before any information can be secured. Because of this code, even after spending vast sums of money over a long period, the federal government was never able to convict Al Capone on the charges which the public felt were self-evident. Instead, he was sentenced for income tax evasions.

The chasm which separates the underworld from the rest of society is further evident from the difficulty with which people change from an outcast occupation to a socially approved one, in contrast with the ease with which they may change from one outcast occupation to another. Gangsters, pickpockets, and prostitutes often turn to begging in old age with no greater loss in status than comes from senility and financial decline. And a member of the underworld may take up any of the numerous rackets and occupations with equal facility. In other words, members of the underworld may change from one outcast occupation to another without changing their friends or social world, but a transfer from an outcast occupation to a socially approved occupation or vice versa entails a radical change in the person's social world. In numerous respects the underworld is a distinct segment of society, set apart from the remainder but preying upon it.

Since begging is one of the occupations of the underworld and its practitioners are "citizens" of this segment of society, it cannot be understood apart from its relation to this sphere of life. Briefly speaking, beggars come from two sources, those who are reared in the underworld and those who are born in organized society but at some time in their lives are forced out of organized society into the underworld.

The underworld is, in a sense, a settling basin for misfits in organized society. Society is a competitive process with a constant sorting, sifting, and reclassifying of the members of society. Those who meet the requirements are advanced, others are able to maintain their *status quo,* while others who fail in competition move to lower social and economic levels. Generally speaking, when one has been demoted from the lowest levels of organized society, he crosses the chasm into the underworld.

The primary prerequisite for maintaining a status in organized society is economic sufficiency. In modern life, people generally associate and mingle with those on an economic level similar to their own. The person who declines or fails economically is forced to move into a cheaper residential district, change neighbors, and in time loses his old friends and his old status. The person who utterly fails to earn a subsistence through socially recognized pursuits has only two alternatives. He may become the recipient of public relief or he may enter one of the outcast professions.

"Doc" lives in a small city of some 150,000. He is the only surviving descendant of a once aristocratic family. His parents were reasonably well-to-do and he was given a college education. After completing his college work, he attended the medical school of the state university and received the M.D. degree. He set up his office in his home city to take up medical practice, but he did not have the "push" necessary for professional success. He lived with his parents until their death, and he never married. He inherited some money from his parents and maintained his office until this was gone. Even by this time, however, he had not built up his practice to where it was self-supporting. He had to give up his office, therefore, and had to move to cheaper living quarters. Gradually what little practice he had vanished.

As his financial situation became acute he secured loans from prominent businessmen who were former friends of the family. Instead of being able to repay what he had borrowed, he was forced from time to time to seek additional loans. The businessmen, realizing the futility of his condition, cut down the size of their loans to amounts which they could afford to give him. Through this process he gradually became a private charity client of these businessmen. He now lives in a small room in a slum district, and has long since stopped his medical practice. He prepares his own meals, does his own laundry, and spends most of his spare time in the public library. For a livelihood he visits each of these businessmen once every two or three weeks and secures a "loan."

The economic failure, however, is not the only type of person who is ejected from society. The social failure finds life as difficult as does the economic failure. Society is little more kind to those who do not abide by its *mores* and conventionalities than it is to those who cannot earn a livelihood. Those who violate its customs and laws sufficiently are termed crim-

inals and are ejected by force from society. Those who commit
less serious offenses are snubbed or disowned by friends and
are isolated from respectable society. Those who eat with a
knife are denied the company of the elite, the unmarried
mother becomes a social outcast, and the kleptomaniac is
strictly avoided. Others, who have peculiar ideas or habits,
are simply considered queer or eccentric. If sufficiently queer
they may be classed as crazy or feeble-minded and may be
treated accordingly. Those who fail to adjust socially, therefore, may find themselves in the clutches of the law, they may
be sent to an institution for mental diseases, or they may be
cast off to the underworld.

"There is a type of tramp who lives on his bad reputation. He may have been sent away for the sake of the
family, or have fled for safety, or he may have gone volun-
tarily to start life anew. Seldom does he succeed, but
family pride stands between him and his return. He cap-
italizes the fact that his family does not want him to
return.

"Such a man resides on South State Street. He comes
from a good family but his relatives do not care to have
him about. He is fat and greasy and dirty; he seems to
have no opinions of his own; is always getting into people's way and making himself disagreeable by his effort
to be sociable. His relatives pay him four dollars a week
to stay in Chicago. On that amount, with what he can
earn, he is able to live." [2]

Another type of person who frequently finds his way into
the underworld either from his own choice or from the pressure of society is the disorganized person. A person living
normally and peacefully, pushing on toward success may suddenly find that his social world has collapsed. Through some
misfortune or severe disappointment he may find that the
motives which have spurred him on have suddenly vanished.
The loss of a loved one, financial reverses, or disappointment
in a friend may suddenly turn the world sour. Endless toil

[2] Anderson, *The Hobo*, pp. 46-47.

and sacrifice no longer have any meaning. The pleasures and joys which have made life worth living have lost their color. The person has no joy in the present and no future toward which he is working. Disillusioned and bewildered, he wanders aimlessly, taking the course of least resistance. The scenes and friends which were a joy to him become a torment, and he flees them. His mental upheaval may cause financial failure. Whether it does or not, he may seek peace of mind by withdrawing into himself, escaping organized society, and hiding from his former world in the anonymity of the underworld.

"At middle age I thought nothing could disturb the delightful tenor of my life. But alas, man proposes and it is God who disposes.

"A young man—a boarder—came to live with us. I was often absent from the city, on business, and the usual happened. I forgave her, of course; it was not in my nature to be revengeful. But from that time my happiness was gone. It took life from my energy. My business went from bad to worse. I took the path that many discouraged men take —I drank heavily, and grew to care only for my poetry. I became, indeed, so depraved that I did what, perhaps, you cannot understand—I deserted my children, and went to New York, already an old man. But the other fellow remained and somehow all that was good in me had gone out, except always my love for my native country, and for its poetry.

"Here in New York, as you know, sir, I live most miserably. This good cafe keeper gives me my meals. I sit here all day and sleep in a hall-bedroom given me by a poor girl who rents the apartment. But when I go home I have one solace—my epic poem—for you know I am writing an epic of Hungary's glorious history." [3]

The process of transferring from organized society to the underworld is usually gradual, whether the person be a financial failure, a social failure, or a disorganized person. The

[3] Hutchins Hapgood, *Types from City Streets* (New York, 1910), p. 150.

process usually begins with a change in residence. Step by step the person moves to cheaper and cheaper residential districts. As he changes residence he changes friends, gradually dropping old ones and taking on new ones. If his difficulties are financial he spends all his savings and then exhausts his credit. He may change from one occupation to another or from one group to another in the hope of finding a satisfactory adjustment. Frequently he attributes his difficulties to the locality in which he lives and he tries moving from one city or town to another in the hope of finding one which will "appreciate" him. Leaving a city makes it easy for him to land at a lower level in the next. Thus, gradually, the failure shuffles down the social and economic ladder from a higher rung to the very bottom.

Mrs. Hobson was born and reared in Alabama. Her father was postmaster and later station agent of the town in which they lived. He provided well for his family and was highly respected throughout the community. Among other organizations in which he was active was the Masonic Lodge in which he received the thirty-second degree. There were six children in the family, and, according to her sisters' reports, Mrs. Hobson was the petted child. She is said to have been quite a favorite of her father and through his lavishness developed very extravagant habits. She went to the seventh grade in school, but was removed by her parents because of severe chills and ill health.

At the age of seventeen Mrs. Hobson married an express agent who was twenty-one years of age. He is reported to have made a good husband, and they got along well together. There were nine children born to them of whom three died in infancy. During this marriage her father and mother died, and a few years later her husband died leaving her with six children and no means of support. She almost immediately distributed her children out among her relatives, and went to Nashville to take training as a nurse. After three months of training, she returned to her home town and married an old man who was getting very feeble. She admits she married him just to get a living, but she was unable to get along with him, and after three months they were separated.

After this separation, Mrs. Hobson moved to Birmingham, where she ran a rooming house. After a few years, she married a stonecutter who was working on a public building in the city and was staying at her house. When he finished this job, they moved to Nashville. For several years after they came here they seemed to get along very nicely. He provided well for them and she kept a very tidy home. Finally, however, he developed an incurable heart disease which prevented his working, and they soon found themselves in financial straits. They appealed to the local social agency and received considerable help. Since she was able-bodied and in good health, the social workers insisted upon her going to work and supporting the family. This she refused to do, saying that she had never worked and she never intended to. Instead she applied to churches and other organizations for aid, and gradually she began to solicit help from individuals. In addition, she began to open her house to couples who wished to have unconventional relations, especially to married men who wished to meet other men's wives. Apparently she herself became a prostitute. She is now a habitual beggar and has continued to be immoral. She has developed a case of venereal disease, which she claims she contracted from a boy eighteen years of age. Though her husband has never outwardly sanctioned her actions, he has not offered objections.

Mrs. Hobson has never kept in close touch with her children since she turned them over to her relatives, and consequently they hardly feel that they know her and will have nothing to do with her. She has gotten whatever help she could from her sisters for many years, so that they have become completely exasperated. In addition, of late years they have gotten the idea that she has become a streetwalker, and have completely ostracized her. Mr. Hobson also has been separated from his relatives for many years. His father died when he was just a boy, and he and his brother were reared by an uncle. This uncle was poor, and they had to go to work at a rather early age. They became separated many years ago and had not heard from each other for thirty years, until the local social agency after several years of searching finally located the brother. This brother was reported to be aged and in poor circumstances, and was unable even to come to see Mr. Hobson, let alone give him help.

In most cases, the period when the person is crossing from the lowest rung of organized society into the underworld is one of his darkest hours. It is the time when he is relinquishing forever his hopes, ambitions, and values cherished from childhood and is entering a world of new values and, one might say, opportunities. The crossing-over comes at the moment when his condition becomes so intolerable that the advantages of the underworld overbalance the compensations of continued struggle in the world of organized society. It is then that he weighs the financial returns of an outcast occupation against the stigma of society, the personal freedom of begging against the routine and supervision of respectable labor, the sympathy and respect of fellow failures over against a status in self-respecting society, and it may be then that he musters all the grievances and injustices which he has suffered at the hands of society.

Mr. Patters is a small, thin, elderly man, slightly crippled, who walks with a cane. He dresses exceedingly well for a man in his circumstances and his manner is courteous in the extreme. For years he was in the newspaper business, provided well for his family, and had quite a normal home. There was apparently very little friction in the home, and the family was well thought of in the southern town in which they lived. Two years ago, Mr. Patters' arches went flat, and he was forced to quit the newspaper business. He has since been unable to find any work which he can do, and his financial condition has been drifting from bad to worse.

He has a son and daughter who contribute to the support of the family, and his brother gives some help, but these sources of income are insufficient to keep the family in its accustomed scale of living. Consequently, he has taken to begging from various businessmen, and he has developed all sorts of deceits to preserve his status. He always asks for a loan, never for a gift. But, of course, the businessman considers it a gift, and Mr. Patters knows he has no hope of paying it back. In addition, he makes every effort to shield the situation from his family. He tells his wife that he is out selling raincoats, and that he buys the groceries which he brings in with his profits. Further, he, in a pleading way, resists all attempts for interviews with members of his family. His son and his brother are quite aware of the situation, and do all they can to relieve the situation without driving Mr. Patters into insanity.

The severity of this last struggle depends to a considerable extent on the suddenness with which disaster comes to the person. If it comes suddenly and without warning the struggle and mental suffering are usually very severe, unless perchance the person is so dazed that he does not realize what is happening. If, on the other hand, the process of failure is a long series of reverses, the last fall may be as welcome as death sometimes appears to be to people suffering from a lingering illness. Indeed, many hover on the brink of dependency so long that they are often mentally prepared for the last thrust years before it comes.

For most people, however, hopeless struggle and mental anguish do not last forever. There usually comes a time when he washes his hands of all responsibility for his failure, and he may turn to avenge himself against a cruel society. Once he has made his decision, he may breathe a sigh of relief and thank Heaven that the struggle is over.

"It's true, Cigarette, that I'm down—'way down—an' I'll never get up again. I've struck the limit. You ask me how it feels. Well, I'll tell you. In general, it feels bad. 'Taint nice to have to think over your recollects, an' wonder what you might 'a' been. Nobody ever got happy doin' that, I don't care who he was. There's one comfort I've got, though, that you haven't—I don't have to worry any more about holdin' my posish, about realizin' my ambitions an' it's a sight bigger relief 'n most people imagine. When I lie down at night, I say to myself, 'you may be a failure an' all that, but you ain't got no headache 'cause you didn't win out, so be happy.' An' do you know, Cigarette, I guess I'm just as contented as you are." [4]

For some, this spiritless contentment is permanent, for others it is only temporary. Most of them have finished their fight and lost. Of their struggle they have only bitter memories, and they have no spirit or desire to start over again. By their decision they have entered a new world, the underworld, a world with different standards, different occupations, and a different life from the one in which they have failed. Here they may start over in a life of a different sort.

Readjustment in the underworld entails two things, securing a profession or "racket," and securing a philosophy of life. Which of the outcast professions the person enters may be a matter of chance or it may be a matter of choice. For success in an outcast profession one must learn the trade just as one must do in a socially approved occupation. The tenderfoot, therefore, often follows the line of least resistance—he enters the profession of those with whom he happens to become acquainted, and he learns the trade from them. Others, however, consciously choose their profession. They may feel that one of the "rackets" brings better returns in proportion to the risks than the others or they may have previously formed attitudes which make it difficult for them to enter one but easy for them to enter another.

Jack is a man some forty years of age. Altogether he has served sentences of about sixteen years in the penitentiary for robbery of one kind or another. At present he is not operating because he believes that operations on a private scale do not pay. He admits, however, that he would be delighted to have a job "gunning" or "slugging" for some gang at $75 per week. He is very short of money at

[4] J. J. Goodwin, "Beggars of New York," *Harpers Weekly*, XLVI (1902), 204.

present, but when asked why he did not turn to begging he said that he did not believe he could bring himself to that even if he were starving to death.

Simultaneously with entering an outcast profession, the person, if he is to become adjusted, must rationalize his actions or must secure a new philosophy of life. Often it is difficult to determine whether the new state of mind constitutes a philosophy or a rationalization. Those entering the begging profession justify begging in many ways. For example:

M. says she begs because her neighbor begs and that she is as deserving as he.

W. says she does not consider her begging a disgrace because Lazarus begged from the rich man's table and went to heaven while the rich man did not.

X. says he thinks begging is wrong, but says he does not consider it begging to just walk along the street with a cup in his hand. He considers he is not responsible if people want to drop coins in it.

T. thinks every one is out to get something for nothing, and he considers himself more honest for outright begging than the "respectable gambler" who plays the stock market.

J. is a blind beggar. He feels that society should support the physically handicapped, and since the government does not collect this support, he proposes to collect his part himself.

Y. claims to be a World War veteran. He believes that he has rendered society an invaluable service and is due any support which he can get out of it.

R. begs only from social service agencies. He claims that the money is put there for the poor and that he deserves it as much as any one else.

In some respects a more ludicrous case than any of the foregoing is one reported by Solenberger. She quotes one beggar as saying, "I don't hold a man up with a gun. He doesn't have to give to me unless he wants to, and if he wants to, I don't see that it is anybody's business but his and mine." [5]

[5] A. W. Solenberger, *1,000 Homeless Men* (New York, 1911), p. 168.

Not all who enter begging are able to make a satisfactory mental adjustment; some never succeed in doing so. Occasionally a person masters the art of begging sufficiently to make a comfortable living but is never able to gain peace of mind in the profession.

Frank is a blind man about thirty-five years of age. Though he had finished a course at a blind school and had later taken special training for a trade, he begged for a living for several years. Finally he was approached by an investigator who asked why he was begging. Thereupon he began to sob, and said, "To tell you the truth, I am not a beggar at heart. I consider beggars the lowest down people there are, and I feel like shooting myself everytime I start out to beg." The fact that he never begged again after other provision was made for him showed that his words were sincere.

Usually the beggar who makes a satisfactory mental adjustment to his profession soon passes the stage of rationalization. He becomes so interested in his new pursuit that he tends to forget whether it is right or wrong. He lives among people who do not question the merit of begging and he ceases to question it himself. The rationalization which he evolves in the beginning he holds in reserve for conscientious givers who challenge his complacency of mind. Whether begging is right or wrong becomes a philosophical question which he discusses with those interested, but it is no longer a burning question related to his own conduct. Consequently, what was in the beginning a feeble mental adjustment to an undesirable situation frequently develops, gradually of course, into a passion for a new profession.

It is the fact that begging can give the person things that he has longed for but has never been able to have that makes it such an entrancing occupation for those who have failed in the social world. Begging is not simply a means of livelihood for those in a state of spiritless despondency or a sort of mental hibernation for failures awaiting death. Once the person has ceased to feel the stigma placed on begging by organized society and has found an adjustment in begging, he frequently wonders why he fought off failure so long.

One of the compensations which begging offers is that of financial security.[6] "Love of money is the root of all evil." Most people can justify their actions or forget the need to justify them, if they bring good financial returns. So it is with the beggar. The person who has struggled along for years at a socially approved occupation, perhaps subsisting on a few dollars a week, is more than thrilled at the five, ten, or twenty dollars a day which he may gain by begging. Old age and physical misfortune no longer haunt him, for he knows that these are the stock in trade of the beggar. The older he gets, the more readily people will give to him. He can expect his income to increase rather than vanish in his declining years. He may revive his youthful dreams of building up a fortune and retiring, and he may succeed in doing so. Many would not under any consideration trade this financial security for the meager social recognition which they were able to secure from organized society.

Many beggars are not primarily interested in financial returns. They love begging because it affords them leisure. They can secure a livelihood with the least possible effort and in the least possible time. They hate rush, routine, and struggle. They love leisure, idleness, rest, and sleep. According to some standards, they are artists at living. Striving for success and status, working for change and perfection in the affairs of the world, worry and the other characteristics of our civilization mean nothing to them. They are the world's leisured poor and are happy in their state.

"His was a nature which preferred ease to anxiety, and idleness to labor. Idleness. Complete physical idleness. That was his joy. To sit and read a good book with nothing to worry about; with his mind dead to the world and its petty difficulties. To walk in the sun of a bright morning. To stand in front of a music shop and listen to a bit of jazz or opera. To lean against a lamp post and watch

[6] See Chapter X.

the troubled people hurrying about as if they were occupied with something actually important. To roll and smoke
a cigarette to the tune of a dream. To listen to religious
fanatics and socialists and smile at their idiocies. To visit
parks with their aquariums and museums. To sit on a
bench and watch young people moving in rhythms of
grace as they play tennis. To walk through a cool fog to
the beach. To climb a hill and look down on dreary
Alcatraz Island covered with its Government Penitentiary
and to realize what a wonderful thing it was not to be
locked up in such a place.... To be idle, to do anything
he liked. To be free to go anywhere he liked any time he
liked. To be nothing but a bum. That was Harry Brown." [7]

For other mendicants begging becomes a sport with many
thrills. Chasing free dollars, acting the role of a paralytic so
well as not to be detected, playing hide-and-seek with the
police, matching wits with scrutinous givers, all give color to
the game. For many, these thrills become a more consuming
passion than playing the stock market, winning at golf, or bet-
ting on the races. The famous German sociologist, Max Müller,
long ago recognized and described the sporting phase of begging. He says:

"Talk of shooting partridges or pheasants, talk of racing
or gambling, there is no sport like begging. There must
always be risk in sporting, and the risk in begging is very
great. You are fighting against tremendous odds. You ring
at the door, and you must first of all face a servant, who
generally scrutinizes you with great suspicion, and declines to take your name or your card unless you have a
clean shirt and a decent pair of boots. Then after you have
been admitted to the presence, you have to watch every
expression of your enemy or your friends as the case may
be. You have to face the cleverest people in the world, and
you know all the time that the slightest mistake in your
looks or the tone of your voice may lead to ruin. You may
be kicked out of the house, and if you meet with a high-

---

[7] William Saroyan, "Portrait of a Bum," *Overland Monthly*, LXXXVI
(1928), 421.

minded and public-spirited gentleman, who does not mind
trouble and expense, you may find yourself in the hands
of the police for trying to obtain money under false pretenses. No, I have known in my time what hunting and
shooting and gambling are; but I assure you there is no
sport like begging." [8]

It is this financial security, leisure, and the sport of begging
coupled with unpleasant memories of a lost struggle in organized society which make it virtually impossible for those
who once enter the profession ever to leave it. Such a tranquil
adjustment does not last forever, however, with all the beggars. Some, even after they have lived happily in the profession
for years, find themselves disconsolate and dissatisfied. The
basis of such mental conflicts is usually ambition, either early
ambitions which they have been unable to satisfy, or ambitions
they have acquired later but realize they can never attain
through begging. Some start out to build up a fortune but as
the years roll on they find that they are unable to do so. Others
build a fortune in the hopes that it will enable them to gain a
place in organized society, but later they find that even with
money they cannot easily cross the chasm that separates the
two worlds and gain a status of respectability. Perhaps the
most common form of maladjustment is that which is brought
about by the ambitions which a beggar has for his children.
The beggar who was reared in respectable society is often
content with mendicancy as a profession for himself, but
usually he cannot think of it as a profession for his children.
As his children get old enough to be conscious of social values
he often begins to worry about the stigma which his profession
will cast on them, and frequently he becomes disturbed by the
attitude his children will take toward him as their father. He
begins to ponder the possibility of changing his profession,
sending the children away to boarding school, or some other
method of removing the taint from their future lives. Red
Crane is perhaps a typical case of such maladjustment.

[8] Max Müller, "Auld Lang Syne," quoted from F. H. Wines, "Max
Müller on Beggars," *Charities*, XIII (1905), 559.

" 'Red Crane,' thirty-three years of age, was to be found almost daily during the first half of 1924 at the angle of the elevated walk leading from Michigan Avenue to the Randolph Street I. C. Station. Before him lay his crutches. His one sound leg was doubled under his body in such a way as to give the impression that he was legless. Bright red hair was always exposed. His features were sharp, eyes keen, and complexion ruddy. When he managed to catch the eyes of approaching persons they rarely passed without dropping a coin into his outstretched hat. He did impress people at first sight and knew it.

" 'Red' invited the inquirer to call at his home and meet his family. The home was a third floor apartment on Ohio street. It was newly furnished, neat and clean. 'Red' set eight dollars as a minimum day's income and worked long hours some days to maintain his standard. There could be no doubt that his standard of living was in keeping with his income. The two children, Lillian aged three and one half and Paul, aged one, were rosy youngsters. Clothes, toys and other baby paraphernalia, the watchfulness of both parents as well as their comments, indicated the pride taken in the well-being of their children. . . .

"For himself Crane felt no shame in his profession, but for the sake of the children both he and his wife were anxious to find other means. They foresaw the insults and ridicule the children of a beggar might receive in school. 'Red' had been considering the matter of training for a job that would pay enough to support his family, even though less than he made begging, and where his physical defects would not interfere. He went to the Chicago office of the State Board of Vocational Rehabilitation for advice and perhaps an artificial limb. He had not been in the state three years, so could not look to them for any assistance. They discouraged his efforts to get retraining at his age and with his dependents. In all he felt that they treated him like a 'bum' and seemed to fear that he would 'work' them for some of their 'boodle' (graft money). Mrs. Crane was optimistic in her hope that some day they might have saved enough to carry the family through the period required for 'Red's' vocational training. Until then they could see no alternative to begging." [9]

As a result of such conflicts beggars, like criminals, frequently try to straddle the chasm which separates the underworld from respectable society and eat the honey of both. They want the status of respectability along with the easy money of beggardom. In an attempt to do both, they sometimes live in a respectable residential section, and beg in disguise, all the time pretending to follow some socially approved occupation. Occasionally in a large city a beggar succeeds in playing such a double role, but seldom for long. Once detected they are the brunt of an indignant society and of the law.

The disorganized persons and the social and economic failures, who are cast off by society, often find in begging a profession with new opportunities. From it they often gain a degree of economic security, leisure, freedom, and interest which they have never been able to secure before. In the end, however, many find that "all that glitters is not gold." The compensations of mendicancy, though satisfying for a time, do not constitute an avenue to the fulfillment of the ultimate hopes which the person has for himself and especially for his children. The tranquil adjustment which at first results is often followed, therefore, by a period of worry, restlessness, and perhaps readjustment.

[9] Freund, "Begging in Chicago," pp. 81-84.

∽∽∽∽∽∽∽∽∽∽∽∽

CHAPTER IX

BORN TO BE BEGGARS

OF a type quite different from the social or economic failure who takes to begging as an adjustment is the person who is born and reared as a beggar. As the royal heir is reared to be a prince or princess, so he is reared to be a beggar. So deeply is the begging culture imbedded in his nature, that he has a poise and an ease in the begging role which cannot be gained by the person who enters the profession as an adult. He has no rationalizations and frequently no philosophy of life which he can state in concrete terms. Indeed he does not need one, for he has no conscience on the subject. He has begged always, his parents have begged before him, and most of his friends are beggars. To him it is the natural way of making a living. None of his intimate acquaintances question the practice, and he sees no reason to question it. Conscientious givers who reprimand him speak in a language which he does not understand. If he answers them, it may be with a rationalization which he has learned from others. Neither the reprimand nor the rationalization have any vital meaning to him. From the standpoint of reform he is usually hopeless.

To understand this type of beggar entails an understanding of the culture in which he is reared. He is a product of the underworld. The peculiar nature of the underworld culture rests to a large extent on the high degree of isolation which separates this strata of society from the rest of the world. This isolation is made possible, and to a certain extent made necessary, by the phenomenon of residential segregation which characterizes modern city life. In the large city, as has been said, people are segregated in different residential areas on an economic basis. The wealthy live in certain sections, the middle classes in others, and the poor in districts to themselves. Through this process of economic classification, the very poor are shunted out of the more desirable residential sections, and eventually most of them land in one or more sections of the city which are the least desirable for living purposes.

A residential district which becomes populated by families who are hanging on the ragged edge of dependency and perhaps most of whom are dependent part or all of the time develops a characteristic scale of values and a culture different from the more substantial districts. Since most of the families are either dependent or fear that they may sooner or later become dependent, no person condemns another for having to receive help. In fact, a certain degree of mutual sympathy develops. A tacit taboo against remarks derogatory to begging arises, and everyone sooner or later comes to accept it as right and proper to receive help. Frequently the poor in such a section lower their scale of values still further. Knowing the straitened financial condition under which many of the families live, the members of the community soon come to justify anything which will bring a financial return. Prostitution is not looked upon with horror, stealing from the wealthy classes is justifiable, and bootlegging is a dignified occupation. Since the whole area is rather thoroughly isolated from the rest of society, the members cease to be conscious of how the rest of the world looks upon these occupations. While the single, dependent family living in a small community is constantly reminded of the fact that begging and indigent dependency are considered wrong, the family in the dependency area seldom has this brought to its attention.

Such a scale of values in the dependent neighborhood is facilitated by the mutual misunderstanding which arises between people of different economic levels as a result of their residential segregation and the consequent isolation. The members of the dependent area, having practically no direct contacts with the well-to-do classes, have little sympathy with or understanding of them. The well-to-do classes likewise have little genuine understanding of the problems of the very poor. Thus, for the middle class, a nice car is something for which a person must save, eventually buy, and then enjoy. The underworld youth has no conception of all this. If he thinks of the matter at all, he assumes that the owner got the car almost for the asking. For such a youth, the car is something to be stolen, enjoyed for a few hours, and then abandoned or sold for a song. Neither party, therefore, understands the other. The members of the underworld ordinarily think life is much easier for the middle and upper classes than it really is, and the members of the upper classes cannot understand why the "underworld characters" are so utterly devoid of conscience as they frequently appear to be.

Once the dependency neighborhood is established, it tends to be a center for a self-perpetuating underworld. The boundaries of the neighborhood may change with the growth of the city but such alterations usually occur slowly. In the course of several years a neighborhood may move a few blocks, but this transfer may take place so slowly that the culture is not disturbed. Although as in any neighborhood the members may change gradually and do change completely with succeeding generations, the morale and spirit tend to remain the same. A neighborhood may retain an underworld status in this way for several years or even for several generations. Through this continuity, the neighborhood tends to become a reservoir for the accumulation of technical knowledge related to the underworld professions. New ideas or methods devised or learned by the members are passed on from one person to another and from one generation to another. The best techniques are thus unconsciously selected and retained. An old underworld neighborhood may have a rich heritage of technical knowledge of anti-social occupations.

Such a neighborhood is not just a reservoir for the accumulation of techniques; it is a training center for recruits for the underworld professions. Children growing up in such neighborhoods take to the underworld professions as naturally as the children in mill towns and in fishing villages take to the occupations of their parents. Not only do the children grow up in the general underworld culture of the neighborhood, but they also have the anti-social occupations commended by their local heroes. It is the bootlegger, not the straggling worker, who has money to flourish and fine cars to ride in; it is the loose girl, not the model of morality, who has fine clothes and many boy friends; and it is the beggar who has leisure and ease along with a comfortable income. To the growing child these are the people who seem to be gaining success, and he idolizes them. He, therefore, not only accepts the underworld occupations but he becomes vitally interested in gaining success in one of them. He does not stop to consider that they may be a means to a merely temporary success.

These underworld areas thus tend to breed a population which takes to them as naturally as the muskrat takes to the swamp. Under the influence of such a community a family may develop begging patterns and pass them on from generation to generation indefinitely. So regularly do such patterns recur in some families that they have at times been mistaken for instincts. In the following family, which has lived mostly in one poverty section for many years, begging has apparently developed into a tradition.

"Some sixty years ago Thomas Jed, a young man in his early twenties, took up residence in a small southern town of three or four thousand population. The fragmentary information available indicates that he came from an adjoining state, though little is actually known of his past. He was at that time a heavy drinker. So far as we are able to learn, he had no communication with any of his relatives, excepting one brother, after he reached this town. This brother lived in one of the prairie states in the Southwest and was apparently comfortably situated. He, in later years, sent Thomas considerable money, and at one time offered to remove Thomas and his family to the prairie section and help him get established, but this offer was rejected.

"Shortly after Thomas took up residence in this town he married into a family, with a large kinship connection in the locality, who were, and still are, of low economic and social status in the community. The men worked at menial occupations and had small incomes. However, these families have always had an exceptional reputation for thrift and for economic responsibility. Their credit even today is accepted without question by the merchants of the town, and it is an unheard of thing for any member to have been dependent on a public agency. A strong familism seems to have prevailed which made of it a sort of self-aid group. All unfortunate members seem to have been provided for out of the family coffers, and loans of one member to another for small economic enterprises have been rather common. In this respect the family seems to have fulfilled almost ideally the family responsibilities imposed by the mores of the Old South.

"The family created by Thomas' marriage became a problem almost immediately. Births occurred in rapid succession. In all, eight children were born, two of whom died in childhood. From almost the beginning the family was dependent. Thomas, because of his drinking, was never able to provide the income necessary to care for the needs of his family. But Mrs. Jed's relatives rose to the occasion and supplied the deficit, so that the family was not dependent on public agencies. Thomas was not able to hold paying jobs and soon confined his productive activities to running a small fish market. As a matter of fact his place of business hardly could be designated by the term 'market,' for it consisted only of a few barrels set out by the sidewalk, and his patronage was principally among the Negroes.

"His drinking habit seems to have been chronic, and as a result the economic condition of his family grew worse rather than better. Each additional child brought greater expense without any additional income. This increased burden fell on Mrs. Jed's relatives, and it is to their credit that they practically supported the family for more than twenty years.

"In the home, Thomas seems to have had the patriarchal

ideal of being lord of all he surveyed, but he seemed much more interested in protecting his rights than he did in exercising them. He resented the interference of his wife and of his wife's relatives in the way he reared his children, but he exerted no great effort to rear them himself. Consequently they grew up with a minimum of training. They attended school only in so far as the law required, and none of them passed the elementary grades. Likewise in the matter of occupational training, the children were never forced to work and never had to contribute to the family income. In the words of Mrs. Jed's nephew, 'In spite of the protests of Mrs. Jed and of the relatives, Thomas never taught the boys to work.'

"All of the children married in their early adult years. One of the girls married a local man and seems to have succeeded very well for a few years. The two boys and one of the girls moved soon after their marriage to a city of about one hundred thousand population, which was located some fifty miles from the town in which they were reared; they were followed shortly by Thomas and Mrs. Jed. The two remaining girls moved with their husbands to other sections of the South. Within a few years, however, all of the girls had acquired children, had lost their husbands through death or through desertion, and, finally, finding themselves widows with children to care for, joined their parents and brothers in the city.

"Thus, in the course of a few years we find the whole immediate kinship group transferred from a small town to a city. It consisted at this time of the aged couple who had always been economically incompetent, of four widows with a total of thirteen children, and of two younger men with families. One of these men had a large and increasing family, and the other had acquired his father's drinking habit, so that he was scarcely able to support himself and his wife even when he tried.

"The whole kinship group, of course, almost immediately fell into dependency, but they no longer received aid from Mrs. Jed's relatives. They now became charges of the public. The old family pattern, however, carried over, and the family solidarity held fast, so that in the new situation the members comprised a compact social group. As Mrs. Jed's family had comprised a co-operating group in maintaining independence, the new group carried on co-operating activities in dependency. Any aid received by one family was readily shared with others who might not have been so 'fortunate.' This, of course, brought them into ill repute with social agencies. Case workers found that they could not treat any family in the connection as a unit, and to reconstruct the whole group was a task of such magnitude as to stagger the most optimistic worker. As a result, the family became a 'bug-a-boo' for family agencies. It became known as 'a bunch of worthless beggars that nothing could remedy.' [1]

"Membership in the family became as much of a stigma among social agencies as certain racial marks are among some social groups. The members, therefore, soon found it impossible to secure aid from social agencies and were forced to resort to other means. They applied to churches and to other social organizations and received considerable aid. Some members tried going back to the town of their birth, but found that they were welcomed no longer by their more distant relatives and that their lot was no better than in the city. At various times members tried moving to other cities, but, since they seem never to have used aliases, their identity was quickly disclosed, and sooner or later all have returned.

"All of this conflict with social agencies tended only to increase the social distance between the family and society which to the family the agencies represented. Accompanied by the familism which already existed, the opposition developed very strong in-group feelings between the members and strong out-group feelings toward society, especially social agencies.

"Blocked from securing help from social agencies, the members showed considerable aptitude for securing aid from other sources. Begging was resorted to by many of the members. Thomas Jed became an ordinary street beggar and Mrs. Jed became a house-to-house beggar. One of

[1] Quoted directly from an old case record on this family which is on file in one of the agencies.

the widows developed into probably the most successful residence beggar in the city. Another member became a habitual church beggar. Other members have secured aid from agencies when they could, received help from churches frequently, and have begged when necessary.

"In their begging activities, the adult members of the family have made liberal use of the children. Children have been taken by their parents or have been sent alone to solicit aid from agencies and from churches. They have been sent out occasionally on the street to beg alone. And almost invariably the adult doing residence begging has carried one or more children along as a sample of the 'half dozen sick children at home.' One of the widows, who does residence begging, carried her youngest daughter, an anemic-looking child, along on these begging expeditions until this daughter was married at the age of nineteen. Since that time she has been taking one of her grandchildren with her.

"As the children have reached adulthood and have gotten married their families have become either constant or occasional public charges. The living members of the kinship group consist of the second, third, fourth, and fifth generations, the original Thomas and Mrs. Jed having died several years ago. A number of the third generation have families, and a few of the fourth generation have married in their teens and have young children. And for every marriage, with the exception of two, there is a case record on file in some relief agency in the city in which they live. The two marriages to which exception is made are those of two women of the third generation who were taken from their mother when they were very young and were reared in an institution. In so far as the author has been able to learn, the families of these two women have a clear record both as regards delinquency and dependency. From the standpoint of relief agencies, the descendants of Thomas and Mrs. Jed represent at the present time an annual case load of approximately fifty individuals. The records of these agencies, however, only represent a small part of the total aid secured by this family. Individuals, churches, and civic organizations have been importuned as persistently as have the relief agencies, and perhaps with greater success." [2]

Being reared in such a family living in an underworld community, the child tends to continue the begging tradition of his family because he has no desire to do otherwise. He so thoroughly accepts the philosophy of the underworld occupations, which he has acquired from his family and friends, that he has no qualms about entering them. In fact, he has a keen desire to enter them. Furthermore, being tutored in these occupations from childhood and living in a community teeming with underworld techniques and attitudes, he can learn one of the underworld professions easier than he can learn any other. And if he comes of a family of beggars he can learn begging easier than any of the other underworld professions. Finally, if he is to have friends and be congenial with those among whom he lives, he must fall in with the begging profession and the underworld. Entering begging, therefore, is for him the line of least resistance. It is the way of life which will bring him into the greatest favor with relatives and friends, though it may be taboo by society at large.

If perchance a child reared in the beggar world does seek to escape, he will find it difficult, if not impossible. Having been reared in such a neighborhood, he has, in society as a whole, an underworld status. He does not have to change friends or social worlds to become a beggar, pickpocket, or bootlegger, but a great change is necessary if he is to become a member of a socially approved occupation. And this change of social worlds is difficult to make. Since he is born in the underworld, he must live down the stigma of his birth, for in cities people are ranked, to a considerable extent, by the residential section in which they live. If a person lives in a middle class section, it is assumed as a matter of course that he is of the middle class socially and economically. So it is with the other residential sections. The underworld neighborhoods, likewise, have their status in the city, and everyone living in

[2] Harlan W. Gilmore, "Five Generations of a Begging Family," *American Journal of Sociology,* XXXVII, No. 5 (1932), 768-71.

such a community is identified with this status. The person born and reared in such a community, therefore, is not only handicapped in the larger world by the habits and attitudes which he develops, but he is handicapped also by the status which the neighborhood bestows upon him.

To escape this social world and status of his birth is a difficult task, and a task for which he is ill-prepared. To effect his escape he must be able to earn a livelihood in the world of socially approved occupations, and his chances of being able to brook the keen competition in these overcrowded occupations is very small. Even his chances of having a sound physique are less than normal. The underworld area is one having a high frequency of tuberculosis, venereal diseases, and numerous other forms of ill health, and it will not be uncommon if the beggar child is a physical weakling by the time his infancy is passed. In addition to his physical handicap he will usually have an inferior education. Even if his area has been fortunate enough to have as good schools as the better sections of the city, his own school work has likely been poor and irregular. He may have been taken out of school frequently by his parents to go on begging expeditions, or he may have worked late on the street at night and gone to school the next day too tired and sleepy to do any work. What is true of his general education is even more true of occupational training. His chances of getting professional training are virtually nonexistent and his chances of getting training even for a skilled trade are poor. If the child of the beggar gets ambitions, therefore, he will find his struggle to get a foothold in a socially approved occupation decidedly an uphill struggle. Since he will hardly be content with an occupation unless it affords him a better income than he could get from begging or some other underworld occupation, his chance of success in his struggle is very meager. With poor health, poor education, and no occupational training he can have little hope of gaining in the "upper world" any economic success which he would consider superior to the one he could gain in the underworld.

Should the person born of a beggar family succeed in overcoming the numerous odds and attain economic success in the world of socially approved occupations, he would still have problems. He, like the millionaire, "does not know how the other half lives," and he would have to learn how this other half lives before he could become a part of it. He would have to reverse most of the habits and attitudes which his childhood world had built up in him, and he would have to acquire a whole new way of acting, thinking, and living. This is hard even for the country boy who "makes good," and it would be doubly hard for the beggar boy. He would have a long and difficult struggle trying to get accepted by "respectable society" and would have a still longer struggle trying to feel natural in that society. If he makes this uphill climb and succeeds in becoming adjusted to organized society, he will be an unusual and a rare person.

As a result of the ease of staying in the underworld and of the difficulty of getting out of it, the children of the underworld nearly always follow in the footsteps of their parents. They go the way of their fathers, not because of heredity but because society dictates that they shall, and so the underworld population replaces itself each generation with its own kind.

The dependency neighborhoods in cities, though important, are not the only source of recruits for beggardom. Industriousness and living "by the sweat of the brow" are ideals of the majority of the workaday world, and any class or group of people who are able to isolate themselves more or less completely from this world may develop a dependency culture. A common and very old way of doing this is to become transient. The transients have always been able to live in and among stable, organized communities without becoming a part of them. To be a part of a community one must become sufficiently acquainted to gossip about friends and neighbors and to be gossiped about. Only by such intimacy can one become responsive to the customs of the community. The transients never attain such intimacy in any community. By continually moving from one to another they remain a stranger in all.

In the Middle Ages the troubadours and minstrels were a

transient type of beggar. In our own country the tramp travels
from one place to another, lives in his jungles, and begs. By so
doing he has remained aloof from the general population, escaped the pressure of its customs, and developed a unique set
of standards and a culture of his own. As has been said, because it is for the most part a male tribe, the tramp world does
not replenish itself by reproduction but by recruiting young
men and boys from the general population. Few of its members were ever born and reared as tramps. The gypsy, however, has reproduced his kind while he lived a dependent,
transient existence. It is this unique class of people which has
roamed through all sizes of communities and in all countries
of the world for centuries, has maintained family and tribal
life, has brought forth and reared children, and yet, few have
ever become a part of any settled community. They have
secured a livelihood from organized society, but at the same
time they have remained unresponsive to its customs and have
developed a culture wholly strange to the communities through
which they travel. Theirs is a truly migratory dependency culture, rich in tricks, devices, and techniques for securing a livelihood while on the move. The gypsy culture perpetuates itself,
generation after generation and century after century, not by
instinct, but by rearing its children to know and love this form
of life.

Another type of dependency culture in which recruits for
begging are reared is found in the master-servant relationship.
Whether this relationship be technically slavery or not, one set
of standards and culture exists for the master class and another
for the servant. Frequently strict morality is expected of the
master class, especially the women, but is not expected of the
servant class. Usually, also, stealing is taboo among the master
class, but petty thievery is tolerated among the servant class.
Likewise the master class is expected to be financially independent and self-sufficient, while the servant class is dependent.

The relationship between the white men and Negroes in the
South is a typical example of this sort of dual culture and dual
standards in the same community. Under slavery, the Negro

was essentially dependent on the white. Technically he gave his labor in return for his keep, but actually most slaves did not recognize this relationship. The "pay" came in such a form that the ignorant slave did not recognize it as a product of his work. He was given a cabin to live in, food to eat, clothes to wear, usually some sort of medical care, and was taken care of during infancy and old age. He did not get these things in return for a specified amount of work; he got them when he needed them. Usually he got the same supplies whether he had done good work or bad, much work or little, and he even got them when he had done no work at all. The ignorant slave, therefore, must have thought that he gave his master work, and his master gave him a living. This feeling was augmented on most plantations by the fact that there was no system of rewarding the slave financially for extra good work and punishing him for poor work. Some of the best plantations did have bonus systems, but ordinarily a uniform and an annual allotment of rations was given to each slave family. The ordinary slave, therefore, could not increase his income by increasing the amount or efficiency of his labor. To increase his income and to gain special favors he had to learn to work his master. To do this, Negroes developed a very efficient technique at an early date. They learned how to be polite, jovial, humorous, flattering, and grateful to their superiors in a very subtle way. They learned to give their masters what they wanted, a glorified reflection of themselves. In addition to this technique for gaining favor, they developed the art of asking for things. They learned to hint or to ask outright for things without being offensive, and they learned to take a refusal with a smile and a joke.

The slave situation thus developed quite different values and standards for the slave class and for the master class. In many things the two sets of standards were diametrically opposite, and supplementary to each other. The master was supposed to be independent, the slave dependent; the master superior boss, the slave humble servant; the master paternal guardian, the slave grateful ward; the master giver, the slave beggar. Thus, though the slave class and the master class lived on the same plantation and were both a part of the same economic system, they lived under a different set of standards. The Negro lived in a dependency status, and to a great extent developed a begging culture.

With the Civil War and emancipation, the Negro's legal status changed. Before the law he was no longer a slave; he was a free citizen. Customs of long standing, however, cannot be changed in a day. In the new relationships which arose, therefore, many characteristics of the slave economy were carried over. The tenant system arose in which the landlord furnished land, tools, work animals, a cabin for the Negro, and supplies. The Negro furnished his labor only. Supposedly there was an annual balancing of accounts and settlement, but frequently the Negro received nothing in cash for his year of work. His system of compensation, therefore, was little different from what it was under the slave regime. In both cases, his income depended greatly on what he could beg the master or landlord to let him have. In domestic service the change was more pronounced. The domestic servant was ordinarily given some cash wage. This wage was usually very small, however, and was understood by both employer and servant to be only a part of the servant's wages. To supplement the cash consideration an indefinite amount of food, old clothes, discarded furniture, and other supplies were given. The domestic servant thus was compensated for her labor partly in money and partly in gifts. The servant, therefore, who could gain good will and could ask for things tactfully could extract larger returns from the household of her mistress than the one who was not so clever. The better her art of begging was, the higher her wages.

Thus in the period following the Civil War, as well as under the slave regime itself, the Negro lived under a different standard and was accorded a different status from that of the white. His moral, educational, and economic standards were on an entirely different basis from that of the white. These differences were recognized and accepted by the Negro and white alike. So strongly has this master-servant tradition persisted that even today many a Negro in the South has some white man who acts as a sort of godfather to him. This white man will bail him out of jail, defend him in a limited way before courts, and give him old clothes and other articles whether he has earned them or not. This white man may be the Negro's employer or he may not. Quite often he is a former but not a present employer. The essential thing is that it is not a business transaction either in form or spirit; it is done in the spirit of paternalism.

Living in the same community with the white, the Negro has developed what amounts to a dependency-begging culture. Being reared in this culture, he falls into this way of life naturally. Gradually learning that both the members of the white race and the members of his own race expect him to play the dependency-begging role, he accepts that as the one proper for him. He becomes disturbed only when he comes in contact with a new set of standards as typified by the New Negro.

Being independent and earning a livelihood by the "sweat of the brow," therefore, are standards of the world of socially approved occupations. Groups or classes who become isolated or "exempted" from the pressure of these standards tend to develop a dependency-begging culture with distinctive standards. The underworld neighborhoods in cities, transient groups, and dependent classes tend to develop standards different from the rest of society. Persons reared in such a culture have the status of their class and acquire attitudes and technical knowledge which predispose them to fall naturally into begging. By birth and rearing they are designed to be beggars.

CHAPTER X

DO BEGGARS GET RICH?

THE question of how much beggars earn has been a favorite subject for speculation for virtually everyone except the beggars themselves. The public has been told on the one hand that beggars are poor people on the verge of starvation, and on the other hand that beggars amass fortunes, and the man on the street is left too puzzled even to guess. The beggar himself is the most active agent for advertising his poverty. His art is chiefly one of portraying poverty and misfortune, and every appeal which the beggar makes is an argument designed to prove that he is poor. In contrast to the beggar's story of poverty, literature contains numerous accounts of the beggar's lavish spending, and current newspapers and magazines publish frequent stories of the fabulous earnings of certain beggars. Courtenay Savage, apparently on a basis of such accounts, published a colorful article entitled, "Beggars Collect Fortunes from the Public." [1] The following brief newspaper story is typical of these accounts which often get into the daily press:

"Danville, Va., Aug. 16. A new kind of a racket came to light here today with the arrest of Joseph Sullivan, who gave his home as Greenville, S. C., on a charge of begging in violation of a city ordinance. Taken to police headquarters, Sullivan's wallet was found to be bulging with greenbacks and he readily admitted that he had been playing the stock market with the money he was given as a beggar. He told police that he had secured $50 in one day by begging and the full amount had been played on the market. He had been here about a week, leading to com-

[1] *Dearborn* (Michigan) *Independent*, October 11, 1924, p. 13.

plaints to the police. He is 83 years old and a German, he said.

"After a warning by Police Chief J. H. Martin, the stranger was released on the understanding that he leave town." [2]

Foreign writers likewise seem to be convinced that their native beggars get lucrative returns from their efforts; for example, the beggars of Japan are reported to make quite substantial earnings. "The report of Mr. Hideo Kusama of the Social Works Bureau in the Tokyo municipal government brings out the fact that beggars make an average of ¥100 a month—and that, to be sure, is a lot more than college graduates frequently make." [3]

If we are to believe Paulian, the beggars of Paris also live well.

"Look about in the Rue du Faubourg Saint Honoré, and you will find there a restaurant frequented by small clerks in government offices who devote themselves every day to a careful study of the menu in order to succeed in making a meal which shall not cost more than 1 franc 25 centimes. These clerks work; they know that the month is long and that money is hard to earn. It is all the harder to earn since they are not allowed to undertake a multitude of small accessory works by which they might augment their income. Were you to see the principal clerk of a Minister keeping the accounts of the coal merchant opposite, what indecorum!

"The Administration do not consider whether the unfortunate clerk has a wife and children to provide for— the poor little clerk often contents himself with a breakfast at 40 centimes and a cup of coffee.

"But go through this same room in the restaurant about ten o'clock at night, what a different picture! The customers no longer choose the cheapest things on the bill of fare. They select what pleases them most; the small

[2] *Greensboro* (N. C.) *Daily News,* August 17, 1932, p. 2.
[3] "Tokyo's Beg Chit 18,000 Yen a Month," *Trans-Pacific,* XIII (1926), 16.

decanter is replaced by a *sealed bottle* of wine; dishes succeed dishes, and the dinner ends with coffee which is again followed by a glass of liqueur. These gentlemen who are dining are the beggars; all the cripples and pretended cripples of the rich Madeleine district are there, consuming the day's gains, and I beg you to believe that their bills are larger than that paid in the morning by the Government clerks." [4]

With the beggar telling one story and the press thus telling another, what may we believe? Is the beggar poor or rich? Does he earn little or much? Or does either account approximate the truth?

The problem of making a true evaluation of the beggar's income is not as simple as it might seem, for, in the first place, there are several ways in which it may be calculated. Since the beggar is free to follow his own schedule, it might at first appear advisable to calculate his earnings on an hourly basis. At best, however, this is difficult because of the fact that there are good periods of the day for begging and bad ones. Whether the beggar does street begging, residence begging, or store begging, certain periods of the day are unfavorable for the practice of his racket and his earnings will be low, while other periods are favorable and during these his earnings will be high. To get any definite conception of the beggar's earnings, therefore, we must use a day's work as a minimum basis for our calculations, and for some purposes we must use much longer periods of time.

Regardless of what period of time we use, the problem of securing accurate information regarding his earnings is a difficult one. Of course, the one who knows best what he earns is the beggar himself, but it is doubtful that he often tells others. He will seldom refuse to estimate his receipts, but it is doubtful that these estimates can be relied upon. If he is talking to anyone outside the begging profession, the beggar is likely to understate his earnings, for he is well aware of the fact that he is supposed to be poor. It is almost equally doubtful that

[4] Paulian, *The Beggars of Paris*, p. 103.

beggars are honest with each other in this respect. Since begging has a certain sporting element, the beggar has the same temptation as the fisherman and hunter to exaggerate his success to those to whom he can afford to boast. One beggar is likely, therefore, to tell another beggar a "fish story." It is interesting, nevertheless, to see what earnings beggars are willing to admit to an outside investigator. Freund questioned forty-three mendicants on the point and has tabulated the replies which he received.

EARNINGS [5]

The accepted statements of forty-three beggars ranged from $2 to $20 as follows:

Approximate Begging Incomes Stated by Beggars

Individual Incomes	Number of Beggars
$ 2.00 to 3.00	3
3.00 to 4.00	7
4.00 to 5.00	18
5.00 to 6.00	6
6.00 to 7.00	0
7.00 to 8.00	2
8.00 to 9.00	2
10.00 to 15.00	3
15.00 to 20.00	2
Total	43

To check these reports of earnings made by beggars, some investigators have practiced begging as an experiment. The stated haul of such experimenters probably is not open to question, but whether their earnings may be considered typical of the average run of beggars is very doubtful. The investigator would be a good actor indeed if he could step into a beggar's role and play it convincingly without much practice. In many cases he would more than likely be awkward and artificial in his acting, or he would be too much the gentleman. In either case he would not be a true beggar. Roy P. Gates, an executive

[5] Freund, "Begging in Chicago," pp. 8-9.

of the Joint Applications Bureau of New York City, on a basis
of his own experiments at panhandling, has estimated that
beggars can earn from $5 to $60 an hour.

> "In order to test begging conditions and to estimate the
> number of professionals at work, Mr. Gates frequently
> does a little panhandling himself. At his last experiment
> several weeks ago at Herald Square he collected $3.32 in
> forty minutes. Conditions are nearly the same in other big
> cities according to Mr. Gates who in a visit to Boston last
> Saturday 'panhandled' for an hour on a street corner and
> picked up $5.31." [6]

Another method of checking the earnings of beggars is to
watch them and count the number of gifts which they receive
in a specified time. Such watching is difficult except in the case
of a stationary street beggar, and even then it is an advantage
if the mendicant is blind. If the beggar can see, he is usually
quick to discern that he is being watched and he is likely to
alter his method or to stop soliciting entirely. Such investiga-
tions, therefore, show the typical earnings of stationary, blind
street beggars more accurately than those of any other kind of
mendicant. In addition, it is seldom possible to watch a beggar
for a whole day, and since his earnings vary from hour to
hour it is difficult to secure a fair time sample. Freund tried
this device in his study of begging in Chicago. His method was
to sample various beggars for fifteen to thirty minutes at a
time and from these samples to derive totals and averages.

> "In all, these ten beggars were watched for ten hours
> and forty-seven minutes, received 420 contributions which
> if computed at 7¢ each, (thought to be a conservative
> average) would give them an income of $29.40. It should
> be stated that although the hour of the day varies from
> early to late, the traffic on the sidewalks was quite heavy
> in every case." [7]

[6] "Panhandlers Who Thrive in Manhattan Crowds," *Literary Digest*,
LXXIII (1922), 52.
[7] Freund, *op. cit.*, p. 10.

Besides these methods which are frequently used by investigators to determine the earnings of beggars, the amount of
money which beggars have in their possession when they are
arrested is often an indication of their income, but it is seldom
possible in such cases to determine just how long it took the
beggar to collect the money. There is even no assurance that
the money was all collected on the day the arrest was made;
the beggar may have started to work with money in his pocket.
If, however, the money which the beggar has on his person
when he is arrested is in the form of small change, it seems
that as a usual rule it would be safe to assume that most of it
was collected on the day of arrest; for, unless the beggar differs
from other people in this respect, he does not enjoy carrying
quantities of small coins around in his pockets. Occasionally,
however, a beggar is caught red-handed, so that it can be
known exactly how much he has taken in during a specified
time. Such a case is reported by John D. Godfrey, mendicant
officer for the Brooklyn Bureau of Charities.

> "Only last week a 'fit-thrower' pulled his little stunt on
> the streets of New York. The 'small change' of passers-by
> began to drop beside the spot where he lay in the apparent
> throes of the attack. A soft hearted policeman gave him a
> half-dollar. Then he was recognized by a 'plain clothes'
> member of the police department, and the game was up.
> In attempting to redistribute their alms to the sympa-
> thizers still standing around, the officer found that the
> young beggar had gathered in ten dollars from less than
> five minutes' work." [8]

The sort of data which is usually considered the most con-
vincing proof of the beggar's income are the records of the
fortunes which mendicants sometimes leave at death. What
appear to be authentic cases of estates of from $30,000 to
$50,000 left by beggars have been reported by numerous
writers, and such cases are sometimes reported in the daily

[8] Godfrey, "A Capable Beggar Makes from $15 to $500 a Day," American Magazine, XCIV (1922), 10-11.

press. The inside story of such a fortune, however, is seldom disclosed. The money may have been made by begging or it may not. The beggar may have been a shrewd investor, and most of his estate may represent the accretion on a small initial investment. What complicates the problem, of course, is the fact that not all beggars beg because they need the money. Some beggars would continue to beg even if they were to inherit a million dollars, and occasionally a person who has an independent income begs for the pleasure of it. For instance, a large ranch owner in Australia is reported to have begged as a hobby, and a former New York racketeer is reported by a friend to have retired with a fortune of about $500,000, to have owned a home in the East and another in the West, to have traveled back and forth with a chauffeur in a fine car, and in spite of all this he engaged in begging as a sport. Fortunes left by beggars, therefore, do not necessarily prove that mendicants garner lucrative returns. Indeed, their fortunes may be no more significant than the estates sometimes left by washerwomen, though it does appear that the former are more numerous than the latter.

If the standard of living of beggars is compared with the earnings which are indicated by these various methods of investigation, the contrast is striking. Most beggars do not live in luxury; the reverse is more nearly true. For example, a study of the living conditions of twelve full-time beggars in a certain city revealed that nine lived in small single houses, one in an apartment, and two in single rooms. Some of the houses were very poor, two were fair, and none was exceptionally good. All were located in very undesirable sections of the city. In one case the beggar had inherited his home, and in another case the beggar was buying his home out of his earnings. The remainder were renters. None of the beggars had a car, but two had a horse each and either a wagon or a buggy. Only three had radios; two of these were small portable models and one was an ancient cabinet model. None of them hired any help except in two cases where boys were employed to lead blind persons on their begging expeditions. In brief, the standard of living of the group appeared to be little, if any, better than that of very poor laborers.

What then is the truth about the income of beggars? In the first place, as far as the writer has been able to learn, no beggar has ever been known to starve, which seems to indicate that even the poorest artists can garner a livelihood. On the other hand it appears that some beggars do accumulate fortunes of considerable size. Between these extremes, the mass of beggars seem to live on a very modest and often niggardly basis. This generally low standard of living becomes extremely interesting in view of the fact that data from numerous sources indicate that the hourly earnings of beggars are surprisingly high. It appears to be fairly common for beggars to collect from $2.00 to $6.00 in an hour, and in some cases they may do much better than that. At such a rate, it would seem that they might easily collect a very sizable daily or weekly income, much larger than most of them seem to do. The question is, why do they not collect more?

Since the hourly income of beggars is so out of line with their daily and weekly earnings, it is quite obvious that they have very short hours. Perhaps four or five hours is an average day's work, and many work less than that. The very nature of begging tends to discourage the beggar's keeping too long hours. As has been said, there are good periods of the day for begging and bad ones. Like the fisherman, therefore, the beggar is tempted to go out only at those times when the "poor fish" are biting good, and to sit in the shade during those parts of the day when he would have to be content with scattered nibbles; for many beggars it is just these hours of "scattered nibbles" which are necessary to bring earnings up to a presentable figure.

Furthermore, many kinds of begging are so strenuous that it does not take many hours to make a day's work. Just sitting on a hard seat or on the sidewalk for hours at a time is little pleasure whether one is begging, waiting for a train, or just twiddling one's thumbs. When the beggar sits, however, he often has to sit continuously in one position, and frequently in a very uncomfortable position. He may keep a good leg folded up under him with a peg extended for the public's gaze, or he may fold both legs and emphasize two stub arms. In addition, he must look hungry, discouraged, or miserable, and if he is inwardly happy, it may not be easy to make his face behave properly. Begging, therefore, is not always easy work even for a strong, healthy person, and as a rule beggars are not choice physical specimens.

In addition to being physically strenuous some of the begging appeals which bring the best returns are of such a nature that they cannot be practiced too often without arousing public investigation and public reaction. Notice, for example, the following case:

> "A young man who simulated palsy with horrifying veri-similitude, was arrested one day after crawling from Fourth to Sixth Avenue, a journey so agonizing that it took him three hours. Yet the physical and nervous strain of the performance were well paid for, since his receipts in those two blocks amounted to $28.00." [9]

Three hours of such agony unquestionably would be considered by most people quite sufficient for a day's work. In fact, regardless of returns, not many would be willing to take such an exercise regularly every day in the week. But what is equally important is that no city would permit such a monstrosity, whether real or simulated, to crawl around its streets regularly. A beggar with such a specialty, therefore, would have to be careful where he practiced his lure; he could not work it too often or too long at a time; and he probably would have to move from city to city to avoid suspicion. Consequently he would have to depend on large returns for the time involved, but could not hope to work many hours a week.

In spite of the difficulties involved in getting large returns from begging, the beggar is often accused of lacking ambition, because he does not take greater advantage of the possible earning power of his profession. In a sense, beggars are lacking

---

[9] "Begging as a Fine Art," *The Nation*, LXXIX (1904), 517.

in ambition, but there are usually reasons for a lack of ambition. In the case of the beggar there are several such reasons:
for one thing he is limited in the uses which he can make of
money. Since he lives by feigning poverty, he must maintain a
certain outward appearance of poverty; he must at least be
cautious of tangible evidences of wealth. Materialistic display
and pomp for him are dangerous. The public and the police
are usually very tolerant of a beggar's claims to poverty as long
as outward appearances indicate poverty, and the arrest of
such beggars seldom makes news. Let a beggar be found with
a nice car, an elegant home, or personal servants, however, and
he makes good news copy, he is quickly hauled into court, and
he is forced to bear the brunt of the righteous indignation of
the public. A beggar cannot even give his money away without getting into trouble and making headline copy. Thus when
a beggar in Portugal attempted to turn philanthropist, he not
only got into trouble with local authorities but he got his name
splashed over the papers in foreign countries.

"Lisbon, Aug. 25. A familiar figure throughout the cities
and villages of Portugal was a certain beggar. He was
blind, he said, and had no money in the world.

"Now this beggar has been arrested and will be charged
with obtaining money under false pretenses, for he pos-
sesses excellent sight and a capital of $50,000. Pride in the
little seaside resort where he was born called Pedro de
Moel, caused his downfall.

"Seeing that little was being done in the way of developing it as a tourist center, he went to the local authorities
and insisted that they should build a big, luxurious hotel,
such as he had 'seen' in other places.

"They laughed at him, whereupon he announced that
he was prepared to contribute $25,000 toward the costs of
the new hotel, the construction of which he wanted to
supervise with his own eyes.

"When the authorities expressed doubt he at once produced his bankbook, showing him to have a capital of
$50,000, and also gave proofs of his excellent sight.

"The authorities thanked him for his generous offer to

the town, but at the same time they arrested him for having begged money for over 30 years under the pretense
of blindness." [10]

There is a very definite limit, evidently, to the amount of
money which a beggar can comfortably use. Some do afford
luxuries, but, generally speaking, a fine car or a yacht is about
as dangerous for a beggar as possessing a stolen jewel.

If, then, the beggar cannot use a large income to advantage
in present living, any motivation for working for large returns
must come from plans for the future. In relation to the future,
the usual person works and saves to better his condition at
some future time and to make provision for himself in old age.
Since, however, the beggar may already be living on as high a
plane as is safe unless he ceases to be a beggar, his only hope
for raising his standard of living is to leave the begging world
and attempt to make a place for himself in organized society.
A few beggars do have such ambitions, some for themselves
and others for their children. Most beggars, however, either
consider it futile to hope for such a change or they are happy
in the begging life and do not wish to leave it. They, therefore,
cannot have much ambition to raise their future standard of
living.

Old age, similarly, is quite a different problem to the beggar
than it is to people in the usual walks of life. For most people,
old age is a period of economic uncertainty, of declining income, and possibly of complete financial dependency. The
average person, therefore, strives to provide financial security
for himself in his declining years. For the beggar, however, old
age is not so foreboding. He knows that old age is an asset in
begging. When he is old enough to have a grandfatherly appearance, he can arouse sympathy more easily, his earnings
will likely increase, and he will be molested less by the police.
Unless, therefore, senility makes the beggar physically helpless,
he is assured economic security for old age without having to
strive and to save for it during his younger years.

[10] *The Times Picayune,* New Orleans, August 26, 1935, p. 5.

It appears, then, that the beggar has little reason to work and save for the future, and that his present needs for money are definitely limited. Even so, most beggars probably earn and spend more than their apparent standard of living indicates. Since their money comes fairly easily and since they use it chiefly to satisfy present desires, they are frequently both extravagant and whimsical in their petty expenditures. Food, candy, tobacco, drinks, clothing, and knicknacks of all sorts are often bought with complete abandon by beggars, and, in addition, most beggars are phenomenally poor managers. Many of them give little attention to the price which they pay for things and have a total lack of system in their spending. As a comical example, one beggar who "sells" pencils for five cents each buys these pencils at that price at a drug store, whereas he could get them much cheaper at wholesale, or with less trouble he could walk across the street from his stand and buy pencils two for five cents, which would serve his purpose just as well. The Jantsel family is a very good illustration of how much beggars can spend without having much to show for it.

The Jantsel family consisted of the father and mother, both of whom were blind, and three children from three years to eleven years of age. The parents begged regularly and seemed to be very successful. A very careful study of their earnings indicated that on the average they made from $7 to $9 a day on regular week days and from $12 to $15 on Saturdays. Since they seldom missed a day of work, therefore, their weekly earnings apparently were from $45 to $60, giving a monthly income of more than $180. On this amount they might have been expected to live well. A check of their living conditions, however, showed that they lived in a very modest four-room house, the best of their furniture was mediocre and most of it was "junk," and they had no car, no servant, no radio, and no reading matter. In fact, there was nothing about the home or the clothes which the family wore which indicated any but a very low standard of living. Reasonably definite data were secured on two significant items in their budget;

they paid $40 a month rent for their house, virtually twice
its worth, and their grocer reported that they had a
monthly grocery bill of $90 to $100. How they spent so
much on groceries and how they spent the remaining $40
or more of their monthly income are hard to conceive. In
the case of the former, they had relatives who "sponged"
on them a great deal and must have accounted for much
of this expenditure. Much of the remaining $40 or more
must have gone for unnecessary items since contacts with
the family over a considerable period gave no clues to any
insurance or savings. In fact, there was rather definite
proof to the contrary.

In answer, then, to the frequent query regarding beggars'
earnings, it seems safe to say that on a per hour basis beggars
frequently get very large returns. These earnings are sufficiently large, in fact, for an ambitious and skilled beggar to
make very large weekly earnings if he is willing to work long
hours. If, in addition to being ambitious and skilled, a beggar
is thrifty, he might hope to save a fair fortune out of his income. Some beggars do this. Most beggars, however, are content to live a hand-to-mouth existence, and since the more
pretentious, luxurious articles may embarrass them, they use
mostly petty perishable goods in their daily living. Even with
the abandon with which the beggar often buys such goods, his
living costs do not run to great proportions. As a result, the
beggar may be able to secure all the money he needs during
the few hours of the day when begging returns are highest.
The usual beggar, therefore, does not work long hours, does
not make a huge weekly income, and does not accumulate a
fortune.

CHAPTER XI

SMALL-CHANGE PHILANTHROPISTS

A STUDY of beggars is not complete without a study of givers. The giver is the complement of the beggar. The fact that there are givers is the one universal reason why there are beggars. If the giver did not give, the beggar would not beg. People might go hungry and cold but if no one gave they would not long continue to beg.

The reasons why people give are in many respects as mysterious and as difficult of analysis as the reasons why people beg. Even with almsgiving deprived of its basis in religion and superstition, with the impostors and hypocrites exposed and discredited, with social agencies provided to care for the legitimate needy, and with the begging fraternity outcast and outlawed, people continue to give to mendicants and to give liberally. The reasons why almsgiving continues to flourish after most of its appeals to the intellect have been thus discredited must be complex and deep-seated.

The reasons which people assign for their giving are not always of importance. Many people actually do not know why they give, and many give for reasons which they dare not admit to themselves, let alone to the public. Such givers, if challenged by their own judgment or by others, rationalize their actions, and it is frequently these rationalizations which they assign as their "reasons." The explanations of almsgiving, therefore, must be deducted largely from indirect sources. A study of begging techniques is of aid. Beggars either know some of the reasons why people give or they find out through trial and error the appeals which work. The rationalizations which people assign for their giving and a study of the begging techniques which bring successful results, however, must be supplemented by a broad understanding of the more subtle motives for action, if a complete explanation is to be had.

The reasons for almsgiving today seem to fall into three classes: the lag of custom, appeals to reason, and emotional factors. Many, perhaps the majority, of people give to beggars from force of custom. Customs are ingrained in the habits of men and slow to change. People abide by them without conscious thought or intellectual reflection. Why we have a marriage ceremony, why we eat with a fork instead of a knife, why men wear trousers instead of loin cloths most people do not know and have never thought to ask; the fact that it is customary is sufficient. The beggar and almsgiving are almost as definitely defined and as deeply imbedded in custom as are the clothes we wear and the food we eat. When a man sits on the sidewalk with a cup in his hand, the public does not have to be told who he is or what he wants. Everyone understands that he is a beggar and that he wishes those passing to drop gifts into his cup. Even the size of the gift is defined in custom. The ordinary man seeing a beggar does not think of dropping a dollar or five dollars into the cup; rather he gives a nickel, a dime, or at most a quarter. And this is all that the beggar expects. So thoroughly are these customs established in the habits of many that the sight of a beggar touches off a set mental reaction and a coin rolls out with almost mechanical regularity. "A man comes up to us in the street. He holds out his hand. We look at him; he is of the mendicant type. That is enough: we straightway conclude that he is an unfortunate individual, that he is suffering, and that he is worthy of our charity." [1]

The customs relating to begging and almsgiving have been strongly reinforced by organized religion. For many people the sight of a beggar brings forth attitudes and images built up by religious sanctions. On one theory or another practically all of the major religions have sanctioned almsgiving in some form. "The old Hindu theory is not only that spiritual goods

[1] Paulian, *The Beggars of Paris*, p. 55.

are more valuable than material goods—and it admits both to be indispensable to human well-being—but that those who devote themselves to the production of the former are entitled to live on charity." [2] "In Taoism, nature has become deified and the religion has a pantheon of innumerable gods. Gods to whom the people flock; gods who will cure all ailments from a tooth-ache to paresis. Gods who, in their immobility of carved and painted wood, are the best beggars of China." [3] "The Buddhists have no poor rates but whoever is admitted to the brotherhood has a right to go round the village or town once or twice a day, to hold out his begging bowl and to take out to the monastery whatever is given him." [4] "Mohammedanism is often thought of as a religion of blood and iron. But not even did the Carpenter of Nazareth so frequently enjoin charity as the Camel Driver of Mecca. ... The Koran contains such words as poor, widows and orphans, alms more often than the New Testament." [5] And the sanction given to almsgiving by mediaeval Christianity is well known.

Most of the religions, along with their sanctions of almsgiving, have attempted to place limitations on the practice, and in some the practice of almsgiving is hard to distinguish from the financial support given the religious savants. As a rule, however, the public mind is influenced more by the sanctions than by the limitations. Just as the begging friars of the Middle Ages called forth hordes of impostors and just as the religious sanctions were extended by popular fancy to include many superstitious beliefs, so religious sanctions generally have their influence extended beyond all intended bounds. Myths, legends, and superstitions grow up in time which give alms-giving greater sanction than the official utterances of the religion. It is hard for anyone not reared in an atmosphere seething with such traditions to realize the force which they may have in the minds of other individuals.

[2] N. B. Parulekar, "Brahmans and Beggars," *Asia*, XXIX (1929), 695.
[3] Bennett, "China's Perennially Unemployed," *Asia*, XXXI (1931), 218.
[4] Wines, "Max Müller on Beggars," *Charities*, XIII (1905), 560.
[5] Albert Edwards, "The Beggars of Mogador," *Outlook*, CI (1912), 931.

"All art, all legend, all tradition, tell for the beggar. The splendid background against which he stands gives color and dignity to his part. We see him sheltered by St. Julian,—Ah, beautiful young beggar of the Pitti!—fed by St. Elizabeth, clothed by St. Martin, warmed by the fagots which St. Francesca Romano gathered for him in the wintry woods. What heavenly blessings have followed the charity shown to his needs, what evils have followed thick and fast where he has been rejected. I remember these things when I meet his piteous face and outstretched palm today." [6]

The philosophy of the Protestant faith has discouraged almsgiving as a practice [7] and, in general, has given its support to organized philanthropy. The effects of the Protestant theories are most clearly evidenced by the almsgiving practices of religious leaders. Thus, we find an American beggar complaining that "from the bum's point of view they [Protestant clergymen] are even worse than Chinamen and farmers, for they won't refuse to help. Oh, no! They gravely waste your time and raise your hopes, and then firmly demand either security or labor." [8] While the Protestant philosophy, thus, has doubtless had definite effects on the almsgiving practices of religious leaders, it has not extended its full effects to the laymen. Just as there is a lag in the change of custom, so there is a lag in the change of religious attitudes of individuals with reference to almsgiving. Few persons of Protestant faith today have a strong enough belief in the religious efficacy of almsgiving to go out looking for beggars to whom they may give, but many entertain a vague, indefinite feeling that giving alms will in some way build up spiritual credit for an after life or will bring good fortune in this life. When they face a beggar, therefore, they are haunted by the possible consequences of a refusal to give.

[6] A. Repplier, "Beggar's Pouch," *Atlantic Monthly*, XCIII (1904), 385.
[7] See Chapter I.
[8] Henri Tascheraud, "The Art of Bumming a Meal," *American Mercury*, V (1925), 186.

In addition to these religious and semi-religious sanctions, almsgiving customs have been reinforced by what appear to be pure superstitions, which are in some cases difficult to distinguish from religious sanctions. Myths, legends, and beliefs which often grow up around religious sanctions are essentially superstitious in character and can hardly be differentiated from pure superstitions. The belief, for example, that "bread cast on the water will return again" is difficult to classify. On the surface it resembles a plain superstition, yet it has frequently been clothed with religious sanctions. Since all forms of superstition thrive most among ignorant and illiterate people, their origin and interpretation are frequently obscure.

In the Occident, pure superstitions, along with semi-religious superstitions, were most prevalent prior to the Reformation. At that time they were accepted by ignorant and intellectual alike and were a powerful factor in bringing gifts to the beggar. Since this early heyday, superstitions have been on the decline, but their death has been slow. At the opening of the present century they had not yet been debarred even from the seats of higher learning.

> "Go to the Sorbonne when the bachelors degrees are given. At the moment the young students, the dictionary under their arm, are going to make some famous Latin verse—on the success of which all their future depends; a swarm of beggars bears down on them. A penny, Sir; a piece of bread—it will bring you good luck! If the student passes without giving anything: You will be plucked, Sir! This sinister prediction always produces its effect." [9]

Most superstitions regarding almsgiving today are doubtless relics of earlier periods, and it is difficult to know to what extent such beliefs survive among modern American givers. Superstitions of all sorts have become taboo among the educated class, and those who still harbor pet beliefs must do it as a secret vice. One may still visit a fortuneteller occasionally, but he must pretend to do it only as a joke, and, likewise, those

[9] Paulian, *The Beggars of Paris*, p. 34.

who give to beggars for superstitious reasons dare not admit it to the public. One can only guess at the number of such givers, but it may be larger than many suspect.

A custom is brought into being to fill some need. Once it has become an integral part of the habits and emotions of people, however, it may continue under its own momentum long after the need which brought it into being has ceased to exist. A given custom may not change, therefore, until long after the condition which brought it into being has changed. This tardiness is known as lag. The custom of almsgiving originated sometime in the distant past, and most of the institutional developments and philosophical changes which have discredited begging and supposedly have made almsgiving unnecessary, are matters of recent history. The withdrawal of religious sanctions even in the philosophy of leading thinkers only dates back to the Reformation and has not yet been fully assimilated by the masses; the large-scale provision of agencies for caring for the needy is even more recent and is still in a developmental state; and the so-called "scientific attitude" is distinctly modern. So recent are some of these changes that they have hardly yet been generally accepted by all of the intellectual classes, and their assimilation by the masses has hardly begun.

> "Although the current arguments as to the value of philanthropy (as opposed to almsgiving) are well known to scientists and other thoughtful students of the problem, it must be noted that these are numerically an indiscernible part of the total population. Millions of everyday human beings have neither heard of the scientific attitude nor are they even interested in it except to welcome the leisure-giving inventions which from time to time it produces. These masses still practice charity in the old irrational yet self-satisfying way." [10]

The custom of almsgiving, which has its origin in the past, may be changing, but it is changing slowly. For the rank and

[10] A. Morris, "Some Social and Mental Aspects of Mendicancy," *Social Forces,* V (1927), 605.

file, it has by no means lost its force. Even the intellectual minority who are personally opposed to almsgiving are not wholly freed from the force of custom. If approached by a beggar in a secluded spot where their actions may not be observed by others, they probably will not give. If solicited in the presence of a gallery of spectators, however, they are likely to accede to custom. Thus, many a young man leaving a theater in the company of a lady has, against his will, dropped a coin into a beggar's cup for fear his refusal to do so might not meet with the approval of his companion.

The intellectual, however, does not give to beggars solely from the force of custom; he may use customs to his own advantage. Among other things, custom has defined liberal giving to beggars as a mark of generosity and opulence. A giver who wishes to manifest these traits may create his impression by giving half a dozen dimes to as many beggars. It is a cheaper method than any other he can use and he considers it a bargain. This must be done with caution, however, for custom does not accord equal status to all giving. Giving small gifts to ordinary street beggars is to some extent considered an act of pity, but just as men are not supposed to weep in sorrow or express in other ways the tender emotions, so they are not supposed to give too liberally to beggars; if they do, they may be classed as weak and sentimental. It is women, therefore, whose special privilege it is to be sentimental, who respond most liberally to beggars on the street. "Beggars tell me that the 'easiest' class of people to 'touch' is that composed of women shoppers. Streets where women congregate to purchase in the big stores and well known shops are gold mines during the shopping hours." [11]

While most almsgiving is done either on a basis of custom or on a basis of emotion, and while the leading thought of the day disparages the practice of giving to beggars, it is not to be assumed that there are no longer any intelligent justifications of the practice. Many educated people, who are well in-

[11] Godfrey, "A Capable Beggar Makes from $15 to $500 a Day," *American Magazine*, XCIV (1922), 11.

formed both as to the theories of philanthropy and as to the programs of social agencies, oppose almsgiving as a practice but do not follow an ironclad rule of refusing all mendicants who apply.

Those sufficiently informed know the admirable work which agencies do, but they also know that relief organizations are not infallible. In spite of their trained investigators, their carefully kept records, and their confidential exchanges, they may make a mistake. They may aid a skillful professional who knows how to "work" them, and they may refuse to help a truly needy person who does not know how to present his case. Some, therefore, aware of such possibilities, regard begging as a rightful and necessary veto on the power of the social agency. Such givers recognize that if a person is in desperate circumstances and is refused aid by a social agency, his only recourse is to crime or to begging, and they consider begging as the lesser of the two evils. Such givers usually are not of the ten-cent variety. Those beggars whom they assist, they aid in a substantial way. If persuaded that social agencies have made a mistake in the case, they either try to meet the man's needs themselves or they try to secure adequate assistance for him. Even the officials of the agencies themselves sometimes give; the director of a large relief agency was observed giving rather liberally to a beggar and, when the author expressed surprise, he said that he knew his case workers too well to have much assurance that they might not make a serious mistake.

Other informed persons are opposed to giving to beggars, but they do not class as a beggar every person who begs. They believe, perhaps rightly, that any man may meet temporary reverses or may get into a predicament among strangers and have to ask for aid. For such a case they feel that receiving a gift or a loan from an individual is not such a blow to the man's self-respect or to his faith in humanity as relief from a social agency would be. That many givers have some such theory as this is evident from the multitude of hardluck stories which are built around the "temporary predicament." Indeed, so many professional beggars pose as persons in temporary straits that it would be a genius who could distinguish the really needy from the impostor. Many givers realize this, but with an infinite faith and an undaunted hope they continue to give.

"Many do it with a lingering suspicion that the recipients are not all honest beggars, and would tell you that it is difficult to find a really honest beggar, but they do it all the same, with a far-off hope that possibly the particular one they are relieving is a genuine case of distress." [12]

In addition to the force of custom and intellectual considerations, much giving to beggars is done for emotional reasons (if an emotion can be called a "reason"). Because of their complex nature and the vague form which they often take, the emotions which prompt almsgiving are difficult to analyze. There are several, however, which seem to operate at one time or another. Apparently they fall into two general classes: first, emotional disturbances which are brought about by the beggar's appeal; and, second, fundamental emotional needs of the giver for which almsgiving serves as an outlet.

Perhaps the most common emotional reaction to the appeal of a beggar is that of pity or sympathy. People say that they give because they "feel sorry" for the beggar. That does perhaps describe the feeling which they have, but they get the feeling by imaginatively placing themselves in the beggar's position. They try to determine how the beggar feels by imagining how they themselves would feel if they were in his place. The feeling which they thus experience may not be true sympathy, because they may not actually feel as the beggar feels. Indeed they may feel much worse than the beggar feels. Ordinarily one is entirely in sympathy with another only when he has been through an experience similar to that of the other, and few people who are not beggars, have ever been through the beggar's experience. Indeed, many people have never been poor and cannot even sympathize with the poverty-stricken. As class lines become more tightly drawn and since the members

[12] G. Coleridge, "Little Brothers of the Pavement," *Living Age,* CCLXXVIII (1913), 294.

of each class are "born to the blood," true sympathy between members of different classes becomes exceedingly difficult. To take the place of true sympathy, however, there is what might be called a secondary sympathy. Through drama, motion pictures, novels, newspapers, and the propaganda of social agencies, the members of each class get pictures of the experiences of other classes. These pictures frequently are highly distorted for the purpose of literary effects. They play up one or two characteristics of each class at the expense of other phases of life. They furnish the material, however, out of which the imagination creates its pictures of the feelings of those whose experiences are different from ours. Thus, every poor person has a definite idea of how he would feel if he were wealthy, and his conception of that feeling is perhaps more glorious than the real feelings of any wealthy person and more glorious than he would experience were he actually wealthy. Most wealthy persons likewise have a definite idea of how they would feel if they were very poor, and this likewise is probably more miserable than most poor people feel and more miserable than they themselves would feel after they had become adjusted to poverty. It is such images as these which are called into play by the beggar's appeal and make people "feel sorry" for him.

People do not always imagine themselves in the role of the beggar; instead, they may imagine some of their loved ones in the beggar's place. Thus different givers have their sympathy aroused by different appeals. A man may see himself in a blind beggar, or he may see his wife, widowed, in a begging woman, while an adoring mother may picture her infant in the role of a child beggar or her son in the person of the young man who appeals to her.

"At a bend in the lane along which I was tramping I came upon a dainty, fragile old lady, standing at the gate of a garden, and, plucking up courage, I asked for a glass of water. 'Water,' she said, 'No not water. I feel too sorry for all the poor men who are looking for work to offer that. Will you come inside and my maid will make you a cup of

tea? I am sure you need it.' She took me into the house,
into an old dining room and she herself waited upon me—
treating me and talking to me not as a tramp, but as an
honored guest. I tried to thank her but she would not
allow me.

"'I had a son, and had he lived, and his need was as
great as yours, I should have wished for some mother to
have helped him.'" [13]

Other people give to beggars simply as a release from an
unpleasant situation. Timid souls frequently find themselves
placed in an embarrassing situation by a crafty beggar and
consider a gift the easiest way out. A man can be driven to
his wits end by a weeping woman whether she be beggar or
wife. And there are "weeping Lena" beggars who are conscious
of this masculine frailty and play heavily upon it. Others fall
prey to bullying beggars who follow them for blocks, or who
get them cornered and besiege them with urgent appeals.

"When we reached Herald Square, Frisco immediately
began operations. I crossed the street and, standing on the
curb, watched him work the crowds. His first prospect was
a very tall man with a brief-case under his arm. Frisco
didn't stop him, but, instead, fell into step beside him. The
man ignored Frisco, apparently, and quickened his pace.
Faster and faster he went, taking prodigious strides, so
that Frisco was almost forced into a trot to keep up with
him. All the while I could see Frisco's jaws wagging at
high pressure. Suddenly the tall one threw out another kink
in his legs and outdistanced his obstinate pursuer with the
ease of a jack-rabbit ambling away from a wheezing
dachshund. Frisco paused a few moments to catch his
breath, then darted into the throng and fastened himself
upon another victim who was going in the opposite direction from that taken by the first. Again the comedy of
accelerated pace and the frenzied wagging of Frisco's jaw.
Whether he wagged it to good purpose or not I don't
know, for he was soon lost in the crowd. Presently he
reappeared, this time at the haunch of a perspiring fat

[13] "Hosts of a Tramp," *Living Age*, CCLXXIII (1912), 120.

man, who strove manfully to escape. And on the face of that hunted man was an expression, not of indignation or disdain, but of positive guilt. He was really ashamed thus to exhibit his lack of magnanimity to the tattered wayfarer whose voice was gabbling at his ear. He looked more and more uncomfortable. He was weakening fast. In a trice he had succumbed. His hand went into his pocket, and I saw Frisco depart with an air of satisfaction." [14]

Whether specifically designed to do so or not, the appeal of most beggars places one in a dilemma. One must appear hard-hearted, stingy, or broke, or else he must give. For many people neither alternative is particularly enjoyable, but giving is the least distasteful. The appeal of the ordinary street beggar is not so harassing. His solicitations are directed at the passing throngs and not at any individual. A pedestrian may escape by "failing to see" the beggar or by appearing to be preoccupied with some weighty matter. What is everybody's business, therefore, may become nobody's. But when a single beggar corners a single giver, the person must "face the music" and either give or refuse to give. Thus many give rather than have their altruism questioned, even by themselves and the beggars.

Another way in which the beggar's appeal constitutes an unpleasant situation is that, to many people, it is a reminder of unfilled obligations. Those who have wealth can only enjoy it, for the time being at least, by closing their eyes to the discomforts of those who do not have it. Society has always dictated that a certain portion of the individual's income should go to the public, and the socialized person concurs in this belief, but he is never quite sure just what part should go to the public. So long as custom dictated the tithe, the man who retained for his own use only nine-tenths of his income could shut his eyes to the needs of others with the comfortable feeling that he had already given his share. Today, however, with less ironclad rules to guide him, the individual is never certain

---

[14] G. H. Mullin, "Sidewalks of New York; Further Adventures of a Scholar Tramp," *Century Magazine*, CX (1925), 52-53. Also found in *Adventures of a Scholar Tramp* (New York, 1925), by the same author.

when he has fully dispatched his altruistic obligations. So long as he stays solely within his own class, he can think of the sums which he has given and can console himself that he has done his share. When, however, he comes face to face with a wretched beggar, who, as it were, points an accusing finger at him, doubts begin to arise and he has a sneaky feeling of guilt, a part of what we have vaguely called conscience. To release him from this obligation which stares him in the face, the beggar asks a mere pittance. The man drops a dime into the beggar's cup, and his mental relief is well worth the coin. A wealthy looking woman, dressed in a fur coat, was recently seen dropping a coin into a beggar's cup. Turning to her companion, she said, "I know I should not give, but I could not eat my dinner if I did not."

The reasons for almsgiving so far considered are in one way or another forms of coercion. The force of customs, intellectual recognition of responsibility, and disturbing emotional states produced by the beggar's appeal are all pressures which tend to coerce the giver into parting with his money. It must not be assumed, however, that people have supported beggars for centuries and are continuing to give solely because of coercion. People do not give to beggars for nothing. The old saying that "it is more blessed to give than to receive" is not without a basis in fact. Giving to beggars satisfies certain fundamental emotional needs arising out of the activities of everyday life.

The equilibrium of the normal man consists of varying combinations of a sense of security in his present condition, a feeling of hope for a brighter future, and a lingering fear of failure or misfortune. While the normal man feels some security in his present condition, he does not consider it permanent. His future, he hopes, will be better than his present, but he is aware that it may be worse. For most of the American middle and lower classes, the "millionaire" has been the symbol of a golden future. The estate of the wealthy is the earthly heaven toward which they work either for themselves or their children. So long as they have hopes, however faint, of entering this heaven they do not wish its destruction. Instead of being golden, however, the future may be dismal. Girded with insurance policies and armed with bonds, men try to fortify themselves against a worse tomorrow, but they are seldom entirely confident that the future will not be worse than the present. Their fears of failure and disaster are symbolized in the beggar and in the "poor house." These comprise the earthly hell from which they shrink. Since, therefore, they cannot abolish the possibility of disaster, it lessens their fear of failure if they know that beggars are well provided for.

That many give for this reason may be deducted from the type of beggar to whom each class of givers responds most regularly and most spontaneously. Wealthy men seldom give only from force of custom, and they seldom give to panhandlers and ordinary beggars; they consider the facilities of social agencies adequate to care for this type of failure. They would not wish themselves reduced to the allowance of a relief agency, however, nor do they wish to see any member of the wealthy class so humiliated. The wealthy man, therefore, will frequently give liberally to a "gentleman" beggar or to a woman beggar who poses as the unfortunate widow of a once wealthy business man. The laboring classes, on the other hand, know that in case of unemployment or misfortune they must rely on social agencies or resort to ordinary begging, and many prefer the latter. At least they are consoled to know that they can resort to begging in case the social agencies fail them. The poorer classes, therefore, support the ordinary beggars most liberally while the upper classes respond to those who have the earmarks of "respectability." In other words, each class of givers tends to support the type of beggar most closely associated with it. Of course, this may be due in part to a greater bond of sympathy between those of like class, but back of this sympathy there is, unquestionably, the desire of the giver to make it possible for the type of beggar which he fears he himself or his loved ones might sometime be, to live on the scale which he would desire in case of such misfortune.

Giving to beggars is also an antidote for the grasping, selfish activities necessary for success in modern business life. After all is said and done, the economic world is essentially a selfish and heartless affair. Every man has to think of himself first, and his fellowmen afterward. Sentimentality is a decided handicap. There are, of course, some human considerations and codes of ethics, but much that would be otherwise unpardonable is justified on the grounds that "business is business." The ordinary man in his business life has to be more or less of a selfish, grasping being. While most men wish to gain success according to the terms which society offers, few men wish to be thought of or wish to think of themselves as being heartless and selfish. Having proved themselves able to conquer, they also wish to prove themselves capable of being considerate and generous. To counteract the grasping activities of their business life, therefore, they need an outlet for a voluntary, spontaneous expression of generosity. Gifts to churches, schools, hospitals and other public institutions serve this need to a certain extent, but the support of such institutions has been put on such a business-like basis and has been made such an integral part of social obligation that the giver hardly thinks of his subscription as a gift. Every man of sizable income is expected to give to a dozen or so organizations. He is not thought generous if he does; he is considered a slacker if he does not. Consequently, men have to go out of the range of ordinary social duties to get an outlet for generosity. For many, the beggar furnishes this outlet. Since the beggar is not a friend or relative, and since there are institutions to care for the needy, the business or professional man can give with the clear conscience that here at least he is not performing a duty to family, church, God, or society; he is simply giving to be generous.

In addition, giving to beggars is prompted by the monotony and routine of everyday living. Life in modern society is not entirely a matter of set patterns, but much of it is. One must rise at a fixed hour, go through a routine business day, and in the evening rush to a social engagement. For the poorer classes perhaps the usual day carries even less variety. Against this monotony and continual pressure many people rebel inwardly, but few follow their inclinations to rebel outwardly. There are many, however, who honor and idealize those who refuse to abide by the conventionalities to which they feel themselves a slave and refuse to shoulder the load which they themselves loathe. For such inwardly rebellious spirits certain types of beggars furnish a vicarious relief from the monotony of their existence. It was this which made the hobo-beggar of a few years back a romantic figure. His unlimited leisure, his lack of cares, and his freedom to follow his inclinations to the ends of the earth made him a symbol of that which the working man yearned for but could not afford. The hobo was highly idealized, and many a gift to promote his happiness was never regretted. That he is now reverting to a common unemployed or homeless man is a sign of his waning romance. Nevertheless, beggars in general are a leisured class, and while many of them are far from colorful, there have always been and perhaps will continue to be romantic figures among their number. In the words of H. D. Irvine, "To all who feel the sad world sadder still for such elimination of useless persons, to all who, while they must work, like to contemplate the idle, to all, in fine, who in spite of the Food Controller cherish like a secret vice a preference for roses over potatoes, I commend the beggars. They are the unconquerable, the undying, and the ever ready leisured class of the world." [15]

Finally, for some people, giving to beggars helps to bolster their self-confidence. Custom places givers and beggars in entirely different classes and accords to each a distinct status. The financially independent person has no doubts as to which class he belongs, but the financial failure may not be so sure of his status. After meeting reverses and disappointments he may find himself grasping at the last straw of independence and self-confidence. He doubts his self and he doubts his status. He needs some ·assurance that he is still of the class which gives and not of the class which begs. He cannot afford a donation of several dollars to charity or to a movement, but he can give a dime to a beggar. True, it is much like whistling

[15] H. D. Irvine, "Leisured Class," *Living Age*, CCXCVIII (1918), 624.

in the dark to bolster up courage, but it may mean much to his self-assurance. In this case, what the beggar gets from the gift is of no significance in comparison with what the giver gets from it.

Thus, in spite of the fact that there are social agencies to care for the needy, and in spite of the fact that many consider the average beggar an impostor, people continue to give. They give in part because they are forced to give, in part for the good of the beggar, and in part for the good of themselves, not so much to gain piety as they did in the past, but to gain peace of mind. Outwardly the giver is the benefactor but inwardly he is often the recipient.

CHAPTER XII

∞∞∞∞∞∞∞∞∞∞∞∞

CONTROL OF BEGGING

EXCEPTING prohibition, there is probably no problem in which attempts at control appear to have been a more blatant and universal failure than they have been in the case of begging. Virtually every city in the United States has some sort of an anti-begging ordinance. Yet there is probably not a single city in which beggars cannot be found on the streets, and usually they can be found in quantity within sound of an officer's whistle. It is quite evident, therefore, that either the control of begging is very difficult or the methods which have been used are poorly conceived.

It is impossible to understand the problem or evaluate the methods of control without a clear conception of the causation of begging, for control is an attempt to manipulate the causes in such a way as to avoid the result. This field of causation of social phenomena, however, is a very complicated one. There is general confusion regarding causation in the minds of the public, and many students who have made extensive studies of various forms of causation cannot be said to reflect a comprehensive knowledge of their subject. In the case of begging, the causes can best be understood if they are considered under three categories: (1) the reasons why organized society cannot provide a livelihood for all persons through employment in socially sanctioned and productive occupations; (2) the factors which determine the selection of those who are to be unemployed; and (3) why part of those who are refused employment in the economic system and some who might secure employment choose to beg.

213

With the possible exception of tribal life, there has scarcely been a time or a place in which society has been able to provide a livelihood for all its members through the socially approved channels of employment in that society. The reasons for this failure of society are numerous and complicated, and, most important, they are ever changing. During the period of the feudal system in Europe, most of the land was taken up by the manors, and most of those who were not connected with this system of feudal estates were without a socially approved means of livelihood. During the time of the enclosures in England thousands were thrown off the manors, and the problem of land was paramount. In the pre-Civil War South, most of the tillable land was included in the plantations and there was little industry or trade; hence most of those who were not included in the master-slave economy were dispossessed of a socially sanctioned method of earning a living. So here again the chief cause was land. With the coming of the industrial revolution there was a catastrophic break-up of the crafts and thousands who had been employed at hand labor found their income gone. Almost continually in the western world since the beginning of the industrial revolution machines have been displacing laborers before the economic system could expand to re-employ them, and hence in spite of expansion there has been unavoidable unemployment. During this period, also, we have had the well-known periodic depressions when unemployment mounted decidedly. In recent years in America, machinery has displaced workers at a highly pathological rate, and at the same time foreign trade was dwindling at a precipitous pace and the financial world was gyrating dizzily. These, combined with other factors, produced depression and enforced unemployment on a scale which threatened to be fatal.

The reasons why societies are unable to furnish socially sanctioned employment to all members vary from society to society and from time to time in the same society. It is impossible, therefore, to make any analysis of such causation which will apply to all societies. It is important, however, to recognize that this inability of society to employ everyone is the fundamental economic cause of most social problems, whether it be crime, delinquency, dependency, or begging, and that such problems are likely to continue until some way is found to eliminate this age-old defect.

If we have the reasons why a given society cannot employ all its members, they may give some idea of how many will be unemployed, but they may not give a complete picture of who will be unemployed. If society cannot employ everyone, on what basis are people selected for employment and on what basis rejected? These criteria on which people have been rejected for employment frequently have been called "personal causes," because they are the characteristics which unemployed persons have, and they may be catalogued by making a careful study of the unemployed. Healy has done this for juvenile delinquents; Laubach, for homeless men; and the Gluecks, for criminals.

In studies of "personal causes" there has often been an implication that they are a constant, which, if once completely tabulated, will be applicable to all places and times. This, to say the least, is an exaggeration. Some of them approach being a constant, but others are highly variable. We know, for example, that a society may get into a position in which virtually everyone may be employed. Such was the case in the United States during the World War. Thousands, who during normal times would have been considered to have glaring defects, were pressed into service, and for the time being their defects sank into insignificance.

The greatest variable in the criteria for selecting those who are to be unemployed is related to the reasons why a society cannot employ all its members. And since, as has been said, these reasons vary, the criteria of selection vary. During the enclosures in England, it was the serfs who were cast off the land, but when Virginia changed its inheritance laws in order to break up the landed estates, it was the landed gentry who swarmed the towns. When the industrial revolution occurred, it was the craftsmen who were displaced, but as the middle-

class, moneyed element arose, many noblemen found themselves in difficulty also. An influx of labor-saving machinery
displaces factory workers, and a periodic depression throws
construction workers of all classes into idleness. A crash in the
stock market throws thousands of brokers and their helpers
out of work, and a change in selling methods makes traveling
salesmen obsolete. Rapid social and economic changes displace
the aged in all stations of life. A revolution brings young political leaders; the acceptance of organized labor by the railroads
forces out many a "gray beard" transport executive; new educational theories usually bring young college presidents; many
an aged physician finds his knowledge obsolete, and, if state
medicine comes, many more will be cast aside. Thus, from
time to time different elements of the population go into the
discard.

Because people are displaced in the economic process, however, it does not always follow that they will become dependent or will fall directly into the socially outcast professions.
They may be unemployed without becoming dependent, for
they may have savings, or they may have relatives who will
support them. As still another alternative, they may change
occupations and displace other workers, who will displace still
other workers in other occupations. The more training, however, which is required for occupations, the more difficult it is
to change occupations. Practically every displacement of workers, therefore, throws some former workers into the ranks of the
dependent.

In addition to these highly variable criteria for selecting the
unemployables, there are, as has been said, certain criteria
which tend to be constant. In some relatively static societies
which have a rigid class or caste system, class membership may
be such a constant; those born into the dispossessed class or
classes are themselves dispossessed. In the India of the past
the Brahman played the aristocratic begging role and his
children inherited his occupation; in the old South the children
of the "poor white trash" usually become "poor white trash";
and in Europe during the Middle Ages the child of the pros-

titute, criminal, or beggar seldom rose above the station of its parents. In a country which has a flexible class system, such as America, hereditary class membership does not necessarily have such finality. As has been indicated in a previous chapter, however, even here there is a tendency for the person born in the "underworld" to stay in it and to engage in the "underworld" occupations.

In societies having a flexible class system there is another set of criteria on the basis of which people have been so regularly rejected for employment that they may well be regarded as constants. Extreme youth, extreme old age, and serious illness are so generally recognized as a handicap that no one asks the reason why. Extremely low mentality, marked insanity, and gross physical deformity are equally regarded as liabilities. Physical deficiency is also a handicap. Thus, the blind are seldom given an opportunity to work, those without hands seldom get jobs, and the crippled frequently are rejected. The pathological use of drugs or alcohol is also a handicap. The unemployed and dependent elements always, therefore, contain a large assortment of aged, sick, feeble-minded, mentally diseased, deformed, and physically deficient persons as well as drug addicts and chronic drunkards. And the begging profession gets a particularly liberal allotment of all of these pathological types.

To care for these numerous persons who are consigned to be economic drones, society has provided an elaborate set of social agencies—homes for the aged, relief organizations, and pension systems. As an alternate, it offers the drone the opportunity to earn a livelihood by engaging in one of the outcast occupations. By failing to protect its property, society provides a livelihood for the criminal; by patronizing the prostitute and giving to the beggar, it provides an income for these elements; by buying bootleg liquor and smuggled goods, it makes illegal commerce profitable; and by being gullible, it endows the swindler. The real problem, therefore, is why so many enforced drones and some who are drones by choice, so far as legitimate occupations are concerned, enter begging or one of the other

outcast occupations rather than accept the organized relief
which society proffers.

The causes for people entering begging in preference to
accepting organized relief are closely linked to the system of
rewards and penalties employed by society. Society attempts
to control the entrance to occupations through an elaborate
gradation of awards in the form of financial returns or of social
approval. For exceptional and difficult tasks large awards are
bestowed; and for trivial and easy tasks, small awards; and
supposedly society has its awards graduated from the smallest
to the largest according to the difficulty involved in getting
people to perform the various tasks.

In administering its system of rewards, society has always
had difficulties, but at the bottom of this scale difficulties have
arisen to perplex it in the extreme. For performing the most
menial common labor it has awarded the minimum financial
return and the minimum social approval. This financial return
was usually only sufficient for a bare livelihood. If, then, society
was to keep its enforced drones alive, it had to give them a
financial return approximately equal to that of menial laborers.
However, to get people to perform menial labor instead of
accepting relief, in some way it had to make labor more attractive than relief. To do this it had to rely on its awards of approval. Since, however, it gave a minimum of approval to the
menial laborers, it could hardly give less to those on relief,
and it was forced, therefore, to give the negative of approval,
namely social stigma, to those accepting relief. Thus "the poor
house" and "charity" have haunted the dreams of many a
person when financial troubles were knocking at his door.

In applying this stigma, society succeeded wonderfully in
one respect. It got its menial labor for a very small financial
reward, in many cases less than a living wage, which, however,
eventually caused other trouble by reducing purchasing power
and bogging up the wheels of industry. In recent years, therefore, America has apparently decided to make relief less igno-
minious. Relief has become "an obligation of the state" and
the "charity case" has become a "client." Already this has cre-

ated a new state of mind in those on relief, a state which Dr. E. T. Krueger has aptly called "militant dependency," and already parts of society are wondering how people will be enticed to work rather than accept relief.

In addition to the problem of getting people to do work rather than accept relief, society has faced the task of getting people to accept relief or even accept work in preference to employment in the socially outcast occupations. In this task, it has not been so successful. Here its system of awards has worked very badly, and in the matter of financial awards it has failed almost entirely. People have given liberally to beggars, they have patronized prostitutes, they have made it possible for criminals to garner a rich harvest, and they have made bootlegging and smuggling profitable. It has been possible, therefore, for almost anyone to secure a larger income in one of these occupations than could be gotten on relief, and in many cases these socially outcast occupations offered a more handsome return than numerous socially approved modes of employment.

Having failed to control entrance to the socially outcast occupations through its system of financial awards, society had to rely on social approval and disapproval. It therefore gave slight approval to the menial occupations, attached stigma to relief, and attempted to stigmatize the socially outcast occupations. At times it has been very successful in these attempts and at other times not so successful. In either case it has been in a perplexing dilemma, for, when society stigmatizes the socially outcast occupations sufficiently to control entrance to them, it by the same token makes escape from them virtually impossible. There have been times when the convict, the prostitute, and the beggar did not have a ghost of a chance to secure employment in socially approved occupations and a not much better chance to secure relief. A person having once become stigmatized was virtually condemned to the underworld for life. But that is not all. The children of these lost souls were tainted and were practically consigned to the same fate as their parents. The illegitimate child, the offspring of a prostitute, a criminal, or a beggar, could not avoid the shadow of its tainted ancestry; society would not allow it. To rationalize this "hereditary" stigma, society invented the criminal instinct and other equally fantastic myths. When, therefore, society has succeeded in its attempt to highly stigmatize the socially outcast occupations, it has tended to make membership in these occupations hereditary in the same sense that membership in a caste and succession to a crown are hereditary.

Having failed to prevent its drones from engaging in the socially outcast professions through its system of social approval and disapproval and financial awards, society has employed its final weapon, the law. Sometimes the law has been employed at the same time that strong stigmas were in vogue. As Victor Hugo has so vividly portrayed in *Les Miserables,* legal punishment in such cases was often little different from stabbing a dead enemy. At other times, particularly more recently, when social stigma has been weak, society has attempted to substitute legal action for informal social control. Fancy laws are enacted and put on the statute books but usually their enforcement is virtually nil; today hundreds of cities have anti-begging ordinances while beggars litter their streets, and in these same cities thousands of women live by their sex in defiance of legal statutes.

In brief, therefore, the causation of begging lies in the fact that society at present is unable to employ everyone at a socially approved occupation, it makes begging and other socially outcast occupations financially remunerative, and it has been unable so far to counterbalance this financial advantage by the use of social stigma or legal action. Many, therefore, choose employment in begging or in one of the other socially outcast occupations in preference to relief or even to employment in the less remunerative socially approved occupations.

In its attempts to correct this situation society has used numerous devices and is trying new ones continually. These devices follow the same categories as causation. They include schemes to make it possible for society to employ everyone, programs to correct the personal defects of individuals on the basis of which these persons are culled out of the working population, and devices for manipulating the system of awards so as to discourage entrance into begging. The schemes designed to make it possible for society to employ everyone are seldom thought of as methods of controlling begging. They are nevertheless the most fundamental attempts at control that society has made. In spite of this, however, such programs are too numerous and too involved to be given lengthy consideration here. Generally speaking, every improvement in the methods of production, every change which betters the distribution of income, every factor which retards the increase in population and every discovery which utilizes an additional natural resource contributes toward making employment for everyone possible. During the past century such developments were expected to come and did come largely from the activities of individuals and small groups pursuing their own ends. During the present century this method obviously has worked poorly. Therefore, pretentious schemes involving whole industries, entire classes of the population, and even the whole economic system and the government have been born over night. Some of these schemes are so all-embracing and so universal in their scope that their missionaries travel the world and at times replace the religious missionary of old. Some plans are very simple and some are very complex, but in numbers they are boundless. Fascism, communism, socialism, and a dozen other "isms" have their schemes. Each has its own patent medicine guaranteed to cure the ills of society.

While society has been thus engaged in following a vision of a time when all its members could be employed, it has not been unmindful of the fate of the drones which now exist. As has been said, it has provided relief, economic subsistence, for these unemployed. Relief, however, has been generally considered undesirable and nonconstructive, and society, therefore, has set up an elaborate system of institutions and devices designed to do constructive work with these economic drones. Fundamentally, these institutions have worked on the problem of preventing the development of, or, if they have already developed, of correcting or minimizing the personal defects of individuals handicapped in economic and social adjustment. Such programs are so numerous and so complex that they cannot be described in detail here, but they do deserve more than passing attention.

The preventive programs of society we can only mention. To prevent the development of physically handicapped persons, society has provided free medical services to those who cannot pay, given free milk to babies and mothers in poor families, legally compelled certain medical treatments to prevent blindness, provided health and safety control of working conditions and of public accommodations, systematically conducted physical examinations of children in public schools, controlled the spread of contagious diseases, and many other things. To prevent the development of educationally handicapped persons, it has provided public schools, set up settlement houses, offered occupational courses of various types, given financial aid to individuals for educational purposes, and passed compulsory educational laws. To prevent the development of pathological personalities it has set up child guidance clinics, provided visiting teacher services in the public schools, and promoted the dissemination of knowledge of child psychology among teachers and parents. And finally, to prevent the development of feeble-minded persons, it has enacted sterilization laws and has taken various measures to discourage the marriage and reproduction of the feeble-minded. By all of these measures, society has sought to decrease the number of "unemployables," at least in future generations, by preventing the development of the physical and mental handicaps which seem to make people unemployable.

Since society has never wholly succeeded in preventing the development of handicapped persons, it has developed an extensive system of agencies and methods for correcting deficiencies which are an impediment to the social and economic adjustment of persons. Perhaps the most commonly recognized of these measures are those designed to correct physical deficiencies. Medical science has devised ways to cure some kinds of blindness, straighten twisted legs and limbs, and even lift faces so as to make a person both more capable and more presentable; it has also found ways to cure many diseases which produce physical weaklings. Venereal diseases, malaria, tuberculosis, various heart ailments, and other similar diseases all produce "walking invalids" whom society classes as unemployable, and for all of these diseases medical science has devised partial or complete cures. Even leprosy has partially yielded to the magic wand of medicine. Furthermore, by glandular treatments some types of mental deficiency have been corrected. In addition, medical science has contributed to the cure of such disorganizing habits as drug addiction and chronic alcoholism. In the case of some deficiencies in which a correction is impossible the difficulty is minimized by a mechanical substitute such as a glass eye or a cork leg.

The important thing about these corrective devices, so far as begging is concerned, is that, while they were developed for the most part through the efforts of private medicine, society has made them available to the poverty classes as well as to the upper classes. In fact, it has taken extensive precautions to see that persons in dependency classes have access to the most advanced methods known to science for curing handicaps. To accomplish this, it has free medical clinics, free hospital facilities, free public health facilities, and special funds to provide exceptional treatments. It has attempted, therefore, to use the facilities of science to correct the deficiencies of the enforced economic drones.

It has never been possible, however, for society to correct all the physical defects which people have, not even the most serious defects. With all the advance which science has made in recent years, there is still no known method of correcting many of the physical defects. For those defects which cannot be corrected, therefore, society has developed another and very interesting type of therapy; namely, education for the physically and mentally handicapped. There are jobs in the modern economic system which can be performed satisfactorily even by persons with decided physical or mental handicaps. The blind can do many kinds of factory work; the higher grades of feeble-minded persons can do factory work, household work, or farm labor; those crippled in the lower limbs can do handwork which does not require standing; and the deaf and dumb can do nearly any kind of work which does not entail too much conversation. There are even kinds of work which a person without hands can do. To do such work, however, the person must be trained for the job. It is to offer such training that society operates schools for the blind, schools for the deaf, schools for the feeble-minded, and training facilities for other types of physically and mentally handicapped persons. In the United States, federal and state agencies have made strenuous efforts along this line since the World War, both for veterans and others, and the experience thus gained has been highly valuable in indicating the kinds of work which handicapped persons can do and the training which they need.

Giving the handicapped persons training for jobs which they can satisfactorily perform has not completely solved their employment problem. It has become increasingly evident that the big reason for the handicapped being unable to secure employment is not their handicap, per se, or their training; it is the attitude of the public and more specifically of employers. The public does not believe that certain kinds of handicapped persons can do work satisfactorily. The blind, for example, have always been considered helpless and they are still considered helpless. The average factory operator would not believe his eyes if he saw a blind person efficiently operating one of his machines, and it would be unusual if he gave a blind person a chance to demonstrate his skill. Since, therefore, employers do not believe that handicapped persons can do work satisfactorily, they simply do not give such people a chance to work at all. To make the education of the handicapped remunerative, it is necessary to educate the public. To this end noble attempts have been made, but so far results have not been encouraging.

Having made little headway in securing employment for the handicapped in the field of private industry, society has tried another tack; it has built factories and workshops designed to employ only handicapped persons. Some of these plants are owned and operated by governmental agencies, while others are owned by private, philanthropic organizations. Perhaps the best known of these are the factories for the blind. A so-called "Lighthouse" is to be found in nearly every city in America and many states have government-owned factories for the employment of the blind. As experiments, these plants are encouraging, but they have not been entirely successful. Most of them have to be subsidized; that is, they pay out more in wages than they get from the sale of their products, which from the standpoint of economics is not sound business. This does not necessarily prove, however, that the blind are incapable of producing a livelihood for themselves. Most of these factories are small, and in recent years small factories generally have fallen under the competition of large corporations. In addition, many of these factories are not equipped with the latest and best machinery. In some cases the agency does not see fit to spend the money which such machinery would cost. In other cases the machinery is the monopoly of a large corporation and cannot be secured for small factories. Hence, as business enterprises, they have not been given a fair test.

Even this brief survey is sufficient to indicate that society has set up an extensive system of institutions and agencies to rehabilitate the handicapped. This system, in fact, has become so extensive and so complex that few but the specialists are able to comprehend it. To make it workable, therefore, it is "capped off" with something in a sense much more simple, the case work method of treatment. Virtually every relief agency today attempts to study each of its "clients" individually and to work out a corrective treatment in terms of the needs of the individual. If this study reveals that the individual needs a cork leg, medical treatment, vocational training, or any of the other services which specialized agencies are able to provide, the individual is put in contact with the agency which can meet his needs. It is this individualized study and treatment which is known as case work, and it is this method as practiced by the widespread relief agencies which serves as the connecting link between the legions of handicapped persons and the multitudinous agencies which are designed to correct handicaps.

The large amount of time and of money which society puts into this extensive program for the prevention and correction of physical and mental defects indicates that it has much faith in this approach to the solution of the problem of dependency and its by-product, the underworld occupations. In some respects such confidence is warranted, but in other respects it is probably misplaced. So far as a given individual is concerned it is well justified. Agencies have had a fair, but not too successful, record in their attempts to patch up individuals and place them in employment in the economic system. The humaneness of the approach is not to be questioned, but the efficacy of this program of treatment as a cure for the problem of unemployment in society is, to say the least, highly questionable. During the period when the corrective program has been expanding most rapidly, unemployment has also been increasing rapidly, and during recent years the latter has been pathological in the extreme. If correcting the defects of individuals helps to reduce unemployment, why the apparent paradox? The answer is that unemployment cannot be decreased appreciably by remedying the defects of individuals. Just as rain cannot be stopped by evaporating the water which falls, so unemployment cannot be dissipated by attacking the deficiencies of the unemployed. Periodically the air becomes oversaturated and squeezes out the excess moisture in the form of rain; later it becomes undersaturated and reabsorbs moisture; and always there is an excess in lakes and rivers which is never absorbed. Likewise the economic system becomes oversaturated with workers and periodically squeezes out the excess. Again it becomes undersaturated and takes on additional workers, so that there are showers and sometimes cloudbursts of unemployment, periods of reabsorption, and always lakes of potential workers which are never absorbed.

One particular misconception has been largely responsible

for the belief that unemployment could be solved by correcting the defects of individuals. It has been generally assumed that, because individuals apparently lose jobs or fail to get jobs because of physical, mental, or educational handicaps, these deficiencies are the causes of unemployment. This, however, is false logic. As has been indicated, the real cause of unemployment is simply the fact that society does not have jobs for everyone, and, since some must be rejected, society must have criteria to determine which ones are to be rejected. Personal defects, then, are a part of the criteria which society uses. Thus, if there were no blind, crippled, or sickly persons for society to reject, it would still be compelled to reject someone, and it would have to use some other criteria to make its selection. The situation is very similar to a school which has a rule that a certain percentage of the students must be failed. It may be possible to "doctor up" one or even several individual students who are failing and make them pass their work, but it is not possible to reduce the number of failures by this method. Since a certain percentage must fail, if one student is made to pass another must be made to fail. Thus, in the case of the unemployed, it is highly probable that for every one pushed into the economic system through the process of correcting defects another is shoved out, so the total number of unemployed remains the same as if no treatment had been given.

As is probably evident, the attempts at control thus far considered are efforts to deal with background causes of social and economic failures. As such they are seldom thought of specifically as attempts to control begging. The conscious attempts of society to control begging are generally confined to schemes for manipulating the system of awards of society in such a way as to get persons to accept relief rather than beg for a livelihood. Theoretically this can be done by making relief more attractive, or by making begging less attractive, or by both, and these are just the things which schemes of control have attempted to do.

Some of the devices for making relief more attractive have already been mentioned, but such schemes are far more nu-

merous and far more subtle than is generally realized. The
methods for removing the stigma from relief are particularly
interesting. Even before "charity cases" became "clients" the
institution of outdoor relief, the giving of relief to persons in
their homes, had done much to eliminate the "poor house"
taint. With this practice people could continue to live in society
as other people live and yet receive financial assistance. However, the fact that until recently such relief was usually not
available to "permanent unemployables" limited its usefulness
so far as begging was concerned. This deficiency in outdoor
relief is now being bolstered by two devices which are almost
totally devoid of stigma; namely, pensions and social insurance. From governmental funds of various kinds pensions are
now provided for the blind, widowed mothers, and other types
of permanent unemployables. Since in the United States governmental pensions have been given traditionally to war veterans for the most part, the term pension is a highly respectable
term. As a consequence, those receiving pensions do not consider themselves at all in a class with the old-time "charity
case." Insurance likewise has a highly respectable definition in
American traditions. Virtually everyone carries some sort of
insurance, whether it be life insurance or weather insurance
makes little difference. Government subsidies to the aged,
therefore, when called social insurance have, in the popular
mind, all the respectability of other types of insurance. The
fact that part or all of the premiums are paid by others than
the insured is an obscure technicality which does not disturb
the layman. Through the development of governmental insurance for the aged and pensions for the handicapped, it will
doubtless be possible eventually for the "permanent unemployables" to receive financial aid without suffering under the
stigma which has been attached to relief.

On the financial end, relief has been made more attractive
by increasing the amount and the dependability of the subsidy.
The vast increase in the amounts given for relief since the federal government opened its coffers to the unemployed is such
common knowledge that it need hardly be mentioned. Further-

more, it is becoming recognized generally that the attractiveness of this form of relief does not depend so much on the amount given the individual or family as it does on the fact that people feel that they can depend on receiving the relief regularly. What everyone also knows but generally regrets to admit is that there is almost no stigma attached to such relief, and what gives a sheepish look to those who would like to protest is that they themselves have been in the government's "soup line." The beggars from industry and high finance had already made governmental charity respectable before the unemployed got a hand in the national dole. With the procession thus started, practically everybody filed by the treasury door, and if everyone does it, then it is inevitably considered respectable. The leaders of the procession should be thankful in fact that the unemployed have not raised more strenuous objections at having to work for theirs while others have gotten handouts either as an outright gratuity or in return for a signed agreement not to work.

Making relief more attractive by removing the stigma attached to it, by increasing the financial aid, and by giving it greater financial security, however, has not stopped begging. Society, therefore, has attempted to strengthen its control of begging by making the practice of begging less attractive. To do this it has used two methods principally: it has attempted to make begging unpleasant by the use of legal penalties, and it has attempted to make it unprofitable by influencing people not to give to beggars.

As has been suggested, the attempts of society to prevent begging by the use of the legal "strong arm" have generally been as humorous as they have been futile. In America, where most law enforcement is slovenly, the attempts to enforce antibegging laws have been, as a rule, extremely weak. Since most of such laws are city statutes, the active arm of the law is the police, and they have been quite immune to the pleas of agencies and citizens for enforcement and have often been deaf even to orders from headquarters. The average policeman is not interested personally in the begging law, but he is hired to enforce many laws in which he is not interested. To him, however, the job of arresting a beggar is a particularly distasteful one. The arrest usually must be made in a public place and even with the greatest of tact it may prove to be an unpleasant affair. The beggar is very likely to create a scene and he may get much sympathy from onlookers. If the beggar is blind or seriously deformed, the situation is particularly hazardous. Force such as might be used against a criminal cannot be used in the arrest of a blind, aged, or crippled beggar. The policeman must use tact and restraint even if the beggar resists, and even then sentimental and well-meaning bystanders may accuse the policeman of cruelty. The average policeman, therefore, having more laws to enforce than he can possibly remember, manages to forget the anti-begging ordinance and overlook the beggar. The chief device for overcoming this lethargy of the police is to establish a special mendicancy detail. A few policemen are assigned the job of arresting beggars and are relieved of all other responsibilities. With such a detail arrests can be secured if higher officials really want the arrests made.

Getting the beggar arrested, however, is only the beginning of difficulties in the legal process. The courts are no more anxious to handle the beggars than the police are to arrest them. The judge simply does not know what to do with the convicted beggar. He may fine the mendicant, but if the latter has no money with which to pay he must be put in jail, and that is just what the judge does not want. In the usual city the jail and workhouse facilities are not suitable for the "punishment" of handicapped beggars and the judge knows it. If then the beggar is passed on to the jail or workhouse authorities, he is still a "white elephant" and will likely be released as soon as arrangements can be made to do so. To relieve the courts of this embarrassment, social agencies frequently agree to care for convicted beggars, and the judge thus can sentence the beggar to "three months on relief." This often helps to get court action, but it does not force the beggar to accept relief in lieu of begging. Typical of the court-social-agency arrangement, which is found in many cities, is the plan which was used by Boston for some time. That plan, as it existed in Boston before the depression and the alphabetical organizations, is described by a member of the Mendicancy Committee.

"Street begging in Boston is dealt with by a committee of the Council of Social Agencies. The Committee is composed of representatives of the agencies having facilities for dealing with the type of persons most likely to be engaged in street begging. For instance, on the committee is the Director of the Industrial Aid Society (which specializes in homeless men, particularly on the industrial side), the Director of the Division of Rehabilitation in the State Department of Education, the Director of the State Division of the Blind, a representative of the Overseers of Public Welfare, one from the Federated Jewish Charities, the Chief Probation Officer of the Municipal Court, the General Agent of the Boston Providence Association, and others having a special interest in the problem.

"The Police Commissioner some years ago appointed two special officers, charged with the responsibility for warning all street beggars and directing them to the Industrial Aid Society. Here they were interviewed, and directed to other agencies when the problem was not such as could be handled to the best advantage by the Industrial Aid Society. However, since most of the men were single and their problem was chiefly one of unemployment, most of the work has actually been done by the Industrial Aid Society in co-operation with the Division of Rehabilitation of the Department of Education. Of those with families, some were referred to the Family Welfare Society, some to the Federated Jewish Charities, some to the Overseers of Public Welfare, and some to the Division of the Blind.

"If the person persisted in begging after being warned, he was arrested and taken into court." [1]

Having failed to control begging effectively by working on the beggar, society has attempted to control begging by con-

[1] From a letter to the author by a member of the Boston Mendicancy Committee.

trolling giving. If society can keep people from giving, it can keep people from begging. In this attempt to control givers society has relied chiefly on publicity; through the radio, newspapers, and public speeches it has attempted to persuade the public that giving to beggars is not only unnecessary but also that it is unwise, if not positively harmful. It is unnecessary to give to beggars, so the argument usually goes, because the social agencies have facilities and are willing to care for all needy persons. Having attempted to assure the public of the adequacy of relief facilities, arguments are given to convince the public that relief should be handled through these channels rather than by private almsgiving. The disadvantages of handling relief through giving to beggars, as usually stated, are that the amount which the beggar is able to collect depends on his begging skill and not on his need for the money. In fact, the really needy person may be a very poor beggar and hence may get very few gifts. Furthermore, from begging the mendicant gets only money whereas he may really need occupational training, medical treatment, or custodial care. In other words, giving liberally to a beggar encourages him to continue to beg and does nothing to help him to become rehabilitated so that he can make a living by useful work. Thus giving to beggars solves neither the personal problems of the individual beggar nor the problem of begging in society as a whole. Finally, the more liberally people give to beggars, the more beggars there will be. As someone has said, "Society can have all the beggars it is willing to support." Having thus disparaged almsgiving, the public is assured that giving relief through social agencies has none of these disadvantages.

In addition to general publicity, numerous other devices have been used to soothe the conscience of the giver and deter giving. A rather common device is to supply prospective givers with cards which they can give to beggars instead of giving cash. The card introduces the beggar to some social agency which obligates itself to investigate the needs of the mendicant and give such help as is necessary. Supposedly, it is an easy way for John Citizen to refer the mendicant to a social agency.

In some cases it has worked reasonably well, but in many places today no agency would obligate itself to care for all cases thus referred to it.

We cannot pass by attempts to influence the giver without a mention of the age-old work test. Givers have long had as a part of their basic philosophy the belief that, if a person wants food, clothing, or shelter enough to work for it, he must need it. Conversely it was believed that if a person really needs these things he will be willing to work for them. As a result social agencies have periodically revived the work test for the purpose of showing the giving public that those who are receiving relief really need it and that all who need help badly enough to work for it can get it. The effect on the public is often electric, but as a method of relief-giving the work test is often a farce. The United States got a nation-wide dose of the ludicrousness of the work test in its unhappy experience with C.W.A.[2] From this debacle the public has learned two important things about the so-called work test. In the first place, a person may go through the formalities of working without actually doing much work, and in the second place, even an honest and self-respecting worker resents doing perfectly useless work. None of us could get enthusiastic about raking leaves back and forth until we wore them out, especially when we knew that it would be difficult to find a new supply of leaves. In other words, what appears to be a work test may not be a work test at all.

From the foregoing discussion it appears evident that society has made a very broad attack on the problem of controlling the beggar. It seems equally obvious that very scant success has attended these efforts to control begging. What then is the difficulty? On the economic side there are numerous people whom society cannot employ, and there are multitudes of employed persons who receive a mere pittance for their labors.

[2] Actually providing useful work at a fair wage to all who are willing to work, we should say, is not synonymous with the work test. Such work is simply an extension through governmental channels of the usual employment facilities of society so as to make possible the employment of more people.

Most of these are potential beggars. Practically all of them could be attracted into begging if the financial returns were high enough, the legal interference negligible, and the social disapproval not too severe. In the last analysis, the amount of money which beggars receive, the severity of legal action against begging, and the social stigma attached to the profession depend on the attitudes of the nonbegging public. As long as this public wishes begging to continue, it will continue, but when it wishes it to stop, it will stop. Obviously, then, a sizable part of the nonbegging public sanctions begging, and the question is, why does it do so? The answer is a rather complicated one which has already been discussed at some length. One or two points, however, should be reiterated. The public knows that there are persons who are unavoidably unemployed and must have help. Most of the public approves theoretically of caring for these people through social agency facilities, but for numerous reasons the public does not have complete faith in relief agencies. The agencies in their campaigns to raise funds paint dire pictures of their needs and inadequacies, and the average citizen may well wonder whether in reality there are facilities for caring for all needy cases. In addition, there are many who doubt the infallibility of social agencies in dealing wisely with all cases, and they do not believe in giving the agencies a life and death power over the needy by refusing the latter the recourse of appealing to the public directly for help.

In addition to these more or less purely economic factors, the social and cultural factors which have been discussed must be taken into consideration. There are traditional attitudes and philosophies toward almsgiving which will continue to exert a force long after all reasons for them are gone. There are also social inadequacies in contemporary life for which almsgiving is a partial compensation, and on the beggar's side there is a dependency and begging culture and social world which tend to be self-perpetuating and which cannot be done away with in a moment.

In conclusion, we have had beggars for centuries and we

may have them for centuries to come. Nothing less than a complete reorganization of society can be expected to eliminate them completely, and no one can be certain that that would do it. Because there will be beggars, however, does not mean that the number of beggars cannot be controlled or their more pernicious practices held in check. How much worse the mendicancy situation would have been had not the foregoing measures been taken, it is difficult to say, but in all probability it would have been immeasurably worse. The devices for control, therefore, may work better than they seem to work, and they can be made to work even better when the public brings to their aid the force of its concerted desires and opinions.

BIBLIOGRAPHY

"Abolition of the Mendicancy Detail in New York," *Charities*, XVI (1906), 113-14.

Addams, Jane. *The Spirit of Youth and the City Streets*. New York, Macmillan Co., 1909.

Allen, W. H. "Vagrant: Social Parasite or Social Product," *Conference Charities and Correction*. New York, 1903, pp. 379-86.

"Alms Receiving Licensed in Boston," *Survey*, XXII (1909), 467.

Anderson, Nels. *The Hobo*. Chicago, University of Chicago Press, 1923.

———. "Case Studies of Homeless Men in Chicago." (Typewritten manuscript in the office of the Chicago Council of Social Agencies and in the offices of the Department of Sociology, University of Chicago.)

Anderson, P. E. "Tramping With Yeggs," *Atlantic Monthly*, CXXXVI (1925), 747-55.

Armstrong, Clairette P. *600 Runaway Boys; Why Boys Desert Their Homes*. Boston, R. G. Badger, 1932.

Aydelotte, Frank. *Elizabethan Rogues and Vagabonds*. Oxford, Clarendon Press, 1913.

Barrett, R. T. "Human Wreckage of the China Coast," *Great Britain and the East*, L (1938), 373.

Beecroft, Eric, and Janow, Seymour. "Toward a National Policy for Migration," *Social Forces*, XVI (1938), 475-92.

"Begging as a Fine Art," *The Nation*, LXXIX (1904), 516-17.

Belloc, H. "The Blind Beggars Guild," *New Statesman*, XXIII (1924), 409-10.

Bennett, J. W. "China's Perennially Unemployed," *Asia,* XXXI (1931), 215-19, 268-69.

Benton, J. "Rest for Weary Willie; Life in a Federal Transient Camp," *Saturday Evening Post,* CCIX (1936), 14-15, 87-90.

Binder, Rudolph M. "The Treatment of Beggars and Vagabonds in Belgium," *Journal Criminal Law and Criminology,* VI (1916), 835-48.

Bishop, E. F. F. "Beggars," (bibliography footnotes), *Church Quarterly Review,* CXXVII (1938), 76-83.

Blatchly, C. K. "State Farm for Tramps and Vagrants," *Survey,* XXIV (1910), 87-89.

Bolitho, W. "Beggars of London," *Outlook* (London), LII (1923), 484-85.

Bombay, General Department of, *Report by Mr. O. H. B. Starte on Measures for the Prevention of Professional Begging in the City of Bombay.* Bombay, 1926.

Booth, William. *The Vagrants and the Unemployable.* London, Salvation Army, 1909.

"Breakfast, Bedroom and Bath in the Subway," *Literary Digest,* CI (1929), 54-56.

Brevis, Harry Jacob. "Principles and Standards of Blind Relief Legislation," *Social Forces,* XIII (1935), 391-99.

"Brotherly Love and Professional Beggars," *Survey,* XXII (1909), 105-6.

Brown, Irving H. *Gypsy Fires in America.* New York and London, Harper & Bros., 1924.

Brown, Malcolm, and Webb, John N. *Migratory Families.* Washington, Government Printing Office, 1939.

Carew, Barnpflyde Moore. *An Apology for the Life of Mr. Barnpflyde Moore Carew Commonly Called the King of the Beggars.* London, Grady and Owen, 1765.

Chardin, F. W. "Two Beggars," *Near East,* XXVII (1925), 453.

"Cheerful Dead-beats Who Go Around the World Without a Cent," *Literary Digest,* LXXXIV (1925), 59-61.

"Chinese Women Form Beggars' Relief Society in Shanghai," *China Weekly Review,* LXXI (1935), 294.

Cleland, A. "Time to Deal with Vagrancy," *Survey*, XXXVII (1916), 268-69.

"Clergyman's Study of the Stranded, A," *World's Work*, IV (1902), 2510-15.

"Coin in a Cup, No Charity," *Literary Digest*, CXVIII (1934), 26.

Coleridge, G. "Little Brothers of the Pavement," *Living Age*, CCLXXVIII (1913), 294-99.

Conyngton, Mary Catherine. *How to Help*. New York, Macmillan Co., 1909.

Cooke, J. "Vagrants, Beggars, and Tramps," *Quarterly Review*, CCIX (1908), 388-408.

Cross, William T., and Cross, D. E. *Newcomers and Nomads in California*. Stanford University Press, 1937.

Cross, William T. "The Poor Migrant in California," *Social Forces*, XV (1936-1937), 423-27.

Cruice, L. "Greeks Bearing Gifts; Christmas Eve in Athens," *Commonwealth*, XXIX (1938), 235-36.

Culver, B. F. "Transient Unemployed Men," *Sociology and Social Research*, XVII (1933), 519-34.

Darnier, C. "Les Tuneurs de Bretigny," *Mercure de France*, CCLXXXI (1938), 71-80.

Davies, W. H. "Beggars," Review. *Living Age*, CCLXIII (1909), 630-32.

Davis, William Henry. *Beggars*. London, Duckworth and Co., 1909.

Dawson, W. H. "German Tramp Prison," *Fortnightly Review*, LXXXVII (1907), 282-91.

———. *The Vagrancy Problem*, London, P. S. King and Son, 1910.

"Disappearing Tramp," *The Nation*, LXXXIV (1907), 5.

Douglas, W. H. S. "Hallelujah, I'm a Bum," *American Mercury*, XXVI (1932), 471-76.

"Driving the Beggars Out of Philadelphia," *Survey*, XXXII (1914), 426.

Dubief, F. *Le Question du Vagabondage*. Paris, Charpentier, 1911.

Dunn, M. B. "Philosophy and Tramps," *Atlantic Monthly,* XCVII (1906), 776-83.

"Dutch Society for the Moral Rescue of Beggars and Tramps," *Review of Reviews,* XXXIII (1906), 356-57.

"Educating England's Tramps," *Saturday Review,* CLXI (1936), 499.

Edwards, A. "Beggars of Mogador," *Outlook,* CI (1912), 929-36.

"Five Professional Mendicants and Their Brief Hey-day," *Charities,* X (1903), 622-23.

Forbes, J. "Jockers and the Schools They Keep," *Charities,* XI (1903), 432-36.

———. "Tramp; or Caste in the Jungle," *Outlook,* XCVIII (1911), 869-75.

———. "Work of the Mendicancy Police in New York," *Charities,* XI (1903), 576-78.

"For Hoboes; Hobo News," *Time,* XXIX (1937), 67-69.

Franck, H. A. "Three Hoboes in India," *Century Magazine,* LXXIX (1910), 774-81.

———. "Beggars of India," *Travel,* XXII (1914), 30.

Freund, Roger Henry. "Begging in Chicago." Unpublished Master's thesis, University of Chicago, 1925.

Friedman, Isaac Kahn. *The Autobiography of a Beggar.* Boston, Small, Maynard and Co., 1903.

Fuller, M. L. B. "My Mother, an Alms!" *Catholic World,* CXXXI (1930), 559-67.

Fuller, Ronald, *The Beggars' Brotherhood.* London, G. Allen and Unwin, Ltd., 1936.

Garrett, Constance. "The Poor Ye Have with you Always," *Social Forces,* XV (1937), 519-24.

Gault, R. H. "Pathologic Vagrancy," *Journal Criminal Law and Criminology,* V (1914), 321-22.

"Gentle Art of Hoboing, as Practiced by an Artist," *Literary Digest,* LXX (1921), 40-43.

"Germany's Modernistic Beggars," *Literary Digest,* CXI (1931), 14.

Gillin, J. L., "Vagrancy and Begging," *American Journal of Sociology,* XXXV (1929), 424-32.

Gilmore, H. W. "Five Generations of a Begging Family," *American Journal of Sociology*, XXXVII, No. 5 (1932), 768-74.

————. *The Sociology of Begging*. Unpublished Master's thesis, Vanderbilt University (Nashville, Tennessee), 1925.

————. "Social Control of Begging," *Family*, X (1929), 179-81.

————. "Types of Begging," *Sociology and Social Research*, XIV (1930), 562-66.

Givens, Colonel. "On the Stem," *Saturday Evening Post*, CCIV (1932), 33.

Godfrey, J. D. "A Capable Beggar Makes from $15 to $500 a Day," *American Magazine*, XCIV (1922), 10-11, 119-21.

Godley, M. "Travellers," *Spectator*, CVII (1911), 373-74.

Goodwin, J. J. "Beggars of New York," *Harpers Weekly*, XLVI (1902), 204, 221.

Gordon, M. "Twilight of the Schnorrer," *Menorah Journal*, XVI (1929), 554-57.

Greene, W. C. "Contentment in Poverty," *North American Review*, CCXIV (1921), 648-54.

Guest, E. A. "10,000 People a Week Ask Henry Ford for Gifts," *American Magazine*, XCVII (1924), 5-7, 84.

Guild, June Purcell. "Transients in a New Guise," *Social Forces*, XVII, No. 3 (1939), 366-72.

Hall, J. N. "Tank Town Professors," *Readers Digest*, XXIX (1936), 31-32.

Hapgood, Hutchins. *Types from City Streets*. New York, Funk and Wagnalls Co., 1910.

Harvey, N. "Concerning Casuals; Life on the Roads," *Spectator*, CLX (1938), 742-43.

Hathaway, Marion. *The Migratory Worker and Family Life*, Chicago, University of Chicago Press, 1934.

Hobhouse, A. L. "A Reply" [to Harvey's article cited above], *Spectator*, CLX (1938), 964.

"Hobo Hegemony; Convention to Decide among Rival Kings of Road Knights," *Literary Digest*, CXXIII (1937), 10-12.

"Honesty Among Beggars," *Literary Digest*, LXXVII (1923), 33-34.

"Hosts of a Tramp," *Living Age*, CCLXXIII (1912), 119-21.

Hotten, John Camden. *The Book of Vagabonds and Beggars.* London, J. C. Hotten, 1860.

"How Columbus Prevents Begging," *Survey,* XLII (1919), 255-56.

"How to Prevent Street Begging," *Survey,* XLII (1919), 87-88.

"I Don't Beg, No'm," *Family,* VI (1925), 105-6.

Inglis, W. "Panhandler's Paradise," *Harpers Weekly,* LV (1911), 11.

Irvine, H. D. "Leisured Class," *Living Age,* CCXCVIII (1918), 624-25.

Irwin, Godfrey. *American Tramp and Underworld Slang.* New York, Sears Publishing Company, 1931.

Jackson, H. *All Manner of Folk.* London, G. Richards, 1912.

Jenison, M. C. "Germany's Tramp Workmen," *Harpers Weekly,* LV (1911), 15.

Johnson, D. "Solo: a Screever at Work," *Fortnightly Review,* CXXXIII (1930), 675-78.

Judge, Arthur Valentine. *The Elizabethan Underworld.* London, George Rutledge and Sons, Ltd., 1930.

Kane, H. F. "Brief Manual of Beggary," *New Republic,* LXXXVII (1936), 288-89.

Kelly, Edmond. *The Elimination of the Tramp.* New York, Putnams' Sons, 1908.

Kemp, H. "Lure of the Tramp," *The Independent,* LXX (1911), 1270-71.

Kenny, R. "Hobo Convention," *Survey,* XXVI (1911), 862-64.

Klein, A. M. "Beggars I Have Known," *Canadian Forum,* XVI (1936), 19-20.

Ladoff, Isador. *American Pauperism and the Abolition of Poverty.* Chicago, C. H. Kerr and Co., 1904.

LaSater, M. N. "Nashville Makes a Venture," *Social Forces,* XI (1933), 219-23.

Laubach, Frank Charles. *Why There Are Vagrants: a Study Based upon One Hundred Men.* New York, Ph.D. thesis, Columbia University, 1916.

Laws, Wallace. *The Life of a Tramp.* Chicago, M. A. Donohue and Co., 1910.

Leach, H. G. "Foreword," *Forum*, LXXXVII (1932), 1.

"Leaves from the Diary of a Tramp," *Living Age*, CCLXII (1909), 143-49.

Lescohier, D. D. "Hands and Tools of the Wheat Harvest," *Survey*, L (1923), 409-12.

Lewis, O. F. "National Committee on Vagrants," *Charities*, XVIII (1907), 342-44.

Liber Vagatorum, The Book of Vagabonds and Beggars. Edited by Martin Luther in 1528, republished by J. C. Hotten, London, 1860.

Lidbetter, E. J. "Pauperism and Heredity," *Eugenics Review*, XIV (1922), 152-63.

Lindsay, Nicholas Vachel. *Handy Guide for Beggars, Especially Those of the Poetic Fraternity*. New York, Macmillan Company, 1916.

Loane, M. "Women Supertramp," *Spectator*, CV (1910), 1073-74.

Locke, Harvey J. "Unemployed Men in Chicago Shelters," *Sociology and Social Research*, XIX (1935), 420-28.

———, and Sutherland, Edwin H. *Twenty Thousand Homeless Men: A Study of Unemployed Men in the Chicago Shelters*. Chicago and Philadelphia, Lippincott Company, 1936.

London, J. "My Life in the Underworld," *Cosmopolitan*, XLIII (1907), 17-22.

———. "Rods and Gunnels," *Bookman*, XV (1902), 541-44.

Lopez, J. S. "Scientific Touch," *Harpers Weekly*, LIII (1909), 16-17.

Mabie, H. W. "Old Time Beggars," *Outlook*, XCVI (1910), 201-6.

Macaulay, R. "Marginal Comments," *Spectator*, CLIV (1935), 833.

McDermott, W. F. "Beggars by Mail," *Readers Digest*, XXIX (1936), 87-89.

McGovern, C. M. "Truth about Beggars," *Current Literature*, XXVII (1900), 228.

Marie, A. A., and Munier, R. *Les Vagabonds*. Paris, Giard and Briere, 1908.

Marsh, B. C. "Experiences of an International Beggar," *Charities*, XIX (1907), 983-97.

Maughiman, H. J. "Man with an Idea," *Commonweal*, XXII (1935), 607.

Mears, John William. *Beggars of Holland and the Grandees of Spain*, Philadelphia, Presbyterian Board, 1867.

"Memorandum on Organization of the Council on Interstate Migration," Council on Interstate Migration (1939).

"Mendicancy Project in New York City," *Social Service Review*, IX (1935), 767-68.

Milburn, George. *The Hobo's Hornbook*. New York, I. Washburn, 1930.

Minhen, T. *Boy and Girl Tramps of America*. New York, Farrar and Rinehart, 1934.

Morris, A. "Some Social and Mental Aspects of Mendicancy," *Social Forces*, V (1927), 605-13.

Mount, H. A. "Hoboes of Industry," *Scientific American*, CXXII (1920), 541.

Mullin, G. H. *Adventures of a Scholar Tramp*. New York, Century Company, 1925.

———. "Sidewalks of New York; Further Adventures of a Scholar Tramp," *Century Magazine*, CX (1925), 50-57.

Munier, R., and Marie, A. A. *Les Vagabonds*. Paris, Giard and Briere, 1908.

Myers, G. "Colonizing the Tramp," *Review of Reviews*, XXXIX (1909), 311-16.

"National Vagrancy; Its National Treatment," *Outlook*, LXXXVI (1907), 533-34.

Nimkoff, M. F. "Personality Problems of Beggars," *Sociology and Social Research*, XII (1928), 431-42.

Numelin, R. "Les Tramps," *Les Annales Politiques et Litteraires*, CXIII (1939), 161-63.

Nylander, T. "Migratory Population of the United States," *American Journal of Sociology*, XXX (1934), 129-53.

———. "Tramps and Hoboes," *Forum*, LXXIV (1925), 227-37.

———. "Wandering Youth," *Sociology and Social Research*, XVII (1933), 560-68.

"Organized to Prevent Mendicancy," *Survey*, XXIII (1909), 156.

Outland, George E. *Boy Transiency in America.* Santa Barbara State College Press, 1939.

——. "The Federal Transient Program for Boys in Southern California," *Social Forces*, XIV (1936), 427-32.

——. "The Federal Transient Service as a Deterrent of Boy Transiency," *Sociology and Social Research*, XXII (1937), 143-48.

"Panhandlers Who Thrive in Manhattan Crowds," *Literary Digest*, LXXIII (1922), 52-54.

Parulekar, N. B. "Brahmans and Beggars," *Asia*, XXIX (1929), 692-97, 734-42.

Paulian, Louis M. *The Beggars of Paris.* Translated by Lady Herschell. New York, Edward Arnold, 1897.

Podolsky, E. "Sympathy Racket," *The Rotarian*, XLIX (1936), 27-29.

Poole, E. "Newsboy Wanderers Are Tramps in the Making," *Charities*, X (1903), 221-24.

"Prosperity among Beggars," *Literary Digest*, LXXIV (1922), 42-47.

"Putting Fake Beggars to Work," *Literary Digest*, XLVIII (1914), 509-12.

Raymond, S. "An Attempt to Eliminate Street-Begging," *Family*, VI (1925), 81-83.

"Reformed Beggar," *Charities*, XI (1903), 5.

Repplier, A. "Beggar's Pouch," *Atlantic Monthly*, XCIII (1904), 385-89.

"Revival of Begging," *Spectator*, CXXVIII (1922), 105-6.

Rhodes, Harrison, "Business of Begging," *Harpers Weekly*, LVIII (1913), 13-15.

Rice, S. A. "Vagrancy Problem in New York," *Conference Charities and Correction*, 1914, pp. 457-65.

Ridge, W. P. "London Loafer," *Nineteenth Century*, LXVII (1910), 335-45.

Riviere, Louis. *Mendicants ets Vagabonds.* 2nd ed. Paris, V. LeCoffre, 1902.

Rolleston, C. "Mischievous Charity," *Westminster Review,* CLXIII (1905), 148-55.

——. "Social Parasites," *Westminster Review,* CLXII (1904), 623-32.

Roucek, Joseph S. "The Tramping Movement in Central Europe," *Sociology and Social Research,* XVIII (1933), 158-63.

Sarcey, Y. "Mendigots et Pauvres," *Les Annales Politiques et Litteraires,* CX (1937), 183-84.

Saroyan, W. "Portrait of a Bum," *Overland,* N.S., LXXXVI, (1928), 421.

——. "Portrait of Another Bum," *Overland,* N.S., LXXXVIII (1930), 182.

Savage, Courtenay. "Beggars Collect Fortunes from the Public," *Dearborn* (Michigan) *Independent,* October 11, 1924, pp. 13-15.

Schumacher, Henry C. "Personality and Its Development as it is Affected by Financial Dependency and Relief-Giving," *Family,* IX (1928), 140-44.

Selden, W. B. "Beggars That Play Strange Roles," *Harpers Weekly,* LIII (1909), 31.

Sharp, W. "Hotel of the Beautiful Star," *Harpers Weekly,* CIII (1901), 673-79.

Simpson, V. A. "Beggars and Begging-Songs," *Virginia Quarterly Review,* IV (1928), 40-51.

Solenberger, Alice W. *1,000 Homeless Men: A Study of Original Records.* New York, Charities Publications Committee, Russell Sage Foundation, 1911.

"South Calling a Halt on Tramps," *Survey,* XXXV (1916), 534.

Steele, D. M. "Lovers of a Cheerful Giver," *Ladies Home Journal,* XVIII (1901), 2.

Stein, G. R. "How About Beggars," *Survey,* LVII (1926), 377-78.

Stiff, Dean (pseudonym of Nels Anderson). *The Milk and Honey Route: A Handbook for Hoboes.* New York, The Vanguard Press, 1931.

Stoker, B. "American Tramp Question and the Old English Vagrancy Laws," *North American*, CXC (1909), 605-14.

"Stopping Mendicancy in Baltimore City," *Survey*, XXIX (1912), 89-90.

"Storm Signals Hoisted for Oriental Solicitors," *Survey*, XXXI (1914), 623.

Stott, A. O. "Chinese Knights of the Open Palm," *Asia*, XXVII (1927), 830-33.

Street, J. "Italian Beggars," *Travel*, XIII (1907), 31-32.

Sutherland, Edwin H., and Locke, Harvey J. *Twenty Thousand Homeless Men: A Study of Unemployed Men in the Chicago Shelters*. Chicago and Philadelphia, Lippincott Company, 1936.

Tascheraud, H. "Art of Bumming a Meal," *American Mercury*, V (1925), 183-87.

———. "Passenger Stiff," *American Mercury*, V (1925), 368-71.

Tassin, A. "Craftsmanship of Begging-Letter Writing," *Bookman*, XXXVI (1912), 246-54.

Taylor, Graham. "On the Vagrant 'Elusive,'" *Charities*, XVIII (1907), 575-76.

"There Are Two Kinds of Beggars," *Survey*, LVIII (1927), 410.

"Thin Dimes: Panhandling No Easy Game," *Literary Digest*, CXXIII (1937), 4-5.

Thompson, Bertha. *Sister of the Road*. New York, Macaulay Company, 1937.

Thompson, V. "Vagabonds of France," *Outing*, LII (1908), 52.

———. "Vagabond Showman of France," *Outing*, XLIX (1907), 483-96.

Tillard, J. N. "Criminal Mendicant," *Charities*, XVIII (1907), 746-49.

"Tokyo's Beg Chit 18,000 Yen a Month," *Trans-Pacific*, XIII (1926), 16.

Tully, Jim. *Beggars Abroad*. Garden City, N. Y., Doubleday Doran and Company, 1930.

———. *Beggars of Life*. New York, A. and C. Boni, 1924.

———. "Lion Tamer," *American Mercury*, VI (1925), 142-46.

Turner, C. J. Ribton. *A History of Vagrants and Vagrancy and Beggars and Begging.* London, Chapman, 1887.

"Vagabonds Abroad," *Living Age*, CCCXXXIV (1928), 552.

Van Vorst, B. "Begging a Fine Art in Paris," *Lippincott's Magazine*, LXXIX (1907), 734-40.

"Varsity Hobo Club," *Literary Digest*, XLVIII (1914), 174 plus.

Waters, Theodore. "Six Weeks in Beggardom," *Everybody's Magazine*, XII (1905), 69-78.

Watson, M. "New Policy towards Drunks and Vagrants," *National Municipal Review*, IV (1915), 621-26.

"Weapons of an Expert Beggar," *Charities*, X (1903), 545.

Webb, John N. *The Migratory Casual Worker.* Washington, Government Printing Office, 1937.

——, and Brown, Malcolm. *Migratory Families.* Washington, Government Printing Office, 1939.

Whiting, F. V. "Trespassers Killed on Railways, Who Are They?" *Scientific American* Supplement, LXXIII (1912), 303-4.

Willard, Josiah Flynt (Josiah Flynt, pseudonym). *My Life,* New York, Outing Publishing Company, 1908.

——. *Tramping with Tramps.* New York, The Century Company, 1899.

Wines, F. H. "Max Müller on Beggars," *Charities*, XIII (1905), 559-61.

Wood, Samuel E. "Municipal Shelter Camps for California Migrants," *Sociology and Social Research*, XXIII (1939), 222-27.

Youmans, F. Z. "Childhood, Inc.; Child Beggars," *Survey*, LII (1924), 462-64.

Young, Pauline V. "The Human Cost of Unemployment," *Sociology and Social Research*, XVII (1933), 361-69.

Yuen, Liang Shao. "Homes for Beggars and Outcasts in Ningpo," *China Weekly Review*, XXX (1924), 82.

Zorbaugh, H. W. *The Gold Coast and the Slum.* Chicago, University of Chicago Press, 1929.

INDEX

ALMSGIVING, rationalization of, 196-99; as a response to custom, 197; as cultural lag, 197-98, 201-3; superstitious basis of, 200-1; intellectual justification of, 202-3; as satisfaction of emotional needs, 204-6; as an escape mechanism, 206-7; as a psychological compensation, 208-9; control of, 232-33. See also Catholic church; Protestant philosophy
Ambulatory beggars, 58, 63-64
Ancient world, begging in, 6-8
Athens, begging in, 7-8
Attitude of public, as reflected in status of begging, 15-18; towards begging, 24-25, 149-50, 234-35; begging techniques adjusted to, 27-28; in rural areas, 62-63; towards vagrants, 76-78; towards local beggar, 112-15; towards handicapped, 222-27
"Automobile family," 89-93

"BILLBOARD appeal," 57-58
"Blackhood," 124
Borrowing, as a begging technique, 30-31, 60-61, 70-71
Brahmin caste, and begging, 216-17
Buddhism, and almsgiving, 198

CALVINISM, and almsgiving, 24
Castes and classes, dependent, 179-82, 216
Catholic church, monasticism, 9,

15-16; monasteries, 10-11, 15-16; church councils, 11-12; mendicant friars, 15-18, 23, 25; decline of, 18
Causation of begging, 213-17; in early Middle Ages, 12-15; in late Middle Ages, 18-25; of children, 120-32; personal maladjustment as, 152-63; underworld as, 168-78; dependent castes as, 178-83; society's system of awards as, 218-19; as related to control, 220-21
Charity soliciting, as begging technique, 31-32
Children in begging, prevalency of, 120, 132; early training of, 120-21, 170-71; natural appeal of, 121; abuse of, 122-23, 126-27; rental of, 123-25; motivation of, 132; causation of, 132-33; as product of underworld, 176-78. See also Causation of begging
China, begging in, 123
Christian churches, early, attitude of, 9
Circuses, begging at, 64-65
City, in ancient times, 4, 7-8; as cause of modern begging, 26; beggars of, 99-100; ecological structure of, 134-36; slum areas of, 136-45; residence of beggar in, 141-48
Civil War, and emancipation, the status of the Negro in relation to, 181

9 781469 644509